The Way to Love

The Way to Love _____

Reimagining Christian Spiritual Growth as the Hopeful Path of Virtue

Matt Boswell

FOREWORD BY
Arthur G. Holder

CASCADE *Books* • Eugene, Oregon

THE WAY TO LOVE
Reimagining Christian Spiritual Growth as the Hopeful Path of Virtue

Cascade Books
An Imprint of Wipf and Stock Publishers
199 W. 8th Ave., Suite 3
Eugene, OR 97401

www.wipfandstock.com

PAPERBACK ISBN: 978-1-5326-4036-0
HARDCOVER ISBN: 978-1-5326-4037-7
EBOOK ISBN: 978-1-5326-4038-4

Cataloguing-in-Publication data:

Names: Boswell, Matt | Holder, Arthur G. (foreword)

Title: The way to love : reimagining Christian spiritual growth as the hopeful
path of virtue / by Matt Boswell; foreword by Arthur G. Holder

Description: Eugene, OR: Cascade Books, 2018 | Includes bibliographical refer-
ences.

Identifiers: ISBN 978-1-5326-4036-0 (paperback) | ISBN 978-1-5326-4037-7
(hardcover) | ISBN 978-1-5326-4038-4 (ebook)

Subjects: LCSH: Christian life. | Love—Religious aspects—Christianity. | Chris-
tian ethics. | Virtue. | Spiritual formation.

Classification: LCC BV4511 B68 2018 (print) | LCC BV4511 (ebook)

Manufactured in the U.S.A.   08/31/18

To Joann, Clara, Renee, and Teddy, my ways to love.

Contents

Foreword

Arthur G. Holder

THE WAY TO LOVE is the book that I have needed to read for a long time. As a parish pastor, a seminary professor, and a scholar of spirituality, I have tried to help Christian people—both as individuals and as communities—as they grow and mature in the life of faithful discipleship. But I have found that most writing about spiritual formation is either too theoretical to be of practical value, or else so focused on tactics and methods that we lose sight of the ultimate goal.

Matt Boswell has found the sweet spot where theory and practice meet on the path to love in action through the development of virtues. He reminds us that God doesn't just want us to *do* good, but to *be* good as well. And to be good not just in one way, or two, but in all the different ways that human beings are made in the image and likeness of our Creator.

There is a winsome simplicity in Boswell's creative approach to the work of spiritual formation. Over and over again, in straightforward language and with vivid examples drawn from Christian history and everyday life, he tells us that being a disciple of Jesus is all about love. What could be simpler than that?

Except that, as we all know, loving can be hard even when we know we ought to do it. Even when we are trying to do it well. Even when we have encouragement from our friends and family, and the support of a Christian community. As Boswell says, growing in love day after day, year after year, requires "training, practice, patience, vision, time, and collaboration" on our part, enveloped from beginning to end in divine grace.

This book speaks to a broadly ecumenical audience of evangelical and mainline Christian readers from an interdisciplinary perspective informed by some of the best current scholarship in theology, ethics, and the social sciences. Boswell's approach draws on virtue ethics (both Protestant and Catholic) and the emerging field of positive psychology to develop a model of spiritual formation focused on five key virtues (gratitude, self-care, justice, kindness, and hope), with love as the ultimate goal.

His treatment of each virtue includes consideration of the theological and philosophical background, pertinent insights from social scientific research, and a case study presenting a prominent modern Christian individual as an exemplar of that particular virtue. Most importantly, we come to understand how all the virtues are connected to one another, and how they are rooted in the model and example of Jesus who is the paradigmatic lover of us all.

Readers of *The Way to Love* will be inspired by Boswell's expansive, hopeful, and compassionate vision, but they will also be guided and supported in their efforts to develop practical programs of formation at various levels: personal, familial, and congregational. Much more than a "how to" book, this is a work of deep pastoral wisdom that gives us the "why" and "what for" and "with whom" of Christian spiritual growth. Read it for yourself—or even better, read it with some friends—and prepare to be "transformed by the renewing of your minds, so that you may discern what is the will of God—what is good and acceptable and perfect" (Rom 12:2, NRSV).

I am not aware of any other book in the field of Christian spiritual formation that covers the same ground as Dr. Boswell's work. While he directly engages well-known authors on spiritual formation such as Richard Foster, Dallas Willard, and Robert Mulholland, providing both appreciation and critique of their work, Boswell's project is rooted in a more sophisticated understanding of human development based in C. R. Snyder's theory of hope. The approach throughout the book is positive, encouraging, and realistic, with many practical examples drawn from everyday life. *The Way to Love* would be an ideal textbook for the seminary classroom, but I can also envision it being used in congregational study groups or workshops for Christian pastors of any denomination.

Introduction

It's All About Love, in Theory

DOES LIVING THE CHRISTIAN life make you a better person?

It should. And if doesn't, you're doing it wrong.

But what does "better" mean? In what sense does Christian spirituality make people *better*? Many who are not Christian have a rather wide range of images of Christians, from more to less flattering. It is not clear to the world at large that being Christian makes an individual *better*. And yet the Christian story reveals the secret to true "betterment."

Love.

"Love the Lord your God . . . and love your neighbor as yourself" (Matt 22:37b–39, NRSV). Jesus plainly lays out with tantalizing simplicity the point of the spiritual life.

But what is love? And how do we "do" it?

Love is a frequently stated rallying cry for Christians. Whatever we mean by it, love is central to the Christian experience. The love of God for humans. The love of humans for God. Humans' love for one another. Love, however, does not necessarily come naturally.

A member of the Quaker meeting I pastor recently lamented the lack of tolerance and inclusion she had been encountering through social media. She exclaimed in frustration: "Why can't people just love each other? I don't get it, it's so simple!" While quiet empathy rather than verbal critique better fit the moment, I thought to myself: "Because it is difficult to love!"

Christian preachers err if they assume that simply reminding their parishioners to love will effectively create a love revolution. Love requires training, practice, patience, vision, time, and collaboration.

But attempt to love we must, because, as I will suggest in this book, the true Christian life is the movement toward love. So then, how do we move?

xi

And toward what do we move? These are questions of spiritual formation, though a survey of various approaches to Christian spiritual formation does not provide the kind of answers these questions demand.

In some cases, Christian spiritual formation seems aimless. Authorities on formation may emphasize the practices that form and/or the domains of the self that warrant formation. Yet by being either cautiously respectful of individual authenticity or hesitant to "push" Christians for various reasons, these leaders can neglect the pursuit of a shared spiritual goal or flat-out reject the quest as futile or imposing.

Goals are crucial in many domains of life, from workplace to education to personal health. Having a goal brings clarity about what to do, here and now. Often such goals reflect deeply held values. Many churches possess articulated goals such as Christlikeness or love.

And while the congregations (and authors who influence these congregations) prescribe various practices and programs as elements of a dynamic spiritual life, they hinder their formative efforts in two significant ways. Either they display an ambiguous or underdeveloped vision of love or Christlikeness (the goal) or they fail to place the cultivation of relevant virtues at the center of their visions of spiritual development (the path).

For example, these congregations and authors commonly promote worship, preaching, prayer, private Bible reading, collective action for justice, and classic spiritual disciplines as means of spiritual formation. These practices are potentially fabulous tools for spiritual growth—insofar as they are conducive to growth in virtue. Without love and its facilitative virtues at the center, such practices risk becoming commodities for spiritual consumption rather than transformative elements of a larger, love-centric spiritual project.

What This Book Is About

Four key concepts dominate this book: hope, love, virtue, and spiritual growth. If the vision of the spiritual life presented here is to take root, we need to understand and embrace these four concepts, perhaps reading them with new eyes to prevent our preconceptions from stifling new learning.

Hope. To actively pursue spiritual growth, you must hope. Hope facilitates spiritual growth. But hoping is not waiting. Hoping is not wishing. Hope is not dependence on external forces or other people. Hope is about the power of the future to transform the present. Hope is about growing into this future. Hope is about imagination. Hope is about goals and movement toward these goals. The spiritual life is a movement of hope. In fact, humans themselves are fundamentally hopers. But for what do we, as hopers, hope?

Love. We hope for love. But what is love? How do you love? Is our love like God's love? Why or why not? Is love fundamentally about me? About you? About both of us? Trying to keep our definitions of love "spacious" is admirable. Yet if love is the goal of the spiritual life, we have to know what we are talking about when we talk about love. This book will offer an energizing and inviting definition of Christian love and clarify the path toward such love—the path of *virtue*.

Virtue. The primary focus of Christian spiritual formation—spiritual *training*—ought to be the cultivation of virtue. But which virtues? What is virtue or a virtue? How do you know when you have a virtue? And why be concerned with *my* virtue when many others who suffer in a variety of ways would benefit from my attention? I will answer these questions by explaining the distinctives of virtue ethics and why your virtue and others' well-being are inextricable. Simply put, virtues are the pathway to love. Traveling this path is the subject of spiritual growth.

Spiritual Growth. What does it mean to grow spiritually? How do you know when it is happening? What do you do to make it happen? What do others do? What does God do? I will examine common understanding of spiritual growth in chapter 1 and identify the way in which these approaches, despite their varied contributions, are ultimately inadequate.

This book highlights the inextricable relationship between virtues and love. It emphasizes that God's grace and human effort to cultivate virtue are not opposed but complementary. It prioritizes social justice while underscoring the necessary undergirding of virtues for effective social change. It articulates an accessible virtue-centric vision of the Christian life that can inspire churches to focus their formative efforts on nurturing this virtuous life. Its vision of the spiritual life, if truly lived by you and me, will facilitate greater peace, greater joy, and greater freedom—for us as individuals and for the relationships and communities of which we are a part.

Two dialogue partners in this journey include *virtue ethics* and *positive psychology*—two distinct fields with differing methodologies yet united in their emphasis on the God-created and God-nurtured potentialities of the human person. A third dialogue partner is what you might call *love theory*, based on the work of theologians and psychologists alike.

Virtue Ethics: Character Over Rules and Choice

James Keenan has abridged Alasdair MacIntyre's argument for the recovery of virtue ethics in three interrelated questions: Who am I? Who ought I to become? How ought I to get there?[1] These questions indicate the basic concerns of virtue ethics.

"Who am I?" Virtue ethics emphasizes human agency and the capacity for personal transformation, expressed in enduring character traits or good habits that enable a person to perform a virtuous act "to the right person, in the right amount, at the right time, for the right end, and in the right way."[2] To be fully human is to be virtuous: to function rightly and harmoniously. Here, morality is not located in an elaborate system of rules or universal laws. Moral behavior is not done out of duty to divine commands or "pure reason." Morality is also not a calculated assessment of the "ripples" of a possible action. Rather, morality is rooted in the characteristics of the human person and precedes or prepares one for particular moral dilemmas. To affirm my agency is to recognize a trajectory to my life formed both by external forces and my own choices: I effectively engage in ongoing self-creation, the development of my story. My individual acts are therefore better characterized not as "right" or "wrong" as though I have offended a lawgiver or betrayed a code but as "helpful" or "harmful"—either leading me toward or away from the person I feel called to become.

"Who ought I to become?" Virtue ethics has a forward-looking, teleological focus; it articulates an end goal toward which individuals and communities ought to strive (typically some form of flourishing or well-being). A strong sense of my *telos* or purposeful end clarifies the nature and purpose of my life, thus clarifying the kind of character that needs cultivating and the particular virtues that constitute this character. Knowing the end of my story—through reason or revelation (or both)—guides the way I live as an agent within that story. Such narrativity is both individual and shared—an important reminder that I am accountable for my actions not only because they impact my character but because my story interlocks with others' stories.

"How ought I to get there?" The ethical life, a quest-like movement of agents toward a goal, is marked by the ongoing development of habits of character—i.e., virtues—shaped by lived experience. MacIntyre defines virtues as those

---

1. Keenan, "Proposing Cardinal Virtues," 711.
2. Aristotle, *Nicomachean Ethics*, 29.

dispositions which will not only sustain practices and enable us to achieve the goods internal to practices, but which will also sustain us in the relevant kind of quest for the good, by enabling us to overcome the harms, dangers, temptations, and distractions which we encounter, and which will furnish us with increasing self-knowledge and increasing knowledge of the good.[3]

Virtues deepen the quality and efficacy of our spiritual practices (and are simultaneously formed through such practices). Virtues strengthen our resistance to obstacles, deepen our self-understanding, and enable us to attain our most sacred goals. Virtues are not values, preferences, beliefs, or opinions, but embodied dispositions, the growth of which reshapes us and implicates our relationships with others, whether they be individuals, communities, structures, or the natural world. How particular virtues are named and connected will vary between communities, traditions, and theorists. Good models that propose a set of essential virtues tend to be comprehensive (have virtues to counter all ills and enhance all goods) and interrelated (operate in distinct but complementary domains). I will later examine how such constellations of virtues have been historically and uniquely constructed before ultimately making a case for a set of cardinal virtues that fits the model I propose in this book.

I am, of course, not the first to suggest that Christians make the cultivation of virtue central to their spirituality, as a survey of relatively recent literature reveals. N. T. Wright, an Anglican bishop, urges the formation of character as a means to Christian worship and mission.[4] Gilbert Meilaender, a Lutheran, encourages Christians to cultivate virtues—traits of character that suit us for life, shape our vision of that life, play a corrective role, and aid us in actualizing our potential.[5] Stanley Hauerwas, uniting virtue with Christian formation, writes that "the Christian life is more a recognition and training of our senses and passions than a matter of choices and decisions."[6] Jennifer Herdt, whose sketch of virtue acquisition is especially informed by Erasmus and the Jesuits, maintains that the imitation of Christ is not only about modeling oneself after an exemplar but also a divine action that

---

3. MacIntyre, *After Virtue*, 219.

4. Wright, *After You Believe*, x. Wright reads the New Testament through the lens of virtue ethics and argues that Jesus and the New Testament writers are deeply concerned with virtue and character. Through following Jesus, the working of God's grace, and the transformative work of the Holy Spirit, we reflect God's image and become genuinely human.

5. Meilaender, *Theory and Practice*, ix–x, 12–13.

6. Hauerwas, *Peaceable Kingdom*, 142.

grows our love for God and others.[7] William Spohn argues that Christian spirituality ought to transform our character through deliberate spiritual practice (not simply spiritual experience).[8]

David Perrin accentuates virtues, clarifying that "the spiritual practices of Christians are not meant solely to stabilize their lives as they are, or to affirm the way they view the world, themselves, or God" but to "transform and reform who they are."[9] Richard Foster insists that we accentuate character formation in our formative efforts, which he believes is a remedy for widespread Christian tendencies toward a pessimistic anthropology, a lack of emphasis on the moral life, and busy church involvement that fills people's time but leaves them untransformed.[10] Despite some of its self-directed violent rhetoric, *The Imitation of Christ* does convey the urgency of dealing with deep-seated habits and attitudes and cultivating "a richer life, a wider repertoire of responses to people and events."[11] The liberating spiritual vision of Gustavo Gutierrez underscores the social dimensions of virtue, challenges individualistic spirituality, and emphasizes community as both the joy of the Christian life and its primary "laboratory" that exposes and refines our greatest vices.[12]

In one sense, Christians should engage in spiritual practices because they are lovers, seeking means of realizing this love. In another sense, practices ought to be shapers of virtue, intended to stretch and challenge, for the sake of deepening one's love and the efficacy of the practices. These two understandings of practice—the more MacIntyrian practice as collaborative endeavor for good and the more Fosterian approach of practice as discipline—will remain in dialogue throughout this book.

---

7. Herdt, *Putting on Virtue*, 6.

8. Spohn, "Christian Spirituality," 270–71, 275.

9. Perrin, *Studying Christian Spirituality*, 274.

10. Foster, "Spiritual Formation Agenda," 29.

11. Miles, *Practicing Christianity*, 24. Miles says that the imitation of Christ is based on the presumption that the image of God is within us; to actualize our nature is to develop our similarity to the divine. Miles helpfully addresses the relationship between women and the imitation of Christ, noting how traditional exhortations to women to imitate Christ's gentleness and self-sacrifice have been damaging. Instead, women should imitate "Christ's anger at injustice, Christ's practices of self-remembering and centering, Christ's rejection of the social role expectations of this day, and the creativity with which Christ met difficult situations" (40).

12. Gutierrez, *We Drink From Our Own Wells*, 133.

Positive Psychology: The Science of Goodness

Think of positive psychology as the more empirically minded twin to the philosophically minded virtue ethics. Positive psychology seeks to identify the emotions, characteristics, and practices that can enable individual, communal, and institutional flourishing. In most classic, therapeutically oriented psychologies, interventions focus on a deficit; the intervention reaches completion when the patient returns to an adequate level of functioning. Positive psychology interventions, in contrast, aim to move people to a more optimal level of functioning, whether they are experiencing depression, anxiety, etc., or are apparently functioning at an adequate level. The goal is to cultivate lasting positive emotions and habits rather than simply "fixing the problem."

The core concerns and areas of research of the positive psychology movement are encapsulated in the acronym "PERMA": positive emotions, engagement, (positive) relationships, meaning, and achievements.[13] *Positive emotions* are an essential component and facilitator of human flourishing. *Engagement* indicates the utilizing and application of talents and strengths in a kind of self-forgetful experience—similar to some conceptions of "vocation" and comparable to what we mean by "getting lost" in something. *Relationships* emphasizes the benefits of healthy connections to others. *Meaning* is about participation in a self-transcending project—something greater than oneself. *Achievement* highlights the satisfaction of personal success.

Substantial, emerging data support the human capacity for flourishing or happiness. Such happiness is not trivial or fleeting but a stable, enduring sense of meaning and well-being, echoing Aristotle's *eudaimonia*. And while much of the work being done is descriptive, some of it is also prescriptive: positive psychologists tend to not only affirm the capacity of persons for emotional, cognitive, and behavioral change but enthusiastically offer practical guidance toward this end. While its goals include self-improvement, positive psychology holistically approaches human flourishing, ultimately taking us outside of ourselves and turning us toward others.[14]

13. Seligman, *Flourish*, 16–20, 24.

14. Good introductory texts abound. See Seligman, *Flourish*, for a nice blueprint of the field. For a good text on "engagement," creativity, and "optimal experience," see Csikszentmihalyi, *Flow*. For the evolutionary and biological underpinnings of positive psychology, see Keltner, *Born to Be Good*. Some good texts on emotions include: Davidson and Begley, *Emotional Life of Your Brain*, which demystifies the brain and demonstrates the physicality of our emotional selves; see also Goleman, *Emotional Intelligence*; Gross, "Emotion Regulation," 3–25; and Fredrickson, "Role of Positive Emotions," 218–26. Compassion is an often-researched characteristic in positive psychology and

Two voices from the field of positive psychology ring loudest in this book. The primary voice is that of the late C. R. Snyder, arguably the leading theorist on the topic of hope among positive psychologists and a central influence on the model of the spiritual life presented in this book. While hope theologians have offered compelling future-oriented theological narratives, I believe that Snyder's model of hope—with its emphasis on the human capacity to set and pursue self-transforming goals—can fruitfully ground this theology in the form of a model of spiritual development. I will devote much of chapter 2 to expanding on this point.

A secondary voice is that of Christopher Peterson and Martin Seligman's *Character Strengths and Virtues: A Handbook and Classification*—the foundational piece of literature on virtue in positive psychology. Their classification is "the social science equivalent of virtue ethics, using the scientific method to inform philosophical pronouncements about the traits of a good person."[15] In the *CSV* classification, six core virtues provide the structure for twenty-four "character strengths."[16] Their classification also introduces a wide range of psychological research on the virtues, making it an excellent starting point for further research. Their taxonomy does have its limitations: its definitions occasionally disappoint, its overarching goals are somewhat contradictory, and it lacks a coherent theory of virtue that addresses how virtues interact with one another.[17] A more comprehensive approach to virtues

---

is explored nicely in Gilbert, *Compassionate Mind*, which makes a theoretical contribution and provides practical guidance for overcoming negative emotions like anxiety and anger and cultivating positive habits like courage and self-control. A nice synthesis of the concerns of positive psychology and its relationship to virtue ethics can be found in Haidt, *Happiness Hypothesis*.

15. Peterson and Seligman, *Character Strengths and Virtues*, 89.

16. Peterson and Seligman, *Character Strengths and Virtues*, 13. For example, the core virtue of courage includes the character strengths of bravery, persistence, integrity/authenticity/honesty, and vitality/zest; the core virtue of justice includes the character strengths of citizenship, fairness, and leadership. While these strengths would be considered virtues or "sub-virtues" in a philosophical taxonomy, here they are not simply more specific forms of cardinal virtues but have a different function and availability.

17. To elaborate: 1) The *CSV* definition of "justice" feels weak, not about the will nor about doing good to particular others but limited to one's participation in society and distributive justice. "Leadership" does not seem a truly universal quality. "Transcendence" seems like a catch-all that means little as a virtue. "Love" is tragically shallow. "Hope" seems undersold as merely a character strength rather than an essential virtue. 2) The direction given to would-be users of the handbook seems conflicted, possibly a problem of nomenclature (e.g., the use of "virtue" vs. "strength"). The *CSV* advocates the cultivation of good character as exhibited in these six universal virtues while also emphasizing that one focus on one's *top* character strengths (effectively virtues) at the expense of one's non-strengths (weak virtues). This could mean one lacks strengths from multiple virtue categories, theoretically leaving significant character deficiencies

that considers their interrelation and posits a theological or philosophical narrative that clarifies which virtues are important and why would enhance or extend their project. This is, of course, my objective here.

In short, *I will use the resources of virtue ethics and positive psychology to construct a model of Christian spiritual development where the goal of love is realized through the increasing presence in the individual Christian of virtues of gratitude, self-care, justice, kindness, and hope.*

What Is Love? The Challenge and Necessity of a Theory of Love

Two objections may arise to deeming "love" the goal of the Christian life: "love" may seem too platitudinous to be a useful goal, or too spacious to be defined in a way that is helpful without being reductive of a wide range of experiences and cultures. I sympathize with these concerns and so respond with a definition of love that is accessible but demanding. Yet I also make a case for a particular understanding of love. I do this with the confidence demanded by real participation in a living tradition but with the humility appropriate to a pluralistic context with competing metanarratives that recognize themselves as "extended, embodied arguments"[18] rather than overconfident and oppressive truth claims.

Love is one of the most ubiquitous Christian, even religious, ideals. While its flavor may change (e.g., relationship with God, oneness with all beings, justice for all, selflessness, etc.), there is a common undercurrent linking these seemingly disparate aims together. Love is also a relatively palatable religious goal. It lacks the theological baggage and ambiguity of "heaven" as a goal. It overcomes the overly cognitive nature of the goal of "mature, reasonable faith." It counters the isolationist tendencies of "authentic self." It eschews the agenda-laden nature of the self-replicating "disciple-maker." Even if definitions diverge, "love" is a good starting point for identifying what the Christian narrative suggests that truly spiritual

that would effectively act as foils for other facets of one's character. The failure of the *CSV* to address the interaction of the virtues means it does not address how a strength like "bravery" can lose its efficacy or benefit if one does not also possess a strength of kindness or wisdom.

18. MacIntyre, *After Virtue*, 222. MacIntyre describes a tradition—applicable to Christianity—as "an historically extended, socially embodied argument, and an argument precisely in part about the goods which constitute that tradition" (MacIntyre, *After Virtue*, 222). Tradition implies a continuity between members amidst generational turnover, a lived ethic, and an ongoing dialogue about what practice and virtues best move a tradition toward its vision of the good.

development ought to entail: the increasing presence of love for God, for others, for the world, for the self.

I offer a clear and specific definition of love—not to limit it but expand it. Such clarity is intended to aid persons in assessing their own movement toward love, like the articulation of clear learning outcomes in the classroom as a means of guiding pedagogical practices. What are called "pathways" to love in this model—i.e., virtues—are both means to love and love themselves; this differentiates them from practices. For example, one might suggest that reading the Bible leads to love but would not say it is love in itself; however, justice (a pathway or virtue) both leads to love and is an expression of love. You move toward the goal by living out the goal in real, tangible ways.

The Christian journey therefore becomes an integrated movement toward love that considers all facets of how humans experience love. As I create a dialogue between one particular theological and one particular psychological approach to defining love, the outcome of this interaction will be a vision of how to more easily access this love.

What to Expect and When to Expect It

Your journey through this book may feel something like the stages of home construction. Once a broad blueprint is sketched, we can make it inhabitable by developing all the component parts.

In the first chapter, I analyze some of the current literature on spiritual development in order to identify the foundations upon which I build and to pinpoint the shortcomings of existing models of spiritual growth. I then present one classical Christian reflection on the spiritual life that is particularly supportive of my argument that will also introduce the themes of the rest of the book. Chapter 2 will explore the meaning of "hope" and present a hope-based model of spiritual growth. Simply put, hope propels Christian spiritual growth. Hope enables us to move toward our ultimate spiritual goals.

Chapters 3 and 4 begin to fill in pieces, in a manner of speaking: a definition of love that can serve as the goal of the Christian life and a definition of the human person that is compatible with this goal. Because my intent is to provide a vision of formation for realizing love, the model takes on a distinctive relational character. With love as the goal, formation becomes a matter of how individuals become more lovingly related to others.

The subsequent subject of investigation then becomes the virtues that ought to be targeted as means of developing our capacity for love. There is emerging consensus in the social sciences about the nature of the human person: we are relational beings, inclined toward meeting others' needs. A model of spiritual formation is needed that develops this capacity—a model that not only helps realize human potential but is also thoroughly Christian. In chapters 5–10 I will propose five cardinal virtues that ought to be the focus of the Christian life in light of the quest for love. The concluding chapter offers some preliminary suggestions for how Christian "formators" ought to reconceive Christian practices in light of my model.

Sandra Schneiders, in her classic summation, defines spirituality as "the conscious involvement in the project of life integration through self-transcendence toward the horizon of ultimate value one perceives."[19] This definition underscores that spirituality is not primarily accidental but intentional; it is explanatory, unifying, and meaning-creating; it concerns the relationship between one's self and an alternative, possible self; and it is goal-directed, shaped by an ideal that is either self-created or informed by a community or religious tradition.

Expanding this definition, I argue that the Christian spiritual life should be seen as the conscious cultivation of virtues in a life-integrating narrative of what I am calling "lovers pilgrimaging toward Love via virtues" through transcending one's *current* self (through grace-enabled personal agency) toward the ultimate value of Love, existentially realized in our character and relationships.

In other words, it's all about love. We are lovers: made by love, for love, to love. Our destination is love. The journey itself is love. It is the journey on which Jesus—the exemplary lover—embarked, loving God and others as he pilgrimaged toward his own destiny: love.

This book maps out the way to love, in two senses. It imagines the Christian life as a path one travels (a "way") toward the ultimate goal of love, a goal which, in turn, illuminates the path. It also suggests a somewhat systematic way of thinking about what love is, how to practice love, and how to grow in one's capacity to love, thus showing the way (or *how*) to love. May this book be a guide so that you might better join Jesus on this pilgrimage toward Love, with Love.

---

19. Schneiders, "Approaches to the Study of Christian Spirituality," 16.

Part One

Reimagining the Christian Life

Chapter One

Spiritual Formation: The Limitations of Popular Approaches

All the way to heaven is heaven, because Jesus said "I am the Way."[1]

—CATHERINE OF SIENNA, 1347–80

Life means growth—and development toward a final complete maturity and perfection. What is this finished perfection for the Christian? The full manifestation of Christ in our lives.[2]

—THOMAS MERTON, 1915–68

WHAT ARE WE TALKING about when we talk about spiritual development and spiritual formation? If spirituality is your conscious involvement in a self-transcending movement toward your horizon of ultimate value, then spiritual growth is the movement. The change. Becoming what you ultimately value.

The use of two distinct terms—development and formation—may seem redundant but is deliberate. I use "spiritual development" to describe what happens as persons grow spiritually as well as the consequent philosophical reflection on this growth. Complementarily, formation is the deliberate

1. Day, *Duty of Delight*, 52. Dorothy Day attributes this phrase to Catherine of Siena, though it may be apocryphal.

2. Merton, *Life and Holiness*, 82.

3

effort to facilitate spiritual development. A question of spiritual development might be, "How does self-care facilitate my ability to meet the needs of others?" while formation asks, "How do I cultivate self-care?" These two terms are often used interchangeably in the literature, so I will help navigate this linguistic murkiness by clarifying terms when appropriate.

Mulholland: Being Conformed to Christ for Others' Sake

Let us start by examining an accessible existing definition. Robert Mulholland, an oft-cited and oft-studied voice on spiritual formation, describes Christian spiritual formation as "the process of being conformed to the image of Christ for the sake of others."[3] A few key and expandable points are contained in this concise definition.

First, spiritual development is a process. It is not instantaneous. This process is experienced by everyone, whether self-identifying Christian or not. Our development is constant; Christian spiritual formation consciously, actively responds to this constancy in a Christ-centered manner. Humans are spiritual beings, fundamentally oriented to become; Christians should deliberately realize this potential through goal-directed energy and action.

Secondly, spiritual development is about "being conformed." This deliberately passive construction may divulge Mulholland's pressure, whether external or self-imposed, to appeal to those of us who insist that *we* do not transform ourselves—*God* does. While a noble attempt at humility, we hamstring our spiritual growth by maintaining that "there is nothing we can do to transform ourselves" but to "make ourselves available for God to do that work."[4] This kind of thinking—perhaps a lingering and exaggerated Protestant fear of works-righteousness—does not facilitate growth but undermines it. The spiritual life should not be conceptualized as two separate movements: the initial stage of readying ourselves to be transformed, and the second stage of being-acted-upon by grace. This dichotomy does not fittingly describe experience and ruptures what is continuous, with devastating consequences for our potential spiritual growth.

Thirdly, spiritual development should form us into the image of Christ. While the image is singular, the expression is plural: our likeness to Christ

---

3. Mulholland, *Invitation to a Journey*, 15. While I resist his terminology (I would call this development, not formation), his four-part definition is the right balance of fixed but spacious, a useful skeleton easily appropriated (though I take issue with the way Mulholland enfleshes this skeletal definition).

4. Mulholland, *Invitation to a Journey*, 26.

is analogical, lived out in ways that honor our personal and contextual uniqueness. Jesus is a kind of template for fully realized humanity, an ideal that then sheds light on particular areas of our present reality that are not yet in line with this ideal.

Finally, spiritual development emphasizes that humans are intended for relationships with God and others. Here, Mulholland's approach is rather compatible to my own, where authentic spiritual growth cannot be divorced from our lives with others. Our relationships are a school for spiritual growth; the quality of these relationships is an indicator of our spiritual maturity.

Mulholland's outline is a fine starting point, little of which I reject in terms of its broad strokes. I propose that spiritual development be tentatively understood as *the self-transforming movement toward and increasing realization of a self-transcending, ultimate goal.* Christian spiritual development, specifically, ought to be conceived of as *the movement of lovers toward Love through the cultivation of Love's constitutive virtues,* following the spiritual path of Jesus.

My Approach to Formation in Relationship to Other Approaches

A "model" of spiritual development is an integrated set of concepts that clarifies how humans progress toward a spiritual goal and that addresses the nature of the goal, the nature of the human person, the stages or movements in development, and the relationship between these components. My proposed model is in multiple ways a divergence from popular models of Christian spiritual development that are influential in the lives of ministry leaders and engaged practitioners. While elements of these models can support my proposed model, I believe some facets of these models are worth rejecting—or at least de-emphasizing. Authentic spiritual growth ought to emphasize 1) goodness over badness, 2) construction over discovery, 3) behavior over thinking, 4) Christ-centeredness over Christian exclusivity, 5) God as friend over God as superior, and 6) quality of character over quantity of practices.

1. Christian Spiritual Development Is More About Growing Good than Holding Evil at Bay

The language of brokenness to wholeness—characteristic of such authors as the illuminating Henri Nouwen and the popular John Eldridge—can be useful but will not be the primary image of growth in this book.[5] A conception of the spiritual journey in which one moves from brokenness to wholeness might be useful for particularized guidance in areas of trauma, but presumes that the human problem is one of getting from a pathological state to a normalized one. In such a model, the journey ends with the absence of negative traits rather than the presence of positive ones.

I think we can do better than a model of spiritual development that attempts, for example, to reduce greed rather than cultivate gratitude, or eliminate lust rather than cultivate a healthy sexuality. "Brokenness" can be a useful concept in clarifying the obstacles on the spiritual path, but the eradication of such obstacles should not be the primary aim. We ought not only to be removing something bad but cultivating something good.

Related, the movement from sinfulness to purity or holiness also does not characterize the movement of my proposed model. John Wesley, an important eighteenth century English theologian, explains "Christian perfection" as the sanctifying process of being filled with love and recognizes justification as our initiation into a process in which God synergistically works with human effort.[6] While I am sympathetic toward this model and Wesley's occasional appeal to virtue, I resist the individualism that frames sin as primarily a barrier to my personal salvation. This individualism does not necessarily manifest in Wesley's *methods* of spiritual growth (which, for example, prioritize small group meetings). Yet his vision of corporate discipleship nonetheless seems to support the growth of "individuals before God" in a way that does not recognize holiness in terms of increasingly right relatedness to others.

For example, Wesley believes that perfection—the fullness of love—can coexist with ignorance or errors in judgment, suggesting a fallible mind and a fallible soul are different matters.[7] Perhaps Wesley felt the need to

5. See for example Eldridge, *Waking the Dead*, and Nouwen, *Reaching Out*.

6. Wesley, "Plain Account of Christian Perfection," 316, 320, 373. My model does share a certain kinship with John Wesley's doctrine of Christian perfection (or at least one understanding of it, as Wesley at times seems to vacillate on its meaning).

7. Wesley, "Plain Account of Christian Perfection," 315. Wesley's context in the Enlightenment period, while informing his stress on the interiority of the Christian life (certainly characteristic of my model) also creates an individualistic tone to his vision. Positively, Wesley's apparent reaction to both an overemphasis on justification

clarify to his contemporaries that erudite reason and fact accumulation do not constitute holiness. Yet right judgment and awareness are not simply failures of reason but of will, heart, and character. The person who stereotypes, fails to attend to minutiae, acts without consideration for distant others (such as those who in oppressive conditions manufacture the products one obliviously purchases) should not so easily be let off the moral hook. If perfection, for Wesley, is love (or the increasing presence of or movement toward it), such love should be accompanied by an ever-improving cognition that works itself out in improved imagination, contextual sensitivity, judgment, and creativity.

The concept of sin is important to my understanding of spiritual development. However, sin is not a collection of isolated "naughty" acts but an underlying human sickness that inhibits the growth of what is most true about us—our goodness. Sin should not connote failures to satisfy an adjudicating God but, instead, inabilities to love others well. Sin should not be combatted because it separates us from God (can anything do that?) but because it separates us from others.

Sin is the not-as-it-should-be-or-could-be of the world. Sin is whatever thwarts the expression of and movement toward love. This would encompass everything from individual closed-mindedness to corporate greed to poor eating habits to indecisiveness—all of which can seriously stifle our ability to love others and collaborate with God.

2. Spiritual Development Is More About Constructing the Self than Finding It

Figuratively speaking, the spiritual quest ought not simply be about clearing the clutter in one's house but building the house from the ground up.

Richard Rohr emphasizes the discovery of a "true self" and reveals his indebtedness to Jungian psychology.[8] Rohr, a Franciscan who is particularly popular in mainline Protestant congregations, affirms the spiritual journey as the progressive elimination of "false selves" until illusions and external or self-imposed pressures to be something fade away and you discover "who you really are."[9] This quest for one's true self might be instructive but aims at

---

and to reservations about "works-righteousness" spirituality is countered by his vision of a personal, devoted faith; Wesley reframes religious activity not as favor-seeking behavior or a pointless addendum but as a more personal response of the heart to God.

8. For a basic overview of Jungian psychology, see McLeod, "Carl Jung."

9. See Rohr, *Naked Now*, and Rohr, *Falling Upward*, 156. While virtue is not front and center in this approach, Rohr is heavily concerned with love (See Rohr, "My

the wrong goal. I agree with David Perrin's critique: "the self is not hidden away in the deepest parts of the human body merely awaiting removal of the layers of debris that are piled upon it" but, rather, is "continually being constructed and is susceptible to change."[10]

Many Christians are riveted by Jungian personality types that emphasize birthright personality tendencies, as in the popular but unscientific Myers-Briggs Type Indicator.[11] The risk of Jungian psychology in a spiritual development model is that it can make the quest about "present, inauthentic me" moving toward "true, hidden, yet-to-be-unleashed" me, rather than about moving present me toward love. It can become an insular effort and a needless distraction, especially given the tendency, when taking personality types seriously, to stubbornly insist upon one's personality type at the expense of openness to new experiences, new situations, and new, ongoing formation that occurs as one's relationships, experiences, and context shift. Discovery of "who you are" can be fruitful if it leads to understanding your unique ability to enrich the world around you. Yet your "true self" is not a finished yet hidden product. It is more the mid-point of a story, awaiting further development.

A related type of model might be a recovery model, which assumes that our goodness is lost (possibly *irrevocably* lost) in the past. This way of thinking does not lend itself well to spiritual growth at all, unless such growth is thought of as the increasing awareness that God likes us in spite of ourselves. What I propose in this book is a developmental model of growth, in which our true self is continually created, nurtured by God, and shaped by the choices we make (and forces outside of our agency). My model is in this way resistant to nostalgia: God is taking us not backward to what we once were, nor inward to what is hidden within us, but forward to a place we have never been.

Problem With Religion," 22).

10. Perrin, *Studying Christian Spirituality*,126.

11. While self-discovery, self-awareness, and recognition of one's possible gifts to others are relevant to a spiritual development centered on love, most contemporary personality psychologists reject the MBTI approach as unscientific. See for example: Grant, "Goodbye to MBTI." Oliver P. John, a leading personality psychologist and creator of the "Big Five" personality test has decried Myers-Briggs as being universally rejected by contemporary personality psychologists (Oliver P. John, personal correspondence, August 8, 2013).

3. Spiritual Development Is More About Change in Habit than Perspective

Spiritual development is more than the growth of our opinions and beliefs and perspectives. For example, James Fowler's "stages of faith" model is a useful companion to spiritual development but does not constitute such development.[12] Fowler outlines the development over the course of the life span of one's perspective on life, self, and faith, the timing of which roughly coincides with natural, human development. Here, lifelong perspectival development culminates in the rarely attained "stage six" as an enlightened perspective that may or may not incarnate an ideal of altruistic love in the form of concrete action.

My proposed model is incarnational from the start. It emphasizes progress not in understanding of God or the meaning of life but in the presence of practical love. Fowler's faith journey moves people toward more complex thinking, listening, self-reflection, and ability to recognize injustice; such progression can enhance the cultivation of love virtues. The development of faith might be better understood as the development of a particular virtue in the Christian life that clarifies the grand story in which we live. Increased faith supports spiritual growth but is not equal to spiritual growth.

As another example, the classical "three ways" tradition—emphasizing the process of purgation, illumination, and union—provides a succinct summary of elements of the journey that may be presented in linear fashion but need not be experienced as such; you can be continually seeing, purging, and uniting.[13] The "three ways" tradition *could* be a resource for targeted virtue cultivation if employed with a good deal of interchangeability or circularity in order. For example, the movement from purgation to illumination to union would be a useful order if one needs to purge oneself of prejudices that inhibit the flowering of the virtue of justice. Or, I might, in a moment of illumination, learn things about myself that guide me toward union via purgation.

Negatively, this approach tends to be overly cognitive, transforming one's ideas and affections without necessarily facilitating the cultivation of positive habits that impact our relationships. Furthermore, with the possible exception of Bonaventure, the prominent writers who frame the spiritual life in terms of the classical stages tend to prioritize the contemplative over the active

---

12. See Fowler, *Stages of Faith*.

13. For a useful, brief survey of the history of the classical stages, see Larkin, "Three Spiritual Ways." David Perrin's analysis is also helpful; see Perrin, *Studying Christian Spirituality* 248–57.

in a way that—whether or not it did this for these practitioner-writers—risks making spirituality isolating rather than connective.

4. Christian Spiritual Development Is More Christ-Centered than Christ-Exclusive

Evan Howard speaks to the ubiquitous fear (more present among evangelicals than mainliners) of spiritual practices that are not explicitly Christ-centered. Howard cites the reliance on non-Christian practices like Buddhist mandala meditation as a "temptation" of spiritual formation.[14]

While I agree that Christians should take care when borrowing practices, my caution comes from three alternative considerations. One, am I honoring the full integrity of the practice in a way that recognizes the context out of which the practice emerges? Two, am I borrowing a traditional practice from a group without inflicting cultural violence or does my appropriation effectively rob a marginalized people of their heritage? Three, am I letting the practice truly stretch, undermine, thwart, grow, and transform me or have I, instead, reduced the potency of the practice by assimilating it to my own spirituality? We should not reject such practices out of fear of the "danger" of that which is not explicitly Christian. Practices that support the cultivation of our capacity to love in the spirit of Jesus (and which are lovingly, respectfully borrowed) should be welcomed as allies in spiritual development.

That said, a truly *Christian* model of spiritual development ought to entail explicit participation in the Christian tradition, formation in Christian community, conscious collaboration with the Holy Spirit, creative imitation of Jesus Christ, and movement toward increasing friendship with God.

5. Christian Spiritual Development Is Guided More by God-With-Us than God-Above-Us

While Diane Chandler's work on Christian spiritual formation is impressive and instructive, I resist the language she uses to describe the goal of this process: to "reflect God's glory."[15] This strikes me as a weak motivator.

14. Howard, "Three Temptations," 46.

15. Chandler, *Christian Spiritual Formation*, 24. Chandler suggests we pursue this goal through collaborative development in seven primary life dimensions: "spirit, emotions, relationships, intellect, vocation, physical health, and resource stewardship" (19). While Chandler's operationalization of spiritual growth into particular facets of the human experience is interesting, it is not sufficiently guiding. In my model, each "virtuous

I believe that Christian love comes from being in a mutual, creative, collaborative relationship with God—not from being a tool or ornament of God. It simply does not feel as satisfying nor is it as transformative to obey a superior as to bond with a friend, and I believe hierarchical language, in which God is great and we are but lowly servants, does more to undermine than facilitate spiritual growth.

A recurring theme in the writing of the recently departed Dallas Willard, an important voice in spiritual formation, is *obedience* to Christ. Willard's stages of growth adhere to a teacher/apprentice model, where we 1) trust and rely on Jesus, 2) desire to be his student, 3) obey his teaching, 4) train ourselves to obey his commands, and 5) find power to "work the works of the Kingdom."[16] While the shift in weight from stage one (a characteristic focal point of many churches) to the life of spiritual training is enticing, his model does not sufficiently clarify what difference our spiritual growth makes in the lives of others (or how others contribute to our spiritual growth). Willard's approach may be too individualistic and posit too hierarchical and male-centric of an approach to authority, commands, and the primacy of the intellect. The language of "obedience" creates a hierarchy between Jesus and the rest of us that may feel appropriately reverent to us but does not seem to be Jesus's priority. Obedience too easily suggests Jesus wants to maintain power *over*, rather than share power *with*.

To Willard's credit, his work does emphasize the transformation of character, even if the language of "obedience" is problematic. This concern for character might help avoid the trap of other, more dichotomous approaches to the spiritual life like Mulholland's, in which our spiritual activity is intended to release us to God's transformation and control of our lives.[17] Though Mulholland—noticeably obligated to a more Reformed theological understanding—urges his audience to take more ownership of their spiritual growth, he betrays his project. He essentially externalizes formation, where what is transformed is not one's whole being and character and makeup but rather one's ability to obey God excellently despite remaining totally other from God, a sinner. I do not see, in this approach, how anything of substance is transformed.

---

domain" entails some facet of the goal (love) with the potential to be developed more fully (while certainly incorporating Chandler's seven domains). The divisions in my model more clearly and practically clarify what constitutes spiritual formation (the increasing quality of these domains or virtues) whereas Chandler's divisions point to facets of life that are implicated by spiritual growth but are not themselves the evidence of spiritual growth.

16. Willard, *Divine Conspiracy*, 367–68.

17. Mulholland, *Invitation to a Journey*, 38, 168.

6. Christian Spiritual Development Is About Quality of Character Not Quantity of Practices

While Richard Foster's focus on practices (or disciplines) leaves the goal of the spiritual life a bit undefined (perhaps how he would prefer it), Foster does, to an extent, equate spiritual with character formation and, like a good Quaker, emphasize the inherent and potential goodness of humans.[18] Perhaps more a move by Foster's appropriators than Foster himself, spiritual development should not be identified with an increase in the quantity and intensity of spiritual practices. Spiritual practices ought not simply keep us occupied, spiritually quenched, enthused, nor be mistaken as evidence of spiritual vitality; such vitality comes when these practices effectively reshape us, cultivating the kind of character God seeks to grow in us.

Ruth Haley Barton shares Foster's concern for disciplines but further emphasizes the adoption of a monastic rule, preferring the term "spiritual rhythms" to characterize the purpose and nature of spiritually forming practices.[19] Joan Chittister, tapping into the Benedictine tradition, similarly lauds the transformative power of a rule of life, with the goal being not "great works or great denial" but "connectedness"—to others, self, and God.[20] Barton's and Chittister's works are excellent resources, if aimed at the cultivation of love. Otherwise, such practices and rules are at risk of two shortcomings: either forming people into something other than lovers or not forming them at all and misguidedly encouraging an association of "deep spirituality" with the presence of spiritual practices.

We should be wary of the commodification of spiritual practices. This applies to non-Christian "spiritual but not religious" folks who selectively create a spirituality borrowed from various traditions, but also to Christians whose consumerist mind-set can reduce Christian practices to "fueling up," standing for just causes, or aids to emotional well-being while sapping these practices of their socially and relationally transformative power. As an example, Jeremy Carrette and Richard King note how Western borrowers of

18. See Foster, *Celebration of Discipline*. While Richard Foster does not consciously operate in a virtue ethic framework, his disciplines or practices—which MacIntyre might consider to be sub-practices constitutive of more complex practices—can implicate character. Such disciplines include meditation, prayer, fasting, study, simplicity, solitude, submission, service, confession, worship, guidance, and celebration. The possible relationship between virtues and disciplines is evident: "excellent" prayer requires and produces honesty and compassion; fasting facilitates self-control and mindfulness; simplicity facilitates generosity and gratitude; guidance encourages self-care and humility.

19. Barton, *Sacred Rhythms*, 14.

20. Chittister, *Wisdom Distilled From the Daily*, 4.

Buddhist practices often are turned inward and away from others when, in fact, Buddhist teaching challenges the ego and undercuts self-centered concern by turning persons outward toward compassion and social justice.[21]

Connecting practices to love-virtues locates these practices in a larger spiritual project in which the narrative of a shared tradition and the presence of other people place certain claims on us. I can cultivate "my" spirituality but in light of my relatedness to others. For example, I should exercise not simply to feel better-looking but because my resulting confidence, peace, and energy will benefit those around me. We need an engaged spirituality that connects us to one another, rather than the deficient alternative of a spirituality that makes us feel momentarily happy and important but which ultimately isolates us.

Practices are not ends in themselves but expressions of virtue and incubators of virtue. Love must be the throughline that unifies all of our practices and efforts to build up the various components of ourselves, the thread that ties it all together. Christian spiritual growth is the growth of relational beings who are aware of and affected by the concerns of those around them. Is there a precedent for such a vision of the spiritual life?

An Ancient Yet Relevant Model of Spiritual Development: Gregory of Nyssa

There is! My model is in many ways a recovery of Gregory of Nyssa's virtue-centric vision of the spiritual life, expanded through dialogue with contemporary voices.

Gregory of Nyssa (331–94 CE) wrote *The Life of Moses* in response to a request for guidance on living a life of virtue.[22] Given the contemporaneous turn in Christian theology toward an emphasis on the incarnation, Gregory's grounded approach to the spiritual path emphasizing the cultivation of habits of character is unsurprising.[23] This incarnational accent is evident in that, despite Gregory's acknowledgment of human limitations, he is not pessimistic about human potential. He suggests Jesus's desire was to

21. Carrette and King, *Selling Spirituality*, 149. Their critique echoes MacIntyre's and the problem of losing the formative power and story of a religious tradition.

22. Malherbe and Ferguson, "Introduction," in Gregory of Nyssa, *Life of Moses*, 2. As bishop of Nyssa in the late fourth century, Gregory gave attention to combatting Arianism and writing interpretations of various scriptural texts (2–3). This text in particular is a commentary on Exodus and Numbers; its allegorical style shows Gregory's participation in an exegetical tradition including Philo and Clement of Alexandria (5–6).

23. Malherbe and Ferguson, "Introduction," in Gregory of Nyssa, *Life of Moses*, 2.

liberate humanity and make it more divine through the cultivation of virtue, a journey on which all humans ought to embark.[24]

The lynchpin of Gregory's model is "eternal progress" (*epikstasis*). This concept emphasizes neither stages nor finality but continual movement and newness. From a formative perspective, *apokatastasis*, or the return of all things to God, should not be construed as a soteriological point about universal reconciliation (i.e., the afterlife) but a declaration of God's unceasing lure of creatures toward their full self-realization—communion with God and with one another. For Gregory, love of God and love of neighbor is the ultimate goal.

Gregory states that "we are our own parents," emphasizing the capacity for self-creation through our choices in light of our goals and ideals for ourselves.[25] Gregory grounds, personalizes, and demystifies God's judgment as seen in the Egyptian plagues by noting that humans make their own plagues through their own choices and evil inclinations.[26] One needs a clear vision of the goal toward which one moves (faith) and intentionality in one's actions and choices that move toward this goal. Faith and works thus collaborate in spiritual growth. Furthermore, spiritual growth entails "honoring the divine" within.[27]

Underscoring this positive moral anthropology, Gregory notes that we are drawn by hope toward "what is beyond" and that persons innately long "to be filled with the very stamp of the archetype."[28] This future-oriented impulse entails a perpetual movement, where our goals are never final but provisional: "This truly is the vision of God: never to be satisfied in the desire to see him."[29] Because of Gregory's insistence on the incomprehensibility of God,[30] one never arrives at God but only moves

---

24. Kannengieser, "Spiritual Message," 72.

25. Gregory of Nyssa, *Life of Moses*, 56.

26. Gregory of Nyssa, *Life of Moses*, 74.

27. Gregory of Nyssa, *Life of Moses*, 110.

28. Gregory of Nyssa, *Life of Moses*, 114.

29. Gregory of Nyssa, *Life of Moses*, 116.

30. Gregory's opposition to the Arian theology of Eunomius, who argued for the knowability of God's essence, is part of what makes his vision of the spiritual life dynamic (and eternal). Further, despite Eunomius's noble attempt to preserve the difference between God and creature, he effectively limits God. Gregory rejects a God "reduced to finitude, measurement, limits, and boundaries" (Boersma, *Embodiment and Virtue*, 25). Furthermore, Gregory's apophatic understanding of contemplative experience stresses not light (like Origen) but darkness, stressing our ability to experience God but not know God (Sheldrake, *Spirituality*, 37). Gregory emphasizes the role of darkness in his interpretation of Moses's ascent of Mount Sinai. The entrance into divine darkness challenges potential idolatry, keeping God "beyond all knowledge."

toward God. Movement rather than stasis is essential to this vision, where binaries do not adequately elucidate the spiritual life as much as continua. God or humans, instant conversion from darkness to light, presence or absence of relationship with God are not as descriptive of the spiritual life as are divine-human synergy, gradual progress, and increasing discovery and collaboration with the divine.

The spiritual life, characterized by hope, compelled by love, constituted by virtues, is dynamic and unending. Gregory's model emphasizes goal-directed movement over goal attainment. A life well-lived is a life of continual growth and becoming. Gregory's model of spiritual development encourages the creative pursuit of a goal that is always beyond yet compels one forward, savoring the discovery of God through increased virtue yet never satisfied by and compelled to transcend one's current state. We are not simply God's friend or not, but developing or unraveling our friendship with God through our daily choices.

And we do it together, in community and in the context of our relationships. We cannot reach spiritual completion in isolation from or at the expense of others.

Christian spiritual development ought to be conceived of as *the movement of lovers toward Love through the cultivation of Love's constitutive virtues*. Because it is hope that propels this movement, clarifies the self that moves and the means of moving, and looks to Jesus as the goal and model of the path, our movement toward Love cannot be understood without a more robust understanding of the nature of hope. This will be the subject of the next chapter.

Regardless of God's incomprehensibility, such an experience of God clarifies right conduct for Moses and thus, similarly, clarifies the life of virtue (Gregory of Nyssa, *Life of Moses*, 33–34, 94–96). This approach better supports a spirituality of movement, where spiritual growth is facilitated by the paradoxical combination of desire that is constant and a goal that is unattainable.

Chapter Two

Spiritual Growth: The Life of Hope

Hope is the power behind love. . . . When hope fails, so does love.[1]

—John Climacus, 579–649

Yes, O God, I believe it. . . . It is you who are at the origin of the impulse, and at the end of that continuing pull which all my life long I can do no other than follow.[2]

—Pierre Teilhard de Chardin, 1881–1955

Hope is fundamental to Christian spiritual growth. We grow, in part, because we hope. The spiritual journey can be understood to be constituted by three elements: the journeyer, the destination, and the journey itself. Or in the language of C. R. Snyder's model of hope: agency, goals, and pathways. When we understand the nature of hope—and it is a rich, multifaceted concept, even in its simplicity—we can better answer the question: What do I do? Where and how do I devote my energy in the spiritual life?

Exploring the meaning of hope will lead to several outcomes: 1) a better psychological and spiritual understanding of how self-initiated personal development occurs; 2) an overarching structure for spiritual development; 3) a method or strategy for self-cultivation that is dynamic, effective, and connective; 4) an innovative expansion of Snyder's hope

1. John Climacus, *Ladder of Divine Ascent*, 289.
2. Teilhard de Chardin, *Divine Milieu*, 44.

theory to the realm of character and spiritual formation; and 5) a narrative for explaining the nature of being human that guides how a person expends his or her spiritual energies. Furthermore, as will become clearer in chapter ten, hope is a virtue itself that functions as an actualizing force: hope develops and enacts other virtues.

Hope is not wishful thinking or passive waiting. Instead, we hope by playing an active role in bringing about an uncertain but possible future with a view of self grounded not in naive optimism but in a realistic assessment of personal capabilities and attainable (but not guaranteed) outcomes. Through practice, hope becomes habitual. Hope is not only *a* virtue but *the* virtue for becoming virtuous. We become better people by *hoping*.

The Basics of Snyder's Model of Hope

Thomas Aquinas (1225–74) recognized the virtue of hope as our inclination toward a future good, difficult but possible to attain (and attained with divine assistance).[3] This classic construal contains the elements of Snyder's model: we are future-oriented creatures; a vision of the future motivates us, helping us overcome obstacles; we, to some degree, are agents in bringing about the future.

Hope has been defined as an emotion, a cognition, and an "affective cognition."[4] In contrast, Snyder's hope functions more as an enduring trait or capacity and at other times as a future-oriented framework. It is not "optimism," a matter of self-esteem, or the result of prior achievement.[5] Hope is "a positive motivational state that is based on an interactively derived sense of successful agency (goal-directed energy) and pathways (planning to meet goals)."[6] Alternatively put, "hope is the sum of the mental willpower and waypower that you have for your goals."[7] Snyder's model is constituted by three parts: goals, agency, and pathways.

---

3. Aquinas, II-IIIae, Q 17, Art 4. Thomas elsewhere affirms our hardwired impulse toward growth: "every nature desires its own being and perfection" (Aquinas, I-Iae Q 48, Art 1).

4. Cheavens and Ritschel, "Hope Theory," 397.

5. Snyder, *Psychology of Hope*, 13–23.

6. Cheavens and Ritschel, "Hope Theory," 397. This dynamic movement is characterized by motivation (agency) and deliberation (pathways): self-appraisal to assess capability of goal-pursuit and production of realistic means of goal-attainment (Snyder, "Hypothesis," 8).

7. Snyder, *Psychology of Hope*, 5.

Goals

Goals are "any objects, experiences, or outcomes that we imagine in our minds."[8] Such goals can look both to the near or distant future, whether next week or the end of our lives (or beyond). These can be large goals or small goals (which often function as subgoals for larger goals). Goals can demonstrate varying degrees of concreteness or vagueness. Goals can be set in a variety of domains, including social relationships, academics, romantic relationships, family life, work, and leisure activity (and, as I will argue, the cultivation of virtues).[9] Hope can include goals aimed at correcting negative behavior or improving "neutral" or positive behavior.

The best kinds of goals are those which are specific and also slightly out of reach yet attainable. Ambiguous goals do not as effectively facilitate change (knowing where we are going is important!) and easily attained goals ask too little of us (lest we hardly go anywhere at all!). Our goals reflect the vision we have for ourselves—the things we desire to accomplish and the people we desire to become.

Agency

If goals are the ultimate or provisional end of hoping (future you and me), the starting point is the present state of the agent (present you and me). Agency is our "perceived ability to shape our lives day to day."[10] Agency is the willingness to take responsibility as at least coauthor of one's life. It is the driving force that thrusts us forward, the spark that ignites our movement. Snyder has also called this "willpower"—the determination and commitment needed to pursue goals.[11] Agency is the sense that we can do what we set out to do and is aided by a deep understanding of our capabilities and resources (internal and external).

Our capacity for self-authorship does not exist in a vacuum, of course. Our past influences are present. We bring our negative baggage to any goal-related pursuit in the present challenge, but we also bring our past successes, which may assist us as something like "encouraging memories" or as something more innate—in essence, a habit of hope. In addition, agency should not be seen in an exclusively individual sense; underemphasized in Snyder's model is the collective, interdependent nature of agency. Resourcing our

8. Snyder, *Psychology of Hope*, 5.

9. Cheavens and Ritschel, "Hope Theory," 397.

10. Lopez, *Making Hope Happen*, 25.

11. Snyder, *Psychology of Hope*, 8.

capacities includes recognizing the ways others have aided or can aid us in our goal pursuits. Furthermore, our collective goals require a collective agency that is greater than the sum of its parts.

Pathways

Like the title of Snyder's seminal work, pathways are about getting "there from here." The pathways component refers to the way in which we develop routes that link our present reality to an imagined, possible future. Developing pathways is, however, not a purely intellectual exercise. Emotions, expectations, and stressors all impact our goal-pursuit. Yet for high-hope people, such factors are surmountable obstacles due to strong agency, effective path-making, and quality goal-setting. Creativity, flexibility, discernment, and diligence are crucial, as the attaining of goals may depend on a steady determination to remain on a well-designed path and a willingness to detach, adjust, and embrace "failures" as learning opportunities. As with agency, I argue that effective pathways thinking involves not only personal giftedness but a recognition of and reliance on the people, practices, and institutions that can aid us.

Hope is not optimism: whereas optimism relies on elements out of one's control (others' behavior, luck, etc.), hope enlists, activates, and alters oneself. High-hope people are optimistic, in control, can problem-solve, enjoy competition, and possess high self-esteem and positive affectivity.[12] This kind of hope does not simply come and go but can be learned—as is the case with virtue. You can become a better hoper, with practice.

The hope model has been applied to relationships, where hope provides a "caring and yet active environment where things get done."[13] It has been used to treat depression and other psychopathological disorders.[14] It has been employed in child education and parenting.[15] It has been applied to athletics and physical health.[16] It has relevance to career success and the pursuit of meaning.[17] In the rest of this chapter, I will apply hope

12. Snyder, *Psychology of Hope*, 50. Snyder et al. have provided measurements for determining both "state hope" (present level of hope) and "trait hope" (capacity to hope over time, more of a "habit"). Snyder, Rand, and Sigmon, "Hope Theory," 260.

13. Snyder, Rand, and Sigmon, "Hope Theory," 296.

14. See Snyder, *Handbook of Hope*. Applications include the treatment of trauma, anxiety, depression, eating disorders, etc.

15. Snyder, *Psychology of Hope*, 164–209.

16. See Snyder, Rand, and Sigmon, "Hope Theory," 263–65.

17. See Snyder, Rand, and Sigmon, "Hope Theory," 267.

to a new domain: the Christian life, particularly spiritual growth and the cultivation of virtue.

There are, however, multiple layers to the relevance of hope to the spiritual life. Let us begin to examine these layers, starting with several twentieth-century theologies of hope.

Hope Theology

Hope theology may name humans as hopers because it is philosophically coherent to say so or because God tells us as much. Snyder's hope names what it looks and feels like in lived experience to hope. My goal is to connect the two—theological and psychological hope—in a way that underscores hope as the essence of spiritual development. What, then, is hope, theologically and ethically understood? In short, Christian hope looks to a revealed or imagined future and participates in the coming of this future either through active collaboration with God or passive expectancy of God's action.

Numerous future-oriented theologies emerged in the twentieth century, largely in response to and in dialogue with developments in the social and physical sciences. Process theologians such as Charles Hartshorne, John Cobb, and Catherine Keller have expanded on Alfred North Whitehead's process metaphysics and emphasized the lure of an open future as a kind of theological starting point that guides the becoming of all things, including a collaborative and responsive God. Process theology fundamentally lacks, however, a strong clarity of the end, which might weaken its relevance to a life of hope (yet perhaps soften overconfident claims about what lies ahead and encourage greater creativity and agency because of it).

Wolfhart Pannenberg has characterized the resurrection of Christ as a proleptic revelation, the in-breaking of the future into the present. "The goal of the world is nearer to God than its commencement," suggests Pannenberg.[18] This theology portrays God as the future who is in relationship with history through creative activity (though far less affected or modified by human choice than the God of process theology). Pannenberg is somewhat ambiguous as to what the "goal of the world" looks like or how our movement toward it plays out in history; greater clarity as to the character of the future and how humans contribute to it is important for spiritual development. The more vivid, detailed, and imposing this future can become, the more likely that people will actively respond to this future.

Johannes Metz's *memoria passionis* looks backward to Christ as a motivator for present, political action while simultaneously looking

18. Pannenberg, *Systematic Theology*, 390.

forward to a future freedom, especially for "the suffering, the hopeless, the injured, the oppressed, the useless of this earth."[19] Hope for Metz is liberating and confrontational; hope causes intolerance of the world-as-it-is and motivates just action. Metz's collective vision can support spiritual development. Individuals-in-relationships grow their capacities for love not simply for their own sakes but so that groups and large communities might grow toward the goal of this good, possible future. Despite the stubbornness of systemic evil, increasing social justice is a probable outcome of becoming increasingly loving.

Jurgen Moltmann characterizes Christians, as an historical community, as a "microcosm" and anticipation of the "reconciled cosmos."[20] Our hope for a redeemed future ought to cause discontent with the present, prompting Christians to "contradict it."[21] Such "contradiction" comes through creative and liberating action in the world, thus discouraging any forms of religious escapism or wishful thinking. Moltmann affirms a kind of universal restoration for which we can hope but which ultimately remains God's gift to us, not something we bring about. Moltmann's Marxist influence is present in the urgency of action but less so in the human inability to bring about this future—a future that is not a mere culmination of history but a radical break from it. Moltmann, in a nod to God's sovereignty, credits God as the true transformer of history; human constructive activity (or praxis) in the world is more of an anticipation of this hoped-for reality than a creation of it. Moltmann's hope *can* foster creativity and responsibility. Yet it may undermine a spirituality that stresses the continuity between agents and goals and the manner in which we, as we grow, constitute the future rather than simply anticipate it. It is not clear what difference, if any, we make to God's accomplishments.

Christians ought to believe that God's activity in the world is dependent on humans who, through the power to imagine the future and possible ways of being in the present in unique and fresh ways, advance the Christian story toward its culmination. The more participatory vision of Pierre Teilhard de Chardin's theology of hope aptly supports this movement and provides a fitting theological narrative for a love-oriented, hope-based model of spiritual development.

---

19. Metz, "Future *Ex Memoria Passionis*," 131.

20. Moltmann, *Sun of Righteousness Arise!*, 69.

21. Moltmann, *Theology of Hope*, 21. Julie Clawson notes the influence Moltmann's own experience as a POW during WWII had in facilitating the development of a hopeful theology to counter the oppression and suffering he personally experienced and encountered in others (Clawson, "Imagination, Hope, and Reconciliation," 296).

Teilhard's theology is heavily influenced by his scientific studies, which give his hope a particular emphasis on growth, the progress of history, and the becoming of all things. Humans participate in the "completing of the world" through "ontogenesis"—a "vast becoming what it is" in which humans simultaneously self-create and move toward harmony with everything else.[22] God is present with, as the spark that motivates growth, the goal pulling us forward, and co-participant in the process. The goal of this process is charity (love)—the "cohesion of souls engendered by their communal convergence *in Christo Jesu*."[23] We move expectantly toward an end in which the world's "potentialities" have been fully realized and Christ is in all.[24]

Teilhard names a goal (love) toward which humans are oriented and recognizes that such becoming is communal—not a conglomerate of individual souls progressing toward their personal destinies, but increasing relatedness to one another, to God, and to the earth. The more we love, the more we participate in others and, concurrently, in God's love. Teilhard maintains that "all conscious energy is, like love (and because it is love), founded on hope."[25] Recognizing this future of emergence and unity energizes us to, through loving activity, grow the presence of God in the world here and now. This is a shared journey, as our hope is unifying and "held in common."[26] Teilhard thus affirms what many evolutionary and positive psychologists (such as Keltner) have affirmed: contrary to misconceptions about Darwinian evolution, creation does not compete but collaborates. We are most ourselves when we love.

Following Teilhard, spiritual development should not only be structured by hope but also be constituted by the continual cultivation of human relatedness to and care for others, realized through the presence of virtues. Moreover, a theology of hope that supports Snyder's hope and spiritual formation should show how human action or inaction contributes to God's future. If there is no divine significance to our human activity, our hope and sense of responsibility for ourselves and the world is undermined.[27]

Snyder's psychological hope can ground and enhance Teilhard's hope theology, elaborating on the actual shape of a future-oriented Christian life.

22. Teilhard de Chardin, *Divine Milieu*, 24.

23. Teilhard de Chardin, *Divine Milieu*, 120.

24. Teilhard de Chardin, *Divine Milieu*, 131–32.

25. Teilhard de Chardin, *Phenomenon of Man*, 232n.

26. Teilhard de Chardin, *Future of Man*, 75. Teilhard's "ethics of movement or conquest" expands the focus beyond individual morality to the individual's fulfillment "within" and "on behalf of (a) community" (Genovesi, *Expectant Creativity*, 63).

27. Genovesi, *Expectant Creativity*, 112.

Furthermore, the model I propose prioritizes the three classic theological virtues.[28] If *hope* is the dynamic process of growth toward a future, *faith* means trusting in the goodness of this future and being wholeheartedly committed to it. Finally, *love* is the content of this future, experienced with increasing fullness as we journey toward it.

Humans are hopers or, better, lover-hopers, wired to move toward a future of Love. Where I build on hope theologians is in naming that future more precisely (defining love) while also developing a richer, more concrete picture of the path toward this goal. This requires moving beyond the thematic (Christians should anticipate the future through present activity) to the particular (which virtues are needed, what do these virtues look like in practice, how do they relate to love, and whose lives are positively impacted by these virtues?).

I emphasize that humans grow into this hoped-for future by becoming it. What I do not do here is nail down with eschatological precision how the transition to the end occurs: in the midst of history, as a radical break from history, as a continuation of history, etc. My approach admittedly more closely follows Teilhard than Moltmann (or others). I diverge from those hope theologians whose vision for future-realization tends to be deontological in nature, located either in individual acts that give foretastes of this future or more substantial, orchestrated acts that seek to conform the present social reality to the eschatological future.

Rather, persons as individuals and in relationships are lured toward and *become* this future through living out a narrative of perpetual cultivation of loving character and expression of this character through loving participation in the lives of others—a life characteristic of the end. We anticipate the future by growing into it. Snyder's hope guides this becoming through helping us imaginatively and particularly envision the future, recognizing our potential to become it, and then doing the practices that will grow us (and others) into the realization of it. And while I am responsible for my loving character in a way that I am not for yours, I am nonetheless responsible for you, simply because I am human. I am not truly growing in virtue if my growth is not rippling out to others, transforming both persons and systems.

28. See Aquinas, I-IIae, Q 62.

Hope as a Conceptual Structure (and Hermeneutic)

In one sense, Snyder's hope provides a heuristic—a kind of memorable short-hand—for conceptualizing spiritual growth. Recall James Keenan's tripartite abridgement of virtue ethics: Who am I? What ought I to become? How ought I to get there?[29] It is no stretch to see Snyder's elements of agency, goals, and pathways in Keenan's summary. Such an operationalization of hope also lends itself to an operationalization of spiritual growth. Any discussion of spiritual development and formation likely considers goals (e.g., What is Christlikeness? What is our "purpose statement?"), agency (e.g. Are humans good or evil? Is our "self" hidden or being created?), or pathways (e.g., How should I pray? What actions best help the homeless?).

Such an itemization can help guide reflection on our spirituality and growth, giving some direction to the reflective process. Goal-articulation and goal-reflection warrant a kind of double-vision: a view toward both distant and immediate futures. On the one hand, a strong teleological vision is needed: one's understanding of what it means to be complete, which could come from a particular religious tradition or from one's own self-determined *telos*. For Christian spiritual formation, the questions guiding the articulation of a final goal might be: What is God calling me to be? What is my eternal future? What does Christlikeness look like? Hope theory would suggest that such questions should be answered with as much detail and imagination as possible. The more vivid one's vision of the end, the more likely this end will captivate and lure persons toward it and the more illuminated potential pathways to this goal will become.

On the other hand, the ability to set preliminary goals and recognize immediate applications is necessary as well. To integrate hope theory with the language of discipleship: I should attempt to describe the qualities of a fully-formed disciple, but I should also identify what a slightly-more-advanced disciple would look like as lived out in a particular relationship with a particular person regarding a particular issue or quality. If "patience" (a fruit of the Spirit) is one component of my final goal or imagined future self, patience with my friend John regarding his incessant tendency to interrupt me would be a good immediate goal. If "right speech" (one element of the Buddhist eightfold path) is part of my final goal, saying kind, timely words with empathy and in clear, plain speech to John about his irritating quality would be an excellent provisional goal. In both cases, immediate goals are congruous with final goals but particularized and simplified, both because of the importance

29. Keenan, "Proposing Cardinal Virtues," 711.

of "baby steps" in the spiritual journey and because spiritual growth happens with real people and real situations, not in abstraction.

This three-part breakdown can also guide our assessment of current theories of development as posited by writers of the spiritual life, presented in church mission statements, or actually lived out in practice (assuming that ideals and reality are not inherently aligned). For example, does a church have a clear sense of where it is taking people, or are clear goals lacking so that aimless movement is the norm? While a spaciousness in ends might seem to suggest inclusion and diversity positively, it can also mean that no one is challenged. If authenticity and self-acceptance are prized, people may feel loved but may not grow. If self-deprecation and "leaning on the everlasting arms" in futility at one's incapacity to enact spiritual growth is the norm, people can admire the future but this future does not transform them in the present.

Thus, the way a particular approach to spiritual development articulates what a human is and is not implicates the formative process. The "agency question" challenges models of formation concerning their beliefs about what a human is—depraved or good, neoliberal isolated individual or the nexus of multiple relationships—and to what extent persons are capable of moving toward spiritual goals. If movement is impossible, spiritual formation is futile.

Finally, the "pathways question" asks how well the prescribed practices and programs are set up to cultivate the qualities needed to realize the goal. For example, if Christlikeness is the goal, is a church's worship style geared toward making its congregants more Christlike? Thinking in terms of hope can help us assess the efficacy and value of our practices, corporate and individual.

Hope as Development and Narrative

At one level, hope is a deliberate process that moves persons toward their goals. If I am to enact spiritual growth, the steps I take toward realizing such growth are part of the hope process. Recall my earlier delineation between development and formation. Spiritual development is itself a goal-oriented process in terms of assessment but not necessarily in terms of experience. I offer this nuance to point out that spiritual growth can happen accidentally or incidentally, not necessarily as the result of a self-initiated process. I might pray to grow spirituality, but I do not seek to experience the death of a friend, even though this experience might stimulate my own spiritual growth. How

I respond to such tragedy will affect my growth but my response is only one component: I am acted upon by the event itself.

Hope clarifies our story. It gives us a narrative, providing a framework for determining whether or not spiritual growth is actually happening. A series of rhetorical questions can elucidate this point. How do I know whether I have developed spiritually if I do not know toward what I am supposed to be developing? How do I assess growth without a strong sense of the "I" that is growing? How do I measure growth without a sense of what incremental movement toward the goals looks like and in what kinds of domains growth occurs?

Without clarity of goals, agency, and pathways, it is difficult to measure growth. In a sense, there is no spiritual growth until it is named as such—until it can be shown how particular phenomena reflect the movement of an agent toward a self-transcending goal. Hope theory thus becomes a way of reading phenomena to assess whether otherwise disparate events can be unified in a narrative of growth. You might observe my interaction with another and note various features of the event: the emotions, the actions, the words, the setting, the demeanor of the two parties, and so on. Yet until the meaning-making phase, at which point the significance of this interaction and its relationship to other interactions with other people at various points of time is identified, you cannot draw strong conclusions about my spiritual growth.

Just as there is felt momentum in much great literature as a character moves toward some final outcome through success, failure, friends and foes, so spiritual growth shares this narrative shape. Spiritual development is a plot, characterized by an agent's journey toward a goal that entails the overcoming of obstacles and the right choices and actions and supportive network to rightly move toward this goal. To witness spiritual development in a person is to observe how he or she has become more like his or her ultimate spiritual goal. This movement is one of hope.

The Relationality of Hope

It would be too simplistic to critique Snyder's hope as individualistic, though its applications have been heavily focused on individual improvement. One check against this is to invite others into our hope journeys. Hopers ought to listen to their experience and that of others along the way so that single-minded pursuit of a goal does not prohibit the re-formulation of goals based on lived experience, trial and error, the limitations of our knowledge of what is best for us, and the wisdom of others.

Secondly, Snyder encourages the simultaneous setting of multiple goals as a way to maintain goal-achievement satisfaction, regardless of occasional failure. What is not clear in Snyder's vision is the extent to which he values the integration of such goals. Yet such integration is crucial. This is one consequence of my use of Snyder's hope: an ultimate goal in dialogue with several sub-goals that guide the "on the ground" diversity of personal goals set by individuals. For example, a person might pursue love as an ultimate goal, receptivity to others as a sub-goal, and a greater ease at accepting critique from three particular authority figures in his or her life—no small challenge given his or her complex childhood relationship with his or her father. Here, the goals at each "level" interact with and mutually inform one another.

Furthermore, the goals we set ought to go beyond ourselves. Hope theory can be applied not simply to self-chosen goals but to a religiously articulated goal—the goal of love. Such an overarching goal can then trickle down to and reorient the rest of the elements of the hope model: which goals are worth pursuing, what a human is and/or could be, and how our own self-cultivation relates to the lives of others and the world. Snyder has anticipated this development of his ideas, as he cautions hopers to not ignore how our goal-pursuits impact others. If such goal-pursuits benefit "only ourselves and not others, we advance the forces of unhappiness, divisiveness, fear, aggression, and destruction. If our minds are filled with hope for shared goals, however, our legacy will be a positive one."[30]

In a hope model of Christian spiritual formation, in which a shared, tradition-informed communal goal shapes the activity and priorities of collaborating persons, Snyder's hope takes on several important concerns: 1) hope recognizes that agency is not independent but interdependent—not the result of pure self-fashioning but a product of my relationships and social locations; 2) hope seeks to benefit others, where the cultivation of the self is situated in a larger project of concern for the good of others; 3) hope vacillates between concerns for *my* possible future, *your* possible future, and *our* possible future, as love invites my participation in the journeys of others, not through imposition but through responsive activity.

Summary

Hope is the dynamism of the spiritual life, where spiritual development can be seen as an unfolding plot, following an agent's journey toward a goal facing potential barriers to and aids toward that goal. Hope is the structure

30. Snyder, *Psychology of Hope*, 297–98.

of the spiritual life, in which Snyder's components—agency, pathways, and goals—form an outline that can be filled in myriad ways. Hope is a hermeneutic for "reading" the spiritual life, guiding the analysis of existing models of spiritual development. Hope is a method of self-cultivation, useful for methodically targeting particular virtues by attention to the three components of hope. Hope is also one the five virtues of love, a point on which I will elaborate in chapter 10.

Here, I have used hope in a multi-layered manner (with an additional layer yet to be explored) to reframe the spiritual life in a way more facilitative of spiritual progress, both on a macro level (What is the spiritual life?) and on a micro level (How can hope be extended from its present, documented applications to the cultivation of virtue-based spirituality?). I have also shown how hope theory relates to hope theology. I have, of course, not yet answered an important question, one to which theologians, ethicists, and psychologists have given varied answers: which virtues are worth cultivating? Which virtues are *necessary* for human flourishing— mine, yours, and ours?

This is ultimately a matter of which virtues an individual, community, or tradition deems "cardinal"—a core set of virtues that are comprehensive, complementary, and make an anthropological statement. Whatever the virtues, we need all of them. My efforts toward well-being will be hindered by "gaps" in my character, no matter how far I develop particular virtues. Character formation is comprehensive. We are not creatures of isolated parts but deeply relational beings, within ourselves and with others.

Chapter Three

Love: The Goal of the Spiritual Life

Love is the art above all other arts.[1]

—WILLIAM OF ST. THIERRY, 1085–1148

Come! Spirit of Love! Penetrate and Transform us by the action
of Your purifying life. May your constant, brooding love bring
forth in us more love and all the graces and works of love. Give
us grace to remain still under its action and may that humble
stillness be our prayer. Amen.[2]

—EVELYN UNDERHILL, 1875–1941

"IT'S SO SIMPLE! LOVE!" The angst-filled words spoken by a congregant of
the church I pastor carry layers of meaning. Her exclamation was perhaps
more affective and nonliteral, a response to witnessing an act or series of
acts of exclusion. Another layer might have been the reluctant recognition
that, in fact, it is not so simple, even though it seems like it should be.

What makes love challenging is the same thing that makes completing
a marathon an ambitious goal for a beginning runner. I may have the capacity for a marathon but without the cultivation of my capacities through all
the preparatory steps (finding the right shoes, creating a training routine,
knowing how to ice and stretch, etc.), completion of a marathon remains an
improbability. Love is a potentiality that must be cultivated.

1. William of St. Thierry, "Nature and Dignity of Love," 61.
2. Underhill, *Meditations and Prayers*, 48.

But to cultivate love, we need to imagine it, savor it, and be captivated by it. We need to know what we are talking about when we talk about love. A Christianity that proclaims some form of love as its highest ambition must base its approach to formation on this love. Growth in love must be a deliberate endeavor, not an accidental good consequence of religious activity or a weekly rallying cry from preachers that soothes but does not take root. We must also have a definition of love that is aspirational but realistic, where progress toward and success in love are measurable. While love may be big, mysterious, and in some ways beyond us, love must also be possible and within our grasp, if we are to cultivate it.

Hope theory, generally speaking, insists on clear and specific goals that are salient and energizing. A hope model of love-cultivating spiritual formation necessitates a thorough description of love. Spirituality is about transformation, not placation. Spirituality can be spacious yet specific. Precision and measurability should not overly mechanize the process and rob spiritual growth of its mystery, beauty, or mystical quality but deepen these aspects. Elaborate, technical definitions and the ability to say "Wow!" can coexist in a single spirituality.

This chapter will paint a picture of love for which I'm especially indebted to two related resources: Jesuit theologian and ethicist Edward Vacek's investigation of love and social scientist Lynn Underwood's model of compassionate love. By the end of this chapter, you will gain a much clearer sense of where a Christian ought to be headed in the transformative process of spiritual development. I hope this description of love adequately describes an end for humans that is clear and inspiring, multifaceted (to facilitate significant and diverse reflection and action) yet simple (memorable for quick recall), and coherent with a biblical, Christocentric vision of the future and of God's relationship with creation.

Love in the Christian Tradition

"'You shall love the Lord your God will all your heart, and with all your soul, and with all your mind.' This is the greatest and first commandment. And a second is like it: 'You shall love your neighbor as yourself.'"[3] Reflection on the what and how of Jesus's exhortation pervades the Christian tradition.

St. Paul spoke of the virtues of love: "love is patient . . . kind . . . not envious or boastful or arrogant or rude . . . does not insist on its own way . . . is not irritable or resentful . . . rejoices in the truth . . . bears all things,

---

3. Matt 22:37b–39 (NRSV).

believes all things, hopes all things, endures all things."[4] Origen (185–254) described a "piercing" and "wounding" love as the implanted desire within us—Eros—to return to God.[5] Augustine (354–430) envisioned a peaceful end—the "Heavenly City"—marked by "the perfectly ordered and completely harmonious fellowship in the enjoyment of God, and of each other in God."[6] Augustine anticipates a social harmony that locates love not in acts themselves but in right relations.

John Climacus (579–649) wedded love with development; when we love we "weep for the sins" of another and delight in another's "progress and . . . the gifts given" to him or her.[7] Love thus participates in others' growth, lamenting setbacks and celebrating progress in this journey. Aquinas considered love (charity) to be our friendship with God.[8] Hadewijch (thirteenth century), a Beguine and mystic, affirmed that "virtues and not sweetness are the proof of love" and recognized her human call to "partner" with love.[9] She emphasized the materiality of love: full development of the person and rich experience of the concrete rather than escape from it.

Julian of Norwich (1342–1416) believed she could only be considered "good" if she "loved God better" and also hoped for a future in which "all shall be well."[10] This future and that path to it are love, constituted by virtue "given by grace" by which we love God, ourselves, and "what God loves."[11] Francis de Sales (1567–1622) affirms that "love is the virtue of virtues. . . . we can love God more each day until the end of life."[12] Dorothy Day (1897–1980)

4. 1 Cor 13:4–7 (NRSV).

5. Origen, *Commentary on the Song of Songs*, 29. See also McGinn, *Foundations of Mysticism*, 119. The underlying Neoplatonism (seen in the language of "return") informing Origen's theology and exegesis supports my proposal in terms of movement, though its "recovery" approach diverges from my more developmental approach.

6. Augustine, *Concerning the City of God*, 878. This would have been a consoling and clarifying vision and response to anxieties following the sack of Rome in 410.

7. John Climacus, *Ladder of Divine Ascent*, 106. The *Ladder* is John's attempt to provide a layout for ascetics of the monastic life.

8. Aquinas, II-IIae, Q 23, Art 1.

9. Hadewijch, *Hadewijch*, 66, 162. Hadewijch's audience was young Beguines, whose love she nurtured.

10. Julian of Norwich, *Revelations of Divine Love*, 10, 24. Julian writes before the Reformation but following Anselm and Thomas; her reliance on reason and affect in her theology (rather than directly on Scripture) likely inform her hopeful view of the efficacy of God's love to overcome human resistance to it (and a more optimistic view of human goodness).

11. Julian of Norwich, *Revelations of Divine Love*, 84, 177. There are resonances of Gregory of Nyssa in Julian's thought.

12. De Sales, *Living Love*, 19. De Sales's affirmation of the human capacity to grow in love reflects, to an extent, his rejection of the contemporaneous theological emphasis

notes the quotidian and personalized nature of love: "Love means answering the mail that comes in . . . that person in the hospital, that person suffering a breakdown of nerves, the person lonely. . . . It means loving attention to those around us."[13] Martin Luther King Jr. (1929–68) speaks of what loving enemies entails: a willingness to forgive, a recognition of goodness in the other, and a desire to grow in "friendship and understanding."[14]

These writer-practitioners' spiritual experiences of love set the stage for the discussion of love in twentieth-century Christian ethics. Anders Nygren, a Swedish Lutheran writing in the 1930s, construed love as agape and became the point to many subsequent counterpoints (including Vacek's) on the nature of love. Agape—the "center of Christianity" for Nygren—is "unmotivated and spontaneous" and gives no consideration to the value of the object of love; agape *bestows* value on what is loved.[15] Real love—God's kind of love—is thus blind and impartial, unconcerned with my passions and wishes.

Nygren disparages human love as totally selfish. Following Luther, Nygren notes that human love "seeks its own good and prefers to receive rather than impart its good."[16] Humans can love others with a selfless kind of love, but it is never truly theirs; a Christian "is merely the tube, the channel, through which God's love flows."[17] As a celebration of God's greatness, Nygren's treatment excels. As a guide for improving human love, Nygren's vision is left wanting. It is too passive, too stifling of human agency, and too suspicious of human desire and emotion to facilitate spiritual growth.

Writing in 1972, Gene Outka defined agape, in contrast to Nygren, to include not only the self-sacrifice of the giver but also a respect for the recipient: agape is the "supreme ethical principle" and "regards others for their own sakes."[18] Outka affirmed the dignity of each person and

---

on predestination. Love is "the turning of the heart toward good with a willingness to please," writes de Sales (31).

13. Day, *Duty of Delight*, 407. While Day's ministry through the Catholic Worker movement includes acts large in scale and impact, the heart of her ministry is regularity and constancy. Her practice of the "works of mercy" is sustained by a responsive and often unflashy love.

14. King, "Loving Your Enemies," 45–46. King's context of the American civil rights movement (not to mention the Cold War) informs his sense of urgency, where recognition of interdependence and effort toward collaboration make love a necessity, not a luxury.

15. Nygren, *Agape and Eros*, 48, 77–78. Agape is "God's way to man," a nonreversible direction for Nygren (80–81).

16. Nygren, *Agape and Eros*, 725.

17. Nygren, *Agape and Eros*, 735.

18. Outka, *Agape*, 12, 278, 8.

responsibility to respect all equally.[19] An emphasis on equal regard, however, risks being idealistic but not realistic, as it tends to ignore our actual relationships and the actual, unique responses that real people and real situations might require of us.

Garth Hallett shares a similar agapic focus but diverges from Outka's equal regard. Hallet's love emphasizes self-subordination to the other while downplaying concern for oneself.[20] Hallett does not go to Nygren's extreme of total disregard for self, but does give primacy to the consideration of others, following which one's own needs can be considered (in terms of priority, not chronology).

Stephen Post, a Catholic, diverges from the self-downplaying tendencies of the agape tradition. Post (who, incidentally, has collaborated with Underwood) emphasizes the mutuality of love (rather than unidirectional selfless acts) and the link between love and self-fulfillment or happiness.[21] Agape is "an affection of the heart" that exists in relationships and should not be made into a "superficial universalism" or separated "from its communal grounding."[22] Such love is expressed through care—the ongoing meeting of others' particular needs discerned through relationship with such others rather than blindly applied principles. Post emphasizes that love often demands something of others (rather than accepting them as they are) and "seeks to elevate" those we love.[23] Love respects but also challenges and empowers.

Vacek's Participatory Love

Edward Vacek's theory of love is strikingly coherent with my other dialogue partners. Vacek's love is dynamic and forward moving (as is Snyder's hope). It prioritizes the emotions (as in positive psychology). It is teleological (as in virtue ethics). It emphasizes relationship with God (as in evangelicalism). It values authenticity and self-love balanced with a concern to alleviate suffering (as in liberal Protestantism). It emphasizes particularity over

19. Outka, *Agape*, 17.

20. Pope, "Love in Contemporary Christian Ethics," 169. Pope notes that both Outka's and Hallett's theories of love possess a strong self-other dichotomy and minimize emotions (179–80).

21. Post, *Theory of Agape*, 10.

22. Post, *Theory of Agape*, 116.

23. Post, "Purpose of Neighbor-Love," 186. Vacek shares with Post an indebtedness to Scheler and concern for love's elevating, creative qualities. Scheler affirms the hopeful nature of love: love entails a "movement, an intention, toward potential values still 'higher' than those already given and presented" (Scheler, *Nature of Sympathy*, 153–54).

universality and relationality over individualism (as in care ethics). Vacek defines love as "*an affective, affirming participation in the goodness of a being (or Being)*."[24] What does this mean?

For one, love entails a state of *"active readiness"* or *"openness."*[25] When we love we are attuned to the goodness and needs of others, welcoming of these others, ready to encounter what is good and be transformed by it, and sensitive to the unique demands of a given situation.

Secondly, *love is an "intentional movement"*—we love definite objects.[26] Instead of a universal, detached love, we love particular objects to varying degrees. There are different kinds of love (e.g., sibling love, parental love, etc.); the character and expression of our love is determined by our relationship with these various others.

Thirdly, *love involves an affective perception of higher value.*[27] Love is "directed toward the whole value of the beloved . . . all the good that it is and can be."[28] Love requires that one be forward-looking, imaginative, comfortable with epistemological limits, and increasingly capable of overcoming obstacles to good outcomes and possible futures.

Fourthly, Vacek notes that *love is about "reception of goodness"*—love changes the lover.[29] With echoes of Gregory of Nyssa, Vacek affirms that our loving movement toward another transforms us as beings capable of doing and growing in love.

Finally, *love involves an affirming response.*[30] Love aids others in their self-realization, helping them more fully experience goodness while combatting whatever destructive tendencies or obstacles would hinder this becoming.[31] Love is a "creative movement" that brings new things into existence and enables us to "cooperate with God's creative and transforming love."[32] Just as we cultivate ourselves, we participate in cultivating others—aided by

24. Vacek, *Love, Human and Divine*, 34. Vacek delineates the elements of love in parallel to the four-fold structure of emotion (though he breaks the third movement into two parts). In emotion, "the self (1) as an *openness-to-good* (2) becomes *conscious* of the value of a specific object (3) is *affected by* that valuable object, and (4) *responds* to the object's value (Vacek, *Love, Human and Divine*, 12).

25. Vacek, *Love, Human and Divine*, 41.

26. Vacek, *Love, Human and Divine*, 42–43.

27. Vacek, *Love, Human and Divine*, 44.

28. Vacek, *Love, Human and Divine*, 44.

29. Vacek, *Love, Human and Divine*, 49.

30. Vacek, *Love, Human and Divine*, 50.

31. Vacek, *Love, Human and Divine*, 55–56.

32. Vacek, *Love, Human and Divine*, 57.

careful discernment of their journey and of what our particular role in that journey might be.

While Vacek's definitions of eros, agape, and philia demonstrate continuity with rather than a dramatic departure from their traditional usage, he does distinctively develop each. Vacek advocates for the interaction and role of eros, agape, and, most importantly for Vacek, philia: "the foundation and goal of the Christian life."[33] Philia prioritizes neither others' good (like agape) nor our own (like eros) but the quality of our relationships. Following Vacek, I believe the weight of the Christian life ought to be placed not on self-sacrifice or personal fulfillment (though both have a part) but on our relationships with God and others.

Underwood's Compassionate Love

Lynn G. Underwood, a social scientist, presented her empirically based theory of love in the first book on the topic in 2008.[34] Underwood uses the term "compassionate love" to refer to that "particular kind of love that centers on the good of other."[35] At first glance this echoes Vacek's definition of agape, though her model has a participatory quality that resembles Vacek's definition of philia. Hardly a disinterested observer, Underwood aims to "discover ways to appropriately encourage the expression of this other-centered love in the world."[36]

Underwood defines compassionate love as a *"self-giving, caring love that values the other highly and has the intention of giving full life to the other."*[37] Compassionate love can be a response to suffering though it is more than empathy or compassion (which leaves room for detachment). Rather, compassionate love (echoing Vacek) is active (as opposed to merely responsive), promotes the growth of others (rather than merely relieving

---

33. Vacek, *Love, Human and Divine*, 280. However, each of these loves has a place in human life and corrects deficiencies: agape counters selfishness, eros counters an underappreciation of the self, and philia counters isolation (308–9).

34. Underwood sees her work as supplemental to Vacek's (Underwood, "Compassionate Love," 3).

35. Underwood, "Compassionate Love," 3

36. Underwood, "Compassionate Love," 3. The term "compassionate love" emerged from a meeting of the World Health Organization (WHO) as scientists grappled with how to cross-culturally measure "quality of life" (8). This evolved into a focus on love, ultimately yielding a term—collaboratively determined by diverse cultural and religious voices—that emphasized both human suffering and flourishing (9).

37. Underwood, "Compassionate Love," 4.

their distress), and depends on engagement with others (rather than being blindly given and detached).[38]

Five qualities are necessary for compassionate love to be present. First, there must be "free choice for the other," taking persons beyond instinctual actions and the deterministic influence of environmental constraints.[39] Compassionate love is conscious and deliberate (while taking seriously the limitations and possibilities of one's particularity and location).

Second, one must grasp, with some degree of accuracy, the "situation, the other, and oneself."[40] One must be self-aware and aptly recognize the particular needs of the other.

Third, one must "valu[e] the other at a fundamental level."[41] Compassionate love is not motivated by pity; it affirms the dignity of the other. It also discerns the future possibilities of the other through attentive engagement—who people are becoming or might become.

Fourth, one must demonstrate "openness and receptivity" to the transcendent or "inspired" quality of love—which might be named as divine inspiration or grace though it need not be explicitly religious.[42] The explanation for the occurrence of compassionate love—whether as experienced by giver or receiver—may be suprarational and surprising.

Finally, a *"response of the heart"* must be present, where affective engagement with the other is a necessary motivator for other-benefiting action.[43] Compassionate love is constituted by openness, affective response, respect, discerning awareness, and strong agency. A growing body of explorations and applications of compassionate love clarifies its nature and possibilities.[44]

38. Fehr, Harasymchuk, and Sprecher, "Compassionate Love," 577.

39. Underwood, "Compassionate Love," 7.

40. Underwood, "Compassionate Love," 7.

41. Underwood, "Compassionate Love," 7.

42. Underwood, "Compassionate Love," 8.

43. Underwood, "Compassionate Love," 9.

44. Susan Sprecher and Beverly Fehr have developed scales and measures for the assessment of compassionate love (Fehr and Sprecher, "Compassionate Love," 32–42). Nadine F. Marks and Jieun Song explore the intersection between compassionate love and developmental theories, postulating that compassionate love is a biopsychosocial model, given its intersection of Maslovian self-actualization, Eriksonian generativity (care for future generations), and a sociological affirmation of contextual factors (Marks and Song, "Compassionate Motivation," 121–58). Mario Mikulincer, Phillip R. Shaver, and Omri Gillath examine compassionate love through a behavioral systems lens, noting that attachment and caregiving impulses facilitate the needed security, protectiveness, support, empathy, and helpfulness to compassionately love proximate or distant others (Mikulincer, Shaver, and Gillath, "Behavioral Systems," 225–56). Lisa

The Basics of Love

What, then, is love, the kind of love that ought to be the goal of the Christian life? In a sentence, *love is receptive, ready, fitting, extravagant, and actualizing participation in others' present and potential goodness.* This definition contains no haphazardly chosen words but incorporates the significant elements of Vacek's and Underwood's work while building upon it. I will first look at the noun "participation" before examining the five preceding adjectives. This definition should also provide some clarity on the essential virtues needed to realize this love.

Love Is Participation

Love is neither the loss nor the withholding of self. It treats the other not as distant, impersonal, or valueless. Love unites you with another without losing the distinctiveness of either of you. Just as you participate in an event or group or experience, so you participate in people. People are experiences, ongoing processes of becoming and emergence. They are stories. When you participate, you enter into the story of another. Such participation changes you and changes others. In such participation we do not impose ourselves on others or shape their trajectory to be more like ours. Rather, we attend to and respect their unique qualities, motivations, and needs.

Participatory love is a way of being with others that honors your you-ness and my me-ness (rather than undervaluing you or me). Such love recognizes that the "I" that I bring to all my relationships matters. I can love you in a way no one else can—not because of my extraordinary qualities but simply because I am me. Spiritual formation should explore that particularity and recognize both the assets and liabilities we bring to our relationships. We ought to recognize what compassionate love scientists call our "substrate": the "base of individual variations in personality, biological, and developmental patterns" shaped by "cultural, historical, family, and social environments."[45] In Underwood's cyclical model of compassionate

---

A. Neff and Benjamin R. Karney define compassionate love in the context of marriage as involving an acceptance of the strengths and weaknesses of one's partner (Neff and Karney, "Compassionate Love," 201–21). I address further applications below.

45. Underwood, "Compassionate Love," 11. Following this first component (substrate), the second component of the compassionate love model is the "specific situation" and the "particular relationship" to the person being loved (12). Compassionate love places differing claims on differently situated persons; this component guides one in determining what others are due (and acting accordingly). The third component of the model is "motivation and discernment" (13). The choice to express something

love, the substrate is the starting point with which we love others—a starting point constantly impacted by the experience of loving others. Love is a self-transforming experience.

We participate in multiple objects or "experiences." For one, we love or participate in ourselves. We care for and value our own needs—mental, emotional, physical, and spiritual. We also participate in others, contributing to their story. This directs our attention to individual persons but also to the larger systemic injustices that impinge upon and inform people's moral choices. I could respond to your admission that you are feeling chilly in my home by saying, "There, there," and showing that I sympathize. I could also turn on the heat or lend you a coat or blanket. I can participate in you in a more immediate way (show sympathy) or in a more overarching manner (facilitate a better environment).

Such participatory love echoes the love of God. This kind of love assumes that God is transcendent but not impassible; God responds to and is changed by humans through God's personal involvement in history.[46] This is a crucial point because the kind of God in which we believe implicates our own way of being. A God who gives but cannot receive is too detached. A God who receives but cannot give is ineffective. But a God who loves through giving yet is moved and even changed by humans is not only the God of the Bible but also a model for a participatory love. Such a God thrusts us into the messy, chaotic, but promising worlds of others in a way that retains our individuality yet values the contribution others might make to our own becoming. Love is a mutual experience, even our love for and with God. The model for our love for others is neither a

---

or act for the good of the other considers needs, priorities, "perceived urgency," and possible actions (13–14). The fourth component and provisional culmination of the model is "actions and attitudes" (16–17). Here, the prior movement from substrate to situation to discernment results in an action. This four-part movement is completed by the presence of feedback loops, where our positive experience of loving others sustains this love. Compassionate love is dynamic: feedback and correction from others and/or internal feedback from lived experience contribute to the development of one's capacity to love, thus transforming the self (17–18).

46. Vacek, *Love, Human and Divine*, 87. See Vacek, *Love, Human and Divine*, 118–49 for Vacek's schema of the moral life, based on God's relationship with us. In short, God affirms us through sustaining and uniting with us; God allows us to make a difference to God, receiving us; we are saved through accepting God's affirmation of us (thus salvation is experienced existentially, through our emotions and lived experience, not as a declaration from without or an instantaneous event; we are increasingly saved through participatory love); we affirm God through participating in (rather than just worshipping or celebrating) God's involvement in our and others' histories; we are united with God by loving what God loves and vice versa; we cooperate with God by becoming more loving; we become co-responsible for the world.

pleasure-seeking, needy God nor a self-forgetful, condescending God but a God who wants to be our friend.

Participatory love emphasizes the uniqueness of every relationship of which we are a part. That is, we do not just love everyone equally, as though such love were a greater good. We love people particularly, in a manner appropriate to the needs they express or that we discern. We are wired to be partial; our love is a response to the good we actually experience, not a goodness we impute to others. Preferential love is simply an honest acknowledgement of and response to our relational situation. Recognizing the nature of our relationships and determining how we are obligated to others provides a clearer, more realistic path toward improving the quality of our love for others than does a generic command to "love all." This scintillating ideal is admirable but too lofty and vague to energize people toward cultivating love virtues.

Such participatory love emphasizes relationality and community in a way that counters the otherwise potentially isolating nature of agape or eros (where I can give to you or use you for my fulfillment and still, in the end, remain utterly alone). Participatory (and compassionate) love requires a responsiveness and mutuality that philia may better capture than agape or eros. When we love, we influence and are influenced. We transform and are transformed. We meet needs while finding our own needs are met. Love is a two-way street. Such reciprocity in the context of ministry to the homeless, for example, might be reflected in the desire not only to "do something good" for another or to satisfy one's need to feel charitable but to create mutuality, recognizing the bidirectional flow of "benefits" between parties. When we love, we grow *with* others.

Spiritual formation should emphasize the cultivation of the kind of qualities that will enable me to better "be" in such possible and actual relationships. While I may not be able to control whether or not a homeless person to whom I offer attentive care will actually deliberately offer him or herself to me, I can cultivate the kind of receptivity and generosity that will better equip me to create a mutual relationship with this person.

My relationship with a close friend follows the same logic: can I vividly imagine what a more loving friendship would look like and what virtues are needed to help realize this projected relationship? And what about the earth itself, both as an ecosystem and as the home to billions of humans? We are participants in the whole, a fact from which we can easily insulate ourselves. Learning how our character and actions (or inactions) ripple out to all living things can give us a vision of the kind of global participants we ought to become and the needed virtuous (and strategic) pathways that will help us get there.

Participatory love is more demanding but more rewarding than the alternatives. It is one thing to do something sacrificial for another and have the act itself be the entirety of the love-event. It is another thing to see ourselves in relationships with others in varying degrees of depth and consider both the immediate and ongoing claims these others have on us. We need the virtues of love to sustain and grow such relationships.

To become increasingly participatory, our love must become increasingly receptive, ready, fitting, extravagant, and actualizing. These five adjectives represent entry points to love or an operationalization of love that will become the basis of the five core virtues to be explored in the second half of this book.

Love Is Receptive

People who love well not only give well but also receive well. Receptivity entails openness to the other, such that your needs, situation, and personality implicate the shape of my expression of love for you. Love's receptivity celebrates the particular goodness and beauty of others. This requires a sustained habit of listening and paying attention, such that the specific actions we call "loving" are influenced and guided by the person or group we are attempting to love (rather than by predetermined, cookie-cutter notions of what is fitting). We are transformed by our receptivity to others, such that they become a part of us and we a part of them.

When we are receptive, we let ourselves be loved. We accept that we are worthy of being loved. Receptivity opens us to transformation and influence, human and divine. We are "filled" or empowered by the reality that God loves us. Accepting God's love not only feels nice but also frees us from the temptation to oppressively use others to make ourselves feel lovable and valuable. We are freed to receive others, as they are, for who they are.

Love necessitates emotional and cognitive vulnerability. It means that we let others guide us, help us, and shape us. It is neither debasing nor weak to rely on others but an admission of the way things really are: that we are who we are because of others. Moreover, love requires a receptivity to and appreciation of the goodness of others and goodness in general. Love opens us to be affected and transformed by this goodness—in others, in the world, and in our experiences.

This dimension of love invites the cultivation of a virtue of gratitude.

Love Is Ready

The self is a gift of which we are stewards. To be "ready" for love—and we are of course never fully ready—means taking care of the self. It also means we embrace and act upon our potential to cultivate virtue, since a virtuous self is an actual and potential gift to others.

Our readiness to love is dictated by a dynamic interplay between internal and external forces—both personal effort as well as the impact of our particular set of influences. Being ready to love requires that we know ourselves, our strengths and weaknesses, our triggers, and the limitations and opportunities linked with our substrate or context. We need to be deeply aware of our own needs, problematic tendencies, and various self-centered motives.

Furthermore, each of is shaped by different experiences, genes, and opportunities. Our differences in gender, religion (and denomination), wealth, region, and the various groups to which we belong are not inconsequential. We love non-generically: despite common, broadly shared qualities of love, the expression of love is perpetually unique. To ready ourselves, we have to know and value ourselves. We must *love* ourselves.

Self-love is not selfishness. Our love for self is not an evil to overcome but a responsibility to be embraced. Because we do not live our lives in a vacuum but in constant contact with others, the way we honor and nurture ourselves has positive or negative consequences for others. Love for self and love for others are inextricable. The dichotomy exists only in particular, discerned acts but not in general: love builds up and mutually reinforces both the self and other. The self is an entity to be known, nurtured, and resourced. To be *readied*.

This dimension of love invites the cultivation of a virtue of self-care.

Love Is Fitting

We are in relationship with everyone, including groups. Nobody is outside the purview of our love. Yet we are obligated to different persons in different ways. Love discerns what others are due and guides us toward the proper meeting of needs. Because love is participatory, what we owe people is more than a series of isolated good acts; there is a continuity to our obligations, usually extending over time. Love is thus caring and faithful.

Love responds to the particular value of particular things and people. For example, I would be demonstrating a weak or incomplete kind of love if I gifted you with a bottle of wine (seemingly a generous and conventional gesture) but neglected to consider your perpetual struggle with alcoholism.

Such activity is unfitting, blind, and imposing, and thus not love. Our love for others will increase when, for example, "immigrants" become particular persons with names, faces, needs, and hopes. We *can* love groups and act on their behalf but we ought not love generically. Love requires paying attention to who is before us and acting in a manner fitting to that person or group (and acting *well*).

The kind of love that ought to be the goal of the Christian life and to mark our relationships is a dialogical love that is always giving and receiving, attentively taking in the needs of the person or group and responding with relevant, timely, and fitting action. Such love is caring and compassionate. This is not a coddling kind of love that prioritizes your comfort, self-esteem, and unreserved self-expression. Love that is fitting is not permissive but combats what is destroying you (whether self-destruction or destruction from outside forces).

This dimension of love invites the cultivation of a virtue of justice.

Love Is Extravagant

Love fulfills obligations but occasionally transcends them. Love is imaginative and creative. Love inspires more love, through acts of seemingly unmerited and excessive generosity and grandeur. The more we participate in others, the more we discern not only how we can meet others' needs but also how we can delight others. Love, occasionally, goes the extra mile.

Love may fulfill existing obligations but can also create new obligations, as in the cases of conceiving a child or forming a friendship. Love is generous. Love can be foolish and lavish. While love should often feel uninhibited and indulgent, love should remain fitting and take its cues from those with whom we are in relationship. Throwing a well-attended surprise party for an introverted friend might not be as graciously received by the recipient as if thrown for an extraverted one, for example.

Love could, on one hand, guide me to not block the grocery store exit while texting on my phone; in so doing I act upon what I "owe" others in that setting according to basic social decency. Yet love could also allow for my walking an elderly man in need of assistance to his car in the pouring rain, holding an umbrella over him to protect both him and his groceries. Particular situations may demand a basic action (or non-action) but are also laden with possibility. Further, while we naturally love those whom our environment and conditioning compel us to love, we can transcend these expected obligations and inclinations. Love is expansive and boundary-transcending.

This dimension of love invites the cultivation of a virtue of kindness.

Love Is Actualizing

Love's actualizing quality enables my apt participation in another. The efficacy of my love for others depends on the overcoming of various obstacles, whether lack of passion, motivation, vision, creativity, courage, or skill. Impediments of all kinds, from life-threating danger to apathy to indecision to competing goods threaten my ability to love. An actualizing virtue (hope) is essential to realizing the fullness of my capacity for receptive, ready, fitting, and extravagant love.

Love actualizes others' goodness. It perceives the narrative of others' becoming, enters into it, and discerns how to appropriately but not overpoweringly aid another in such growth. Love sees the possible, good future of others and participates in its coming, promoting others' flourishing while collaborating with them in overcoming their particular obstacles.

Our love is continually at risk of projecting ideals on someone and even undermining a grace that loves things as they are. Yet a love that does not seek to help others "become" dishonors what others are—dynamic beings wired to grow. Growth is fundamental to the human experience. Love does not merely seek to improve others but invites others to become what they are wired to become. What exactly that is will be taken from two sources held in tension: what our religious and/or communal narratives suggest humans ought to become (e.g., a paragon of love) and the unique trajectory you are on (e.g., your unique capacity to love and the distinct relationships in which you can express such love).

The actualization of love requires not only steady commitment but also creativity and flexibility in the ways we care for others, as people and circumstances change through time. Love is a continual dialogue between fidelity and adaptability and is thus very much alive: in continuity with what has come before but flexible and responsive to new circumstances.

Love is actualizing when it is also discerning, knowing not just how to choose "the good" but how to choose between competing goods and balance our varied commitments. Discernment can also reveal our own underlying motivations, which could be obstacles to love. When such motivators as personal gain, prestige, or the hope of reciprocity are present, our efforts to love are potentially weakened. Our love may, in such cases, be a semblance of love—appearing virtuous but ultimately lacking in virtue. Love goes beyond actions to dispositions, which undergird and sustain the tangible things we do on behalf of others.

When we love, we participate in others' present and potential *goodness*. This is not to suggest that there are significant parts of others we ignore because they qualify as "badness" but, rather, to affirm that goodness is primary. Love certainly compels us into the chaos, anxiety, malice, coward-ice, and insecurity of others. Yet we are compelled because, despite these realities, we see and feel value and goodness in others—the good present in them and the good we imaginatively discern may emerge with the assis-tance of liberating, nurturing love. Weeds may hinder the growth of a flower but they are not the flower itself.

This dimension of love invites the cultivation of a virtue of hope.

Cultivating Love

This is the love for which humans ought to strive. It is also God's kind of love. God receives us; God is ready for us; God gives what is needed; God gives more than what is needed; God overcomes obstacles to this love and helps us overcome obstacles as we grow.

But what kind of love is *most important* to God? God's "unconditional love" is a source of comfort to many, a liberation from the anxiety-inducing quest for divine acceptance in favor of a steady, unwavering affirmation of each of us. But "relationship with God," a cornerstone of faith for many, is sapped of its potency if seen in overly hierarchical terms.

God seeks collaborators and friends. God seeks people who will not only appreciate God or receive God's appreciation but who will create a new, third thing: a relationship between God and person where both parties make a difference to one another. God, it might be said, wants to "get lost" in us—to experience an intimate and joyful relationship with humankind. The euphoria some Christian worshippers experience in celebrating the goodness and beauty of God might be enhanced by a consideration of the possible bi-directionality of this movement. God, too, "gets excited" about us—who we are and who we are becoming. Paradoxically, God is both satis-fied and unsatisfied with who we presently are. God's love should not stifle our growth but ignite it.

The definition of love presented here ought to be the goal of the Chris-tian spiritual life. As a goal, it functions to keep us moving forward, grow-ing, and positively impacting those with whom we are in various degrees of relationship. It risks being too abstract as a goal, however, if detached from our actual relationships. How I do know if I am growing in my receptiv-ity without people to receive? How can I tell if my love is becoming more extravagant if no one benefits from this extravagance? The best, most ener-gizing and growth-producing kinds of goals will be derived from particular relationships. It is not simply a matter of envisioning a more receptive "me," in isolation from others, but imagining what receptivity looks like in my relationship with my wife, my father, my doctor, the congregation I pastor, or homeless individuals in my city.

Because we cannot force relationships, our spiritual growth must focus on our own capacity to love. Yet we can form this capacity by more than the imagining of our individual selves loving faceless people. We ought to imagine particular people and consider how to grow the virtues that will enable fuller participation in these others, for our part.

Chapter Four

You and Me: The Self That Grows

We are, by nature, responsive, relational beings, born with a voice and into relationship, hard-wired for empathy and cooperation. . . . Our capacity for mutual understanding was—and may well be—key to our survival as a species.[1]

—CAROL GILLIGAN, 1936–PRESENT

It is costly to say our life means putting on Christ and growing to our fullness in Christ, but at least that offers us an adventure worthy of ourselves and promises a transformation that is stunning.[2]

—PAUL WADELL, 1951–PRESENT

LOVE IS THE GOAL of the spiritual life. In a hopeful approach to spiritual growth, a firm grasp of this goal is essential. Perhaps equally important is a clear understanding of our agency. What is a human? That is, who or what is the "I" that journeys toward the goal of love? Of what is a human capable? What makes a human capable of it?

How we answer these questions can help or hinder our spiritual growth. Evangelicals and mainliners may be enthusiastic about spiritual growth but handicap themselves with some theological and practical

---

1. Gilligan, *Joining the Resistance*, 3.
2. Wadell, *Friendship and the Moral Life*, 13.

limitations. An example of both in a single act might be the singing of a Christian hymn or worship song that emphasizes God's acceptance of us even though we are sinners. Some evangelicals will accept the label "sinner" and take it as permission (or encouragement) to avoid striving. Some mainliners will take "God's acceptance" as the freedom to simply be oneself, without need of personal change. While the language of sin need not be discarded, we should be cautious about how our labels inhibit movement toward the goal of love.

Christians generally affirm that humans are made in the image of God. Most basically, the *imago dei* is most fully demonstrated in our love. As God is a lover, so humans are lovers. Humans are fundamentally capable of love. Increasing fullness of humanity entails the progressive realization of love. How we think about what and who we are impacts our ability to cultivate such love. So what kind of self-understanding ought we to have as Christians? Why should we believe that such growth is possible?

A Christian love-facilitating understanding of personal agency should affirm: 1) the self is malleable; 2) the self is situated; 3) the self grows; 4) the self seeks the good; 5) the self transcends itself; 6) the self hopes; 7) the self is a story; 8) the self is relational; and 9) the self is graced. These nine self-conceptions can strengthen our agency as we attempt to cultivate love.

A Human Is Malleable

Humans can change. In fact, humans are continually changing, whether we like it or not. Theologically speaking, God's creation is not simply initial but ongoing. God may have designed and launched the human project but is also with us, now, creating (or perhaps co-creating) us as we live our lives. Transformation does not happen once but is something we should expect, welcome, and recognize as happening, right now, always.

Humans are characterized by plasticity—able to be molded by new experiences, even on a neurological level. We are not inherently stuck, set in our identity or current reality. We are always changing and always becoming. Our environment changes us. Our relationships change us. Our experiences change us. The work of neuroscientists has shown that the brain's structure can significantly change as a result of personal experience or pure mental activity.[3] This work challenges a long-standing belief that brains are fixed, incapable of wholesale change. We are not immovable but flexible, capable of forming new habits no matter our age.

3. See Davidson and Begley, *Emotional Life*, 161–65.

On the other hand, our thoughts and virtues are not disembodied enti-
ties but grounded in our bodies, suggesting we are in some sense bound to our
physical history. Our bodies themselves—not just our ideas and opinions—
are malleable. Learning to love, in regard to our brains, results in material
change. Nonetheless, the physicality of our habits is a reminder that overcoming obstacles to love may require significant work. Unlearning ingrained
habits can be arduous. Instantaneous conversion is an aberration (and even a
kind of violence). Cognitions, emotions, and bodies are interdependent. We
must care for and recognize the sacredness of our bodies in order to grow
spiritually. It is with our bodies that we love other bodies.

A Human Is Situated

While we can change, we are also situated or grounded in a particular place.
This is not to say we are unavoidably "stuck." But our starting points and social contexts do implicate our spiritual lives and movement toward love. We
are afforded both opportunities and limitations by the historical, cultural,
and social realities in which we live our lives; such realities shape our feelings, thoughts, wishes, and bodies—even our virtue. This is an important
point not only for self-understanding but also for understanding those we
love. People are complex, diverse in their needs, opportunities, and limitations; our loving participation will vary from person to person.

Humans experience different obstacles and aids to the cultivation of
love. We ought to be sensitive to the reality of such diversified experience, especially in terms of measurability of growth. For example, two people—one a
victim of neglectful, abusive parents and one the beneficiary of attentive, caring parents—both have an incentive to cultivate the virtues of love. Yet what
"successful" growth looks like for each will differ. For example, humility in
the "victim" might entail the increased capacity to trust in others and receive
their help—no small feat given a history of mistreatment. Humility for the
"beneficiary" might challenge the potential sense of entitlement or excessive
self-confidence that might come from a privileged upbringing, tendencies
that might effectively isolate and insulate such a person.

In addition to positive or negative experiences in our upbringing, what
differentiates our capacities to love might also be social pressures and norms.
For example, some research has shown women to be more empathetic and
men to demonstrate more altruistic (agapistic) love.[4] While such research
should be taken for what it is (an interpretation of data) and not become an
imposition, persons of any gender could consider whether they have been

4. See Smith, "Loving and Caring," 112–13.

conditioned to display one component of love at the expense of another. They could then target those underdeveloped qualities to more completely love in a way that is at once empathetic and altruistic. Given the opposite hazards of either a sympathetic response lacking an accompanying concrete action or a generous and sacrificial act that shows little regard for the recipient's expressed needs, a more holistic love is required that incorporates and needs both movements.

Jean Vanier suggests that "to be human is to accept history as it is and work, without fear, toward greater openness, greater understanding, and greater love of others."[5] Acceptance is about self-awareness, honesty, and recognition of and affirmation of difference; it should not be a license for powerlessness or apathy regarding moral and spiritual development. Knowledge of our history and that of others enables us to delicately and non-imposingly grow love in ourselves and others.

Yet we are not simply self-made persons. While I am personally responsible for myself, and while we might fittingly affirm God as the source of our virtue, such virtue grows in us through participation in our religious communities, in our intimate relationships, and in our varied relationships in the world. A richer understanding of our context and the forces that shape us can help us gain an increasingly clearer sense of who we are and the obstacles and aids we will face on our journey of love-centered spiritual growth.

A Human Grows and Expands

As articulated in chapter 1, we ought to think about spiritual growth as the creation of something new rather than the recovery of something lost. Recovery models of growth send us on a quest to uncover a hidden goodness beneath layers of depravity or, contrastingly, encourage us to accept that such goodness is irrevocably lost and to abandon the pursuit altogether. More developmental models recognize the formative quality of lived experience and the ongoing creation of the self. Rather than attempting to recover something great that we've lost, we ought to recognize that such "greatness" is being cultivated, nurtured by God, others, and ourselves.

Mencius (372-289 BCE), one of the early and most important Confucians, emphasized our potential to become *ren*—the ultimate and multilayered virtue that is something like love, peace, cohesion, harmony, and right order all rolled into one. Mencius felt meaning and satisfaction would only come through "becoming moral people," a process of developing our "moral

5. Vanier, *Becoming Human*, 15.

sprouts."[6] These "sprouts" and their corresponding virtues are not just excellences but a matter of power: the ability to "affect one's self, other people, even the natural world."[7] While void of a personal deity, Mencius's vision acknowledges that we are graced with the capacity for growth—by way of virtues—for the sake of the self's membership in the larger web of life.

My own Quaker tradition underscores this expansive movement of the human person. We affirm, with William Penn, that all possess the "seed of the Spirit . . . to be drawn out and nurtured."[8] Our depravity may be real but is not as fundamental as our goodness or light. The light, or seed, grows through our attention to it in "creative newness," writes Thomas Kelly.[9] Goodness, in the Quaker tradition, is not primarily located in acts or in God's occasional interventions but is fundamental to the human person, regardless of religious affiliation. Christians who recognize this goodness or light as Christ are energized toward growth and action in the world. This more mystical approach that affirms the nearness of Christ can help keep the potentially humanistic tendencies of nontheological models of cultivation grounded in spirituality and grace—in this case, a prevenient grace characterized by God's presence in all.

To draw on alternative language for growth, humans "expand." Self-expansion, a concept proposed in compassionate love literature to explain our motivation for forming relationships, is marked by two human propensities: the motivation to acquire resources to face future challenges and a unifying movement of "including others in the self."[10] Essentially, we are compelled toward others by a desire for connection and by a recognition that others can contribute to our own becoming. In the process of self-expansion, we absorb and integrate others' perspectives into our own. What we acquire from others are their perspectives and ideas. We acquire similar tastes and interests. We identify with others' joys and pains as if they were our own. And we share with others without hesitation because the dividing line between "mine" and "yours" fades as we expand. Prejudice decreases and tolerance increases as cross-group friendships are formed, compelled

6. Ivanhoe, *Confucian Moral Self-Cultivation*, 18.

7. Yearley, *Mencius and Aquinas*, 54.

8. Steere, "Introduction," 49.

9. Kelly, *Testament of Devotion*, 11. Kelly and other Quakers speak out of a tradition that has been strongly anti-establishment from its inception (in seventeenth century England), emerging out of a resistance to spiritual hierarchy and authority that insufficiently recognized the presence of God in all. Their affirmation of Christ within and of human goodness extended to Quakers's recognized justice-work, including historic efforts on behalf of slaves, women, and prisoners.

10. Brody, Wright, Aron, and McLaughlin-Volpe, "Compassionate Love," 286.

by our self-expanding impulse.[11] The more we receive others, the more we grow. The more we grow, the better off others will be.

In short, humans are wired to grow and expand: to become more than they presently are and to do so in collaboration with and dependence on others.

A Human Seeks the Good

Humans are oriented toward goodness. Sin is real, but not what is most defining about humans. There is no denying the complicated mix of goodness and wretchedness in humanity. But the defeatism of emphasizing depravity undermines spiritual growth. The truth of the *imago Dei* is that we are fundamentally good creatures. What is most defining about us is this goodness, particularly our impulse to become better, more loving persons. Sin interrupts—sometimes devastatingly—our natural impulse toward healthy and harmonious relationships.

Developmental and positive psychologists reinforce this affirmation of human goodness. Carol Gilligan, noting trends in human sciences, asserts that we are "hard-wired for empathy and cooperation."[12] Dacher Keltner, a leading scientist of emotions, argues that our emotions, brains, and genetic makeup suggest we "are wired for good," connoting both the growth of our own goodness and the capacity to "bring out the goodness in others."[13] Human evil has often been described as a breakdown in relationships or a turning in on oneself. Yet the more dominant and fundamental force in humans is the good desire to connect with others and contribute to their well-being. We are driven to love not only out of selfless concern but also out of self-care: doing good for others strengthens our relationships and thus, in turn, ourselves. Goodness is fulfilling.

Peterson and Seligman lean heavily on attachment theory to underscore how our capacity to love and be loved is essential for the survival of our species. Here, love concerns the reciprocity of safety and care between individuals, is rooted in our evolutionary history, and emphasizes the needs to survive childhood (and thus have a caretaker), to reproduce (and thus have a mate), and to continue our species (and thus take care of our young).[14] In contemporary research in evolutionary anthropology, ruthless

11. Brody, Wright, Aron, and McLaughlin-Volpe, "Compassionate Love," 301.
12. Gilligan, *Joining the Resistance*, 3.
13. Keltner, *Born to Be Good*, 4, 269.
14. Peterson and Seligman, *Character Strengths*, 304–5.

competition is trending downward. Goodness expressed through prosocial-ity and collaboration is trending upward. We are "born to be good."

A Human Is Self-Transcending

We are characterized by the ability to aspire and to be transformed by our ultimate values. We can transcend our present selves and becoming that which we are not yet. We can also transcend our agendas, concerns, and self-preoccupation and become "ever more involved in the lives of others."[15] The same impulse displayed in those characters in stories who set off on some sort of quest characterizes each of us. We want to be a part of something greater than ourselves. We want our lives to matter to others.

This propensity is essential to Sandra Schneiders's conception of spirituality itself: a movement away from "isolation and self-absorption" and toward ultimate value and, subsequently, toward others.[16] Francis de Sales maintains that "in every human soul God implanted a desire to seek the divine. . . . Our happiness depends upon recognizing and acting upon this."[17] Karl Rahner affirms that we are "oriented toward God" and recognizes Christ as the emblematic example of transcendence.[18] Vacek asserts that love is self-transcending because it frees us of "physical, bio-logical, and psychological determinisms" and allows us to "participate in beings other than [ourselves] for the other's sake."[19] We are compelled to transcend our self-absorption to participate in God and others. Spiritual formation must nurture this impulse.

Growth and self-transcendence are related but distinct. Our capacity for growth emphasizes the continuity with which we build upon the past. Our capacity for transcendence emphasizes the possibility of radically breaking from what would otherwise restrain us.

A Human Is a Hoper

Vacek's approach to the three loves affords new language with which to expand on the relationship between hope and love. Hope, as examined

---

15. Perrin, *Studying Christian Spirituality*, 146. God evokes and answers our self-transcendence (Vacek, *Love, Human and Divine*, 51).

16. Schneiders, "Theology and Spirituality," 267–68.

17. De Sales, *Living Love*, 9.

18. Rahner, *Foundations of Christian Faith*, 53.

19. Vacek, "Scheler's Phenomenology of Love," 175.

in chapter 2 and as it has been most frequently used by appropriators of Snyder's model, was heavily focused on the development of the self. I have argued that this need not be seen as a selfish pursuit, as a larger love-centric narrative can situate self-development in a way that moves it beyond self-absorption to something more like good stewardship of a gift.

If hope paired with eros concerns self-development, hope paired with agape could be seen as our involvement in another's development. Similarly, hope paired with philia would concern our ability to be involved in the realization of the higher value of relationships. Each movement has a place in spiritual development. Hope aids my becoming a better lover. Hope aids me in helping you become a better lover. Hope helps us—friends, coworkers, fellow citizens—better realize the fullness of our relationships and communities.

Hope is about humans becoming human. We are human from the start, of course, but more fully realize the possibilities of this humanity as we progress through life. The goal of our lives is love, but not a love we obtain with any kind of finality. Movement, not completion, should characterize the spiritual life. Our love-oriented movement itself consti-tutes a life well-lived. As hopers, we are, to an extent, fulfilled when we obtain love goals in the present, whether we finally eliminate our use of plastic bags or we collaboratively end the implementation of an oppressive national policy. In another sense, as hopers, humans never arrive. Fortu-nately, love is limitless. Hopers always have something for which to hope: "because God's love is without limit, and because being human means sharing in the image of God, we can never in our human loving reach the limit of our ability to love."[20]

Just as Snyder's hope allows for evolving goals, so the limitless goal of love will also change as our love grows, continually reformulated and better grasped in light of our lived experience. Our perceived *telos* (goal) ought to be vivid but not inflexible; this would indicate both a lack of humility and a misunderstanding of the way experience educates and clarifies. The life of virtue is a life of hope, where an end goal—whether understood as the future or as the timeless purpose of a thing—is in continual transformative dialogue with my growing self.

20. Bondi, *Love as God Loves*, 23. Bondi explores the theme of love in the early church (especially the fourth to sixth centuries), highlighting the pervasive emphasis on the centrality of love in the spiritual life. "Love is the *goal* of the Christian life," she suggests. "But love is not a goal in the same way that the destination of the journey is a goal. I may never fully get to love the way I would when I complete a journey to a geographical location" (33).

A Human Is a Story

We make sense of our experiences, in part, through storytelling. When we recall an interesting event, we do not just list a series of bullet-points. We present these events in a unified form, maybe even interpreting the motives of those involved and filling in the gaps as best we can. We narrativize. In the same way, humans themselves are narratives: a unified continuity of events, each building on what came before and implicating what comes next. We are shaped by our past. We are shaped by our interpretation of the past. Our past clarifies our present. Our past and present contribute to the development of our future, guiding our decisions and actions. Our future—promised or desired—shapes our present trajectory. We are stories.

A narrative understanding of the self provides a way to speak of enduring qualities (virtues), to recognize growth, and to experience progression and momentum. The Christian life should not consist of simply doing the same things, learning new rules, or living in a stifling dependency on "grace" that weakens the impetus to grow. Rather, like a character in a good book, there is an arc that takes us through various obstacles toward some end which, as we move toward it, transforms us.

In such a narrative conception, as in Snyder's model of hope, the past is recognized as a continual influence and focus of reflection. No person is a blank slate. Practically speaking, if I determine that gentleness is a virtue demanding extra attention, I need to do more than simply absorb multiple definitions of gentleness and discover gentleness-producing practices. I need to understand past instances of being harsh, rough, rude, or neglectful, and articulate the causes for such tendencies. Understanding my "subnarrative" of gentleness and the relationships involved in this subnarrative can clarify the path toward becoming gentler.

We have our own unique plot in a larger story that is distinct from others, yet our stories intersect. Like a figure in a multi-character story, I have distinctive strengths but also limitations. My journey is different from that of others, though at some level unified in a common quest. If humans are created to love and God is at work in the world to move all creation toward love, this movement is our narrative. Yet my own narrative, in light of my unique conglomeration of relationships, sociocultural setting, genetics, and even luck, will be distinct. We live a narrative of ever-increasing participation in relationship with God and others in which our combined stories do not negate our differences but enhance them.

There is no end to this narrative, no final stage of moral development or final harmonious interaction of virtues, only the continual progression of the narrative. Even if such a claim, echoing Gregory of Nyssa's *epikstasis*, must be accepted in faith, there is a practical immediacy to such a narrative view: it offers a more dynamic, energetic, restless, and relationship-enhancing approach to the spiritual life that avoids the potential complacency or impotence of an approach emphasizing a false finality. There will always be more of God and others to be experienced, valued, and nurtured. There will always be more of the story to be written.

A Human Is a Nexus of Relationships

We do not grow and live in test tubes, isolated from the world and one another. Even if there is, visually speaking, a point where I stop and you begin, we are in reality much more integrated. I am who I am because of others. Consequently, love cannot be learned in private study. Virtues cannot be acquired in unending solitude. Love needs others to help it grow. Love does not grow abstractly in our minds but through our experiences with others and the unique events that occur in our personal histories. Our agency is relationally and contextually formed.

Vacek and Underwood affirm that our agency is highly context-dependent, our love is informed by those we love, and the loving process is bi-directional or cyclical, allowing those we love to shape our own agency. Catherine Keller observes that humans are not "skin-encapsulated subjectivities, not of atoms and substances, nor of any fixed natures. . . . We are processes of relationship, members of multiple collectivities, human and non-human."[21] David Perrin argues that the human self is not "autonomously self-constituting or self-creating but molded, shaped, and reformed within the context of multiple relationships, enlivened by the Spirit of God."[22] Miroslav Volf insists that humans are "embedded in a network of multiple social and natural relationships" and that we integrate others "into our own personality structure."[23]

You influence me whether I welcome it or not; yet I can deliberately increase my receptivity to you, allowing a part of you to become a part of me. Our isolating and self-promoting tendencies, more than just making us unlikable, cut us off from the source of our life, being, and becoming—others.

21. Keller, *On the Mystery*, 106.

22. Perrin, *Studying Christian Spirituality*, 146.

23. Volf, *After Our Likeness*, 182–84. Volf's vision of personhood echoes Vacek's unity-in-difference but is more derived from Volf's theological understanding of the Trinity. Rather than sacrificing particularity in a social view or community in an individualistic one, Volf's Trinitarian anthropology affirms God's unique relationship to each person, whose dignity follows from his or her shared humanity but whose uniqueness follows from this exclusive relation to God (182).

The Confucian vision of the human person can further illustrate a more spiritually forming relational anthropology for the Christian life and deserves our extended attention as an interfaith dialogue partner.

Confucian "person making" is a process of "taking in of other selves to build a self" (this sounds a lot like Volf).[24] In the Confucian worldview, improved relationships are the mark that one is moving toward the goal of sagehood. The sage—"the profound person"—is conscientious (*zhong*) and altruistic (*shu*): his or her feelings are "in tune with the circumstances in which they are aroused" allowing for fitting responses; he or she listens well, is cognizant of personal limitations, and is flexible, open-minded, and considerate.[25]

Li is an essential Neo-Confucian concept that is often translated as "principle" but which Stephen Angle uniquely translates as "coherence"—the "valuable, intelligible way that things fit together."[26] Coherence is personal and shared: the integration of our feelings, ideas, abilities, and actions can reflect *li*, as can the presence of peaceful and mutually dignifying relationships with others. Neo-Confucians recognize *li* as a universal goal, drawing us toward it. Concurrently, my growth is a contribution to universal growth—the shared becoming of all things. Such "things" are not static but dynamic, captured in the Neo-Confucian principle of *qi* or "matter-energy." All is in flux, constantly moving and adapting. Contemporary neuroscientists take this understanding of reality for granted, even suggesting that such plasticity extends into old age. You *can* teach an old dog new tricks, because reality is vibrant and ever-changing.

Each of us is a convergence of multiple relationships. What any given person experiences of me is the conglomeration of all of these other "absent" persons. Past wounds from others can be triggered in present interactions, arguably allowing the relationship I share with another to impact the

24. Hall and Ames, *Thinking Through Confucius*, 118. This parallels Aron's self-expansion model (see above). Many Western conceptions of personhood emphasize individuality, a dichotomy between the public and private, and fear the loss of freedom that comes with an interdependent vision; in the Confucian perspective, "'sociality' is at the very root of existence" and our equality is not "abstract" but tied to our "sameness" (152–54). The philosophy of Confucius (551–470 BCE) emerged in the context of warring Chinese states struggling to gain power, an era that subsequently led to the decline of etiquette and good manners (Cen and Yu, "Traditional Chinese Philosophies," 30–31).

25. Tu, *Centrality and Commonality*, 26, 35. Tu Weiming is a twentieth-century Confucian commonly seen as representative of "third wave" or New Confucianism.

26. Angle, *Sagehood*, 32. Neo-Confucianism is marked by a return to classic wisdom and opposition to the "dominance of Buddhism and Daoism" and best represented by Zhu Xi in the Song Dynasty (960–1279 CE) and Wang Yangming in the Ming Dynasty (1368–1644 CE) (4).

relationship with the person before me. This precursory influence would extend not just to an individual (like a parent or a former romantic partner) but also to communities or social realities that have shaped me (e.g., my social class or religious community).

This is not a denial of personal responsibility. It is rather a recognition that there is no isolated "I" who encounters another but a connected "I" who brings all of my existing relationships to every new event. Confucian-inspired spiritual formation may therefore call a person to practice, for example, mindfulness (How do I carry the presence of others with me?), discernment (What particular relationship is implicating the present moment?), and fidelity (How can I manage my own negative baggage to prioritize a steady commitment to this person's needs?).

The Confucian relational vision of the self challenges a self-centered understanding of virtue as it becomes evident that the presence or lack of virtue in our lives profoundly impacts the flourishing of others, whether individuals, groups, or society at large. This vision can aid the measurability of our growth in virtue, as the (increasing) health and harmony of our relationships are indicative of virtuous growth, not to mention whatever small but significant impact we have on society at large.

Li reminds us that things function best when they fit together rightly. This could mean more attention to how what we eat affects our emotions and capacities. It could encourage us to recognize the connection between our own happiness and right relationships, encouraging expressions of forgiveness, affirmation, and a humble dependence on others in their areas of strength and our areas of weakness (or a willingness to aid others where the roles are reversed).

Societally, there is no shortage of abuses of power, laws needing revision, unrestrained greed, and tragic ignorance or indifference, all of which create substantial social disharmony. The Confucian vision of the self can encourage Christians to look for possible harmony and actualize it or find budding harmony and cultivate it.

A Human Is Graced

Grace is essential to the spiritual life as I have presented it. If there is any suspicion that such an agent-focused and initiative-dependent spirituality is graceless, it is possible that the question to which "grace" is the answer is misunderstood. For example, grace is commonly presented as the solution to the problem of sin. Humans deserve nothing from God and should be left to their own entropic trajectories. Consequently, God gives us grace, which effectively bridges a gap that enables us to be in God's good "graces" and ultimately receive eternal life.

But the problem to which my model responds is much different. The problem is that we are not as loving as we ought to be and could be. We need help growing in love. Grace is God's presence with us, aiding us in this journey. God's friendship with us is grace. God takes initiative and we take initiative in a collaborative partnership. In this interaction, we do not just receive grace—we *are* graced.

Jennifer Herdt uses the clarifying term "grace-enabled agency" to reconcile the apparent conflict of human and divine initiative. Herdt argues that grace enables but does not displace human agency.[27] Put differently, we *are* saved by grace but not overwhelmed by it, such that who we are ceases to matter. Grace should not be a license for passivity but a call (and aid) to initiative. Grace-enabled agency unites God and humans in a more intimate, transformative partnership than do some more traditional ways of understanding grace that seem to effectively stifle spiritual growth. Love requires intentionality. Love should not be a matter of "coasting" or accident, but something God grows in us through our efforts to improve at it.

In such a divine friendship, we act and are acted upon. Even our conscious imitation of Christ—something we do—can be simultaneously experienced as something being done to us. Jesus did not simply cultivate this virtue, but through his virtue opened himself to the transformative power of God and others, letting his relationships transform him. When we participate in Christ by imitating him, God participates in us and in others through us.

Yet the working of God's grace and the presence of Christlikeness transcend the Christian church. This book proposes a Christian way of conceiving the development of humans-who-are-spiritual-beings, not simply a description of how Christians uniquely develop. While conscious participation in the Christian tradition may successfully facilitate the realization of love through the cultivation and practice of virtues, it also may not. Love is love, wherever it manifests. Christians would do well to celebrate such love—if it is truly love—and not fear it.

---

27. Herdt, *Putting on Virtue*, 113–14. Herdt especially lauds the spacious approach of Erasmus—a sixteenth century Christian humanist—whose moral vision does not precisely demarcate divine and human contributions. Despite her begrudging efforts to defend Aquinas's distinction between infused and acquired virtue, Herdt opts for a simpler, less dichotomous approach. Rather than neatly distinguishing between grace and nature, Herdt prefers a "messier interpretation" of this relationship, affirming that all reality is "fallen-and-in-process-of-redemption, fallen nature shot through with grace" (Herdt, *Putting on Virtue*, 163).

Grace-enabled agency, like Vacek's articulation of the love between God and humans, gives God ontological and sequential priority. Just as our being depends on God's being, our love depends on God's initiating love. Humans did not create love but have received it: our capacity to love, our movement toward love, and the reality of love itself are gifts to us. God's affirmation of us is grace, a truth that might provide the initial spark for our spiritual growth. Yet God's continued presence with us is also grace, a presence characterized by mutuality. We are co-responsible and codependent (in the best, non-pathological sense of the word).

Without undermining our personal responsibility to act in the world, this synergistic conception suggests, in a sense, that the line between where God's action stops and ours begins is amorphous. This synergy, of course, goes beyond our individual growth and applies to our existence in the world and in relationships, as we participate in the growth and becoming of the world. In a growing, collaborative relationship with God, grace and agency are inextricable.

Summary

This chapter and the one before it have expanded on two of the necessary elements of the hopeful spiritual growth: clarity of goals and agency. I have acknowledged the Christian prioritization of love but challenged the often vague articulations of love by providing a thorough definition that is at once theologically rich, scientifically grounded, tenable in the contemporary situation, and responsive to real problems.

The problem of sin is that it separates us from the God who is Love but also, more perceptibly, from others. Virtues, antidotally, are connective and liberating. They equip us to overcome our isolation from others and our bondage to an uncultivated self—a self that is closed rather than open to others, that acts in self-preservation rather than self-giving, that cannot make space for others' needs, that is unable to notice and celebrate particularity, and that lacks the imagination needed to properly empathize, imagine a possible future for others, see the good in others, and creativity overcome obstacles.

The integrated picture of the spirituality and morality for which I am pleading is undeniably demanding. But morality should not be easy. Morality is not simply a matter of rattling off bullet points or avoiding some key, obvious vices. Cultivating virtue demands much of us. We should lovingly accept ourselves and accept the love of God yet also allow a perpetual restlessness with ourselves and our world invigorate the quest to become more loving. We ought not to shortchange ourselves and others with frivolous self-acceptance and cheap grace but collaborate with God and others in helping us more truly becoming ourselves. Our identity, after all, is a combination of who we are now and who we are becoming.

I will now turn to the pathways component of the model: the virtues. To reinforce a point, the term "pathways" should be understood spaciously. Virtues are not simply means to an end, even if they facilitate the increasing presence of that end. Virtues might lead to love but also constitute the actual expression and realization of this love. As we hope for love, we experience love. As we hope for God's kingdom, we experience God's kingdom. Virtues are the *way* to love, but also the way *to* love.

Part Two

The Virtues of the Christian Life

Chapter Five

The Path: The What, Why, and How of Virtue

> Ethicists and moralists have several tasks: to critically reflect on the contemporary situation to see whether existing anthropologies and the coordinating constellations of virtues inhibit or liberate members of our global community; to perceive new horizons of possibility; to express the possible ways that virtue can attain these horizons; and to make politically possible the actual new self-understanding and self-realization.[1]
>
> —JAMES KEENAN. 1953–PRESENT

ALASDAIR MACINTYRE DESCRIBES VIRTUES as "dispositions which will not only sustain practices and enable us to achieve the goods internal to practices, but which will also sustain us in the relevant kind of quest for the good."[2] Virtues are *dispositions*—habits, propensities, patterns of responding to situations. They are *sustaining*—the backbone of something larger, without which the something larger would be poorly realized or not realized at all. They are means to an ultimate *good* and combat potential threats to that good.

Building on MacIntyre but with particular attention to my project here, I define virtue as a *pathway to love*. To elaborate: *virtues are those qualities or habits that enable future-oriented agents to increasingly realize*

1. Keenan, "Virtue Ethics," 123–24.
2. MacIntyre, *After Virtue*, 219.

their goal of love by becoming more loving, experienced through the increasing presence of the essential dimensions of love and visible in the context of one's varied relational and social obligations.

So why the five virtues proposed in the five subsequent chapters? Models of cardinal virtues are comprehensive and conducive to quick recall. What is needed in our Christian quest toward love is a set of cardinal virtues that is complete and memorable for the sake of practice and constructive elaboration. These virtues should also enable us as practitioners to assess our spiritual growth—whether or not our love is effective and growing.

Consequently, the proposed five virtues are an operationalization of love: a dissection of love into more tangible measures or virtues that can clarify whether or not one is loving and guide a deepening spirituality—i.e., deeper participation in God's love. Whereas "love" may be a difficult phenomenon to measure, the five virtues of love more easily lend themselves to assessment, especially when further separated into sub-virtues.

Yet relationships may be the real key to measuring growth in love, acting as points of reference. Virtues, because of the relevance of each to every possible relationship, become a way to systematically assess the quality of one's love. One might assess one's relationship to a friend: Do I receive her? Am I in a healthy place to meet her needs? Am I meeting her needs? Do I occasionally go above and beyond for her? Am I capable of overcoming obstacles to loving her while also aiding her own becoming? These virtues are the best means or "areas of practice" for growing in love; they respond to the possible question, "where do I start?"

I present these virtues as pathways to love as defined in chapter 3. My choices are primarily informed by both the Christian tradition and positive psychology, often letting one or the other guide the naming of a particular virtue but in dialogue with the literature of both. For example, positive psychology most informs my understanding of "hope," though my description is incomplete without previous Christian conceptions of hope and, more importantly, the particular sub-virtues or integral virtues that I borrow from Thomas Aquinas and others to complete my description. I also tend to give contemporary research priority over classic views but do incorporate the past into the present. For example, I maintain the indispensable virtue of justice but define it in light of recent literature on care. Relatedly, I emphasize the role of self-care to, perhaps paradoxically, emphasize a recurring contemporary focus on our relationality.

The role these virtues play in love is not linear but circular. There is no starting point. For example, self-care may seem like a starting point, as being "ready" to love may feel foundational in the way that having fuel in your tank is essential if you are to drive anywhere. But the movement from readiness to actual encounters with others is multidirectional. I do not learn about myself or recognize my needs in a vacuum. My openness to others is self-illuminating. My active meeting of others' needs reveals how others might meet my needs and how I might care for myself to sustain my love for others. My impulse to treat others lavishly reveals my unique talents and resources and opportunities. My participation in others' becoming and in the fight for love highlights my own growth trajectory, clarifies my own goals, and pushes me toward greater awareness of my agency or substrate. The virtues inform and strengthen each other.

As I define love and its constitutive virtues, I am mindful of what Arthur Holder has written about definitions of spirituality: "The value of any such definition must be judged by its heuristic quality: does it stimulate research, offer insight, and raise interesting questions to be explored?"[3] I would concur and would add, in light of my project: do these virtues give an effective roadmap and create a sense of hopeful energy among Christians to increase their deliberate efforts at spiritual growth? Jonathan Wilson writes that "no account of the virtues is independent of a community and particular vision of life."[4] I will subsequently explore this point.

Methods of Cardinal Virtue Construction

Without disingenuously denying my agency, my five proposed virtues have in some sense been chosen for me: by my definition of love, my dialogue partners, and the needs (as I perceive them) of the Christian communities I have in mind. I have also observed the methods of prior virtue theorists and their articulations of essential virtues. Let's examine a few of these to more fully understand the function of virtues and how they can fit together in a coherent whole.

Plato—The Classic Four

The four "cardinal virtues"—as they have long been designated in the West—are central for Augustine and Aquinas but originated in Plato's vision of the ideal, good city: wisdom (prudence), courage (fortitude), moderation (temperance), and justice. As the ideal city is a just one, where every person—guardian, metal-worker, etc.—fulfills his or her proper function, so the virtuous person is a just one, where the "rational," "appetitive," and

3. Holder, "Introduction," 5.
4. Wilson, *Gospel Virtues*, 24.

"spirited" parts of the soul are ordered.[5] To be just or "balanced," one's prudence guides the exercise of courage and moderation. Plato is foundational for any discussion of essential virtues, though his voice is faint in this book. Plato's dualism and disdain for materiality make his vision difficult to reconcile with a model that intends to grow our loving participation in concrete, valuable, embodied relationships. Plato's model, aimed at lessening the encumbrance of the body, is instructive but antiquated.

Thomas Aquinas—Four Plus Three

Thomas retains the classic virtues (or "moral" virtues) but supplements them with three theological virtues or means to heaven—faith, hope, and love. By suggesting virtues have "parts," Thomas can include numerous other supportive or allied virtues in this scheme—a move I mimic though less systematically than Thomas. For Thomas, the goal of virtues—habits that perfect us and lead to good actions—is happiness, found in God or the "vision of the Divine Essence."[6] Unlike Plato (though echoing Aristotle), prudence takes precedence over justice for Thomas. Reason is crucial for Thomas; in a sense, moral failures result from the failure to be reasonable. As the virtue of prudence perfects practical reason, such reason guides our ability to act justly—give others what they are due—while warding off what would otherwise thwart such good actions, whether pleasurable obstacles (overcome by temperance) or dangerous or fear-producing ones (overcome by fortitude).

As obstacle-overcoming virtues, I will incorporate courage and prudence into my virtue of hope. While a similar move could be made with temperance, I will argue for this self-protective virtue as a part of self-care. For Thomas, the intellect is distinct from other parts of the soul. One effect of making hope the overarching virtue for two of Thomas's four natural virtues is to link body, emotions, and cognitions as collaborative forces in actualizing other virtues.

While Thomas believes the four cardinal virtues can be acquired, God must infuse faith, hope, and charity/love. Unlike the natural virtues, which follow the mean (as in Aristotle), theological virtues are more nuanced: while we all have natural limitations, the expression of these three virtues is in another sense limitless (you cannot have too much faith, hope, and love). Among the

---

5. Plato, *Republic*, 115–18.

6. Aquinas, I-IIae, Q 2, Art 8 and Q3, Art 8. The body, initiative, and friends help us cultivate virtue but are ultimately inadequate in attaining this end which is, in its fullness, a gift of God (Aquinas, I-IIae, Q 4, Art 6, 8, Q 5).

theological virtues, charity remains after death while faith and hope do not, having outlasted their usefulness.[7] Charity, as friendship with God, requires that we become good, as "there cannot be friendship of man to God" without such goodness.[8] This is not about meriting God's favor with good behavior but about becoming, in a sense, "compatible" with God.

Thomas posits a universal moral anthropology. He is not simply creating a theory for resolving moral dilemmas but telling the story of the Christian life and what full participation in that story entails.

Mencius—Fulfilling Social Obligations

Mencius's relational cosmology emphasizes interconnectedness in contrast to more atomistic and individualistic understandings of human persons. Consequently, Mencius's virtues and greater project of self-cultivation are more other-centered than Aquinas, concerned not only about personal excellence but about shaping one's social world. Recall Mencius's conception of "sprouts" (chapter 4): gifts from Heaven (*tian*) and potentials to be developed. Humans are defined by four sprouts—"the heart of compassion . . . disdain . . . deference . . . [and] approval and disapproval"—which are developed through four virtues: benevolence, righteousness, propriety, and wisdom, respectively.[9]

The cultivation of these virtues impinges on one's ability to fulfill relational obligations, including "serv(ing) one's parents" and "car(ing) for all within the Four Seas."[10] The tension between self and other is noteworthy. Rather than disparaging the self, as a shallow understanding of a more collectivist approach might sound to Western ears, Mencius's moral vision is rather balanced. While virtues like "propriety" (subordination to others through social rituals and manners) or "righteousness" (a proper shame for one's shortcomings) may seem to denigrate the self, they actually honor it: a functioning, well-ordered society marked by proper etiquette benefits the individual. Furthermore, self-denigration—when juxtaposed with what one knows one can be—can motivate personal improvement and ameliorate one's care for others.

---

7. Aquinas, I-IIae, Q 67. While I have little interest in speculating on more concrete details of the afterlife in this book, there is at least a conceptual difference here between Thomas and my model: whereas Thomas affirms a finality to our relationship with God, I (with Gregory of Nyssa) would retain a place for hope and the incompleteness of love.

8. Aquinas, I-IIae, Q 99, Art 2.

9. Mencius, "Mengzi," 130.

10. Mencius, "Mengzi," 130.

These virtues are collaborative and somewhat hierarchical: benevolence or active compassion (*ren*) and propriety or respect expressed through
conventions (*li*) are primary, guided by good judgments (*zhi*), and empowered by the motivation to better oneself (*yi*).[11] Like Austen (see below),
Mencius gives primacy to being properly relational in a particular social
order (though Austen's virtues are more self-advancing than Mencius). To
be moral is to integrate oneself with others, requiring benevolent attention
to others and critical attention to oneself.

Jane Austen—Ladies and Gentlemen

Jane Austen, through her novels, presents an ethic of virtue directed at the
early nineteenth-century English middle class. Austen's central virtues,
demonstrated by characters in her stories, include prudence (thoughtful
planning to protect and further self-interest); amiability (civility to all, giving each person his or her due); propriety (able to act rightly, virtuously);
and dignity (respect for self and one's autonomy).[12] In *Sense and Sensibility*,
for example, characters (politely) rebuke one another. In the midst of John
Dashwood's anxious overanalysis of Mrs. Jennings's financial situation and
pushiness toward Elinor, Elinor responds, "Indeed, brother, your anxiety
for our welfare and prosperity carries you too far," a critique that seems to
jolt and redirect John.[13] In this exchange, John fails to demonstrate all the
virtues by straying from "the mean": too much prudence and too little amiability, propriety, and dignity.

Sarah Emsley argues that the purpose of these virtues in Austen's literary world is individual happiness (an end often supported but not constituted
by marriage).[14] Austen's virtues help her characters navigate their particular
social situations to move toward this happiness. Despite contextual differences, these virtues can shed light on my proposed virtues. Amiability, for

---

11. Yearley, *Mencius and Aquinas*, 39.

12. Rodham, "Reading Jane Austen." Rodham clarifies the relevance of Austen's
virtues for the middle-class: "Unlike aristocrats, the middle-classes are not free from
material concerns, and are thoroughly dependent on the goodwill of others for success.
Unlike peasants, the bourgeoisie are not trapped by a subsistence economy, but have
the resources and time—the leisure—to reflect on who they want to be, and to make
and carry out plans for their future" (Rodham, "Reading Jane Austen"). Rodham raises
an important issue: how to define virtues clearly but spaciously so that Christians of
all socioeconomic statuses can feel empowered by the virtues and not find them either
irrelevant on one hand or an impractical luxury on the other.

13. Austen, *Sense and Sensibility*, 153–54.

14. Emsley, *Jane Austen's Philosophy*, 21–22.

example, could be at worst a kind of inauthentic and self-centered tool yet may at best aid a virtue of justice, the exercise of which underscores our varied obligations to particular people, from intimate to stranger.

James Keenan—Relational Virtues

James Keenan proposes a set of cardinal virtues to fit a contemporary Catholic context and argues that we are relational beings in general (and called to justice), specifically (and called to fidelity), uniquely (and called to self-care), who need guidance in order to navigate between these three virtues (prudence).[15]

Keenan splits humanity's general and specific obligations into two virtues (justice and fidelity, respectively) to resolve the tensions between justice and care. Contrastingly, I prefer a single virtue expressed on a continuum, where our obligations to close individuals and to groups are not different movements but more a matter of gradation and intimacy. I believe my approach enhances both ends of this spectrum, keeping, for example, a heightened concern for those marginalized by unjust structures while similarly recognizing my children are not possessions but persons whose autonomy must be acknowledged and respected.

Moreover, "fidelity"—while useful for Keenan's emphasis on Catholic marriages—seems overstated as a cardinal virtue. Fidelity—as a virtue of commitment and endurance—supports my virtue of "hope" and requires a good deal of prudence in its application, as some commitments are worth keeping and some ought to be abandoned. Furthermore, "prudence" is for Keenan what hope is for me: a future-oriented virtue and the "glue" of the virtues. I prefer hope to prudence (and Keenan might sympathize) for its more imaginative and affective qualities, especially in light of my virtue of kindness, a virtue that often appropriately thwarts prudence. Our visions of the end also differ: whereas Keenan's goal is vague ("faithful, loving Catholic"),[16] mine has been thoroughly and carefully defined. Keenan may deliberately not want a defined "goal" in his model, preferring more general categories of virtues that invite dialogue (though he might welcome my project as a cultural enfleshment).

15. Keenan, "Virtue Ethics," 126.
16. Keenan, "Virtue Ethics," 133.

Melanie Harris—The Lived Experience of a Community

Melanie Harris, a womanist theologian and ethicist, proposes cardinal virtues derived in part through a literary approach: an analysis of the experiences of women of African descent as portrayed in Alice Walker's literary work. What she calls a "womanist virtue method," following Katie Cannon, is motivated by several objectives: to "remedy the omission of African American women's experience," to facilitate justice and "optimal strategies for living," and to combat oppression.[17]

This approach indicates an "ethics from communities of the dispossessed" as a counterpoint to "dominant ethics."[18] Such a distinction helps clarify why a virtue like, for example, "frugality" is absent from womanist virtue ethics let alone any ethics emerging from the marginalized: it assumes a freedom of choice absent from such communities. I continue to be highly mindful of this diversity of experience in constructing my virtues. A virtue like "hope," for example, that so highly stresses goal-oriented activity must be sensitive to the ease with which differently privileged individuals can access resources to aid their practice of "hope."

Harris proposes seven core virtues that arise from Walker's writings: generosity, graciousness, compassion, spiritual wisdom, audacious courage, justice, and good community—all defined in relationship to black women's experience.[19] Such virtues collaboratively sustain a community navigating a world that perpetually marginalizes it, equipping the community in addressing the unjust world outside the community while facilitating flourishing within it.

17. Harris, *Gifts of Virtue*, 52–53. See also Cannon, *Black Womanist Ethics*. Cannon's method proceeds by 1) surveying black women's literature, 2) identifying themes from this literature, and 3) discerning the ethical implications of these themes to determine appropriate virtues (Harris, *Gifts of Virtue*, 55). Harris identifies Cannon's three central virtues: "invisible dignity," "silent grace," and "unshouted courage" (56). Such virtues acknowledge injustice, promote self-respect, and energize agents for social change.

18. Townes, "Womanist Ethics," 91.

19. Generosity helps individuals "stick together" in an oppressive context (Harris, *Gifts of Virtue*, 114). Graciousness allows others to "come into their voice" while subverting hierarchy and domination (115–16). Compassion is at once care for self and for others (117). Spiritual wisdom guides decision-making and helps the oppressed resist replicating the "foolishness" of their oppressors (118–19). Audacious courage is a kind of radical bravery of self-assertion (119–20). Justice concerns fairness, good judgment, and the eradication of obstacles to equality, freedom, and rights (120–21). Good community entails mutuality, accountability, and living harmoniously with all living things (121–22).

A Hybrid Approach

The above six methods inform my own. As in Plato and Thomas, the virtues collaborate with one another and correspond to capacities needing development. As in Mencius and Keenan, the virtues are relational and convey a particular community's vision of the good life for all. As in Austen and Harris, my virtues are relevant to my targeted community in a distinct way and emerge from dialogue with and observation of this community.

The following five chapters will develop the five virtuous pathways toward love and, in so doing, introduce the reader to a variety of resources that will provide a foundation for spiritual formation. I will also present a corresponding exemplar for each virtue. To be fair, it is unlikely that a person exemplary in one of these virtues is strikingly void of the others, given the way virtues collaborate and support one another in our growth in and experience of love. I also run the risk of misreading or romanticizing an individual and forcing them into my definitions. I nonetheless offer five virtuous exemplars, trusting that they can at least provide a starting point for practice and imitation while also prompting the reader to consider other possible exemplars.

My method of identifying virtues in the exemplars I investigate will be informed especially by self-characterization (how do they speak to their own virtues?), by testimonies (how are they described by others?), by attention to narrativity and practice (how might these individuals' religious narratives and practices be expected to shape character?), and by attention to written exhortations, in which case I will generously assume that what these persons call others to do emerges from lived experience and is thus likely to parallel their own character. I thus, in a sense, assume integrity rather than hypocrisy.

I hope the following chapters prompt imaginative and hopeful discussion about how to embrace and apply this theory of spiritual development in one's own life and congregation.

Chapter Six

Gratitude: The Gift of the Other .

It is a strange feeling to be so completely dependent on other
people; but at least it teaches one to be grateful, and I hope I
shall never forget that. In ordinary life we hardly realize that we
receive a great deal more than we give, and that it is only with
gratitude that life becomes rich. It is very easy to overestimate
the importance of our own achievements in comparison with
what we owe to others.[1]

—DIETRICH BONHOEFFER, 1906–1945

To be grateful is to recognize the love of God in everything He
has given us—and He has given us everything. Every breath we
draw is a gift of His love, every moment of existence is grace,
for it brings with us immense graces from Him. Gratitude
therefore takes nothing for granted, is never unresponsive, is
constantly awakening to new wonder, and to praise of the goodness of God.[2]

—THOMAS MERTON, 1915–68

GRATITUDE IS THE VIRTUOUS pathway that develops our receptivity as
lovers. It is characterized by what Anne Lamott describes as the three

1. Bonhoeffer, *Letters and Papers*, 46.
2. Merton, *Thoughts in Solitude*, 42.

72

most essential prayers: "help, thanks, wow."[3] To elaborate, gratitude entails an openness to assistance, a recognition of how the gifts of others have shaped or can shape us, and a self-transforming appreciation of what is good in itself.

In terms of the Aristotelian mean (though gratitude is absent from Aristotle's list of virtues), those with too little gratitude are entitled, presumptuous, or proud. They cannot say "thank you" and are unaware of their social formation. They act as though they are wholly self-made not only in principle but also in practice: they neither need nor want help. Oppositely, a person with too much gratitude may have an unduly low view of themselves, unable to recognize the actual and potential gift he or she is to others. In an interdependent vision in which persons are energetic forces, continually shaping one another, the realization of love depends on the ability to make space for an influx of such energy. This chapter first explores the thankful qualities of gratitude before looking more particularly at the gratitude-like virtues of humility and wonder.

Gratitude

Psychologist Robert Emmons, arguably the world's leading scientific expert on gratitude, posits that to cultivate gratitude is to "sharpen our ability to recognize and acknowledge the giftedness of life."[4] Gratitude, as a receptive virtue, opposes self-sufficiency. It magnifies the contributions others have made to our lives. As Gilbert Meilaender puts it, "To be grateful is to gladly and willingly remain needy."[5] Gratitude challenges the notion that we are self-made creatures and turns us toward the sources of the goodness in the lives.

Gratitude Sees that Everything Has a Story

Gratitude acknowledges what is before us but also recognizes the multiple components, layers, and causes behind what is before us. It looks at the food on the table and considers the people, the animals, the piece of land, the weather patterns, the road to the grocery store, the people who

3. Lamott, *Help, Thanks, Wow.*

4. Emmons, *Thanks!*, 18.

5. Meilaender, *Theory and Practice*, 164. Meilaender characterizes gratitude as an obligation but one that can be expressed in varied ways beyond simple reciprocity, allowing for great freedom in ways to fulfill this obligation.

built the road, the people who funded the building of the road, and so on. Grateful people can "stretch their attributions to incorporate the wide number of people who contribute to their well-being."[6] Gratitude need not undermine personal agency and its affirmation of our power to shape reality, though it should facilitate a more chastened view of the self-causation of our own reality.

Gratitude "remembers," posits Emmons, noting that this is in part why religious traditions can inculcate gratitude so well: their liturgies, sacraments, and rituals emphasize the collective memory of the tradition and experience with God or the Ultimate.[7] Even in our experiences of self-sufficiency, gratitude recognizes our indebtedness. I may thank God for a meal, even though God did not pay the bill nor cook the food when I was not looking. Yet gratitude recognizes all of the many factors, forces, people, and randomness that enabled the exchange of my money for that particular meal. Gratitude is thus a kind of hermeneutic for reading life: it opens us to new and deeper connection with others, to new experiences, and to new growth by looking to how I have received from others in a way that a more self-sufficient reading of life prohibits.

Gratitude Is a Relationship-Strengthening Quality

Gratitude diminishes loneliness, improves relationships, and makes us more likely to "protect and preserve these relationships."[8] Gratitude unites us with others by revealing to our consciousness how we are inherently united with others. Gratitude is enhanced the more deeply we can value the gift and the giver, and even more so if the gift is "gratuitous," going "beyond the receiver's social expectations."[9] In terms of other love-virtues, I can be grateful for justice-gifts—those benefits that emerge from steady, caring others. Yet

---

6. McCullough, Emmons, and Tsang, "Grateful Disposition," 113. McCullough, Emmons, and Tsang emphasize, drawing on attribution theory, that it is not simply externalizing attributions that makes a person grateful but the ability to recognize the contributions of others (113). Balance is important here: a person who cannot take credit but only credits others has probably exceeded the mean of gratitude.

7. Emmons, *Gratitude Works!*, ix–x. Emmons explores the central role of gratitude in Christianity and Islam, identifying this virtue as a proper response to God's grace and noting its expression in various Christian practices; yet even in non-monotheistic spiritualities, gratitude acts as a "compelling force behind acts of compassion" in response to the realities of life's "interdependence" and "mutuality" (Emmons, *Thanks!*, 92–103).

8. Emmons, *Thanks!*, 44.

9. Emmons, *Thanks!*, 38.

I can also be grateful for kindness-gifts—that which is unexpected, super-erogatory, surprising, and coming at a greater cost to the giver.

Gratitude is an embodied experience. There is a connection between gratitude and electromagnetic signals that can mutually influence one another's brain rhythms; such an exchange of energy leads to numerous benefits for both parties.[10] Psychologist Sara Algoe affirms the way in which gratitude serves the evolutionary function of relationship-building with responsive others in "reciprocally altruistic" relationships.[11] Algoe's theory emphasizes the responsiveness of the giver more than the reception of the gift. The experience of receiving a gift signals to us that others care about us and thus has a binding effect between us and our benefactors, facilitating stronger relationships.

Gratitude means noticing not only what others give us but also the potentially significant level of attentive care that may have led to the gift. Gratitude does not merely count blessings (though this is important) but highlights the positive qualities of others and therefore strengthens relationships. Grateful people receive not only "things" but also people.

Gratitude Reciprocates

Grateful people tend to be good givers. Grateful people are also less materialistic and envious, thus less encumbered by such barriers to relationships and more available to others.[12] Gratitude can facilitate a simplicity and contentment that frees people up to fill the "space" of their lives with people rather than "stuff" or the quest to acquire such "stuff." Gratitude prompts us to both repay and pay forward our gifts, thus creating a reciprocity and expansion of gift-giving beyond our initial reception of a gift. As we become aware of what has been provided for us, our awareness of the needs of others can grow.[13]

Gratitude also builds and deepens relationships by encouraging short-term self-sacrificial behavior for the sake of the long-term health of a relationship.[14] In other words, gratitude focuses on the relationship with the

10. Emmons, *Thanks!*, 88–89.

11. Algoe, "Find, Remind, and Bind," 455. In economic accounts of gratitude, repeated gifts indicate trustworthy relationships and emphasize the distributional act of the exchange; Algoe's relational account emphasizes our appraisal of others that helps us determine whether someone will be responsive to our needs over the long-term (461–62).

12. McCullough, Emmons, and Tsang, "Grateful Disposition," 120.

13. Emmons, *Thanks!*, 54–55.

14. Bartlett and DeSteno, "Gratitude and Prosocial Behavior," 324.

benefactor rather than on the gifts alone, prompting not simply debt-absolution behavior but a willingness to enhance the other and our relationship with the other, even at the expense of our immediate good or comfort. The interconnection of the virtues is reinforced: outgoing virtues like justice and kindness ought to be cultivated in tandem with a virtue of gratitude, which provides a significant emotional undergirding for these other virtues.

Gratitude Enhances Well-Being

Grateful people more easily resist "envy, resentment, greed, and bitterness"; they can better cope with daily stress, are more resilient in the face of trauma, and recover more quickly from illness.[15] Emmons and colleagues researched persons with neuromuscular diseases and noted how often overlooked gifts can be a source of gratitude and that one can choose gratitude regardless of the harshness of one's circumstances. While compassionate discernment is needed when encouraging gratitude—which should never be a mechanism by which the oppressed are pacified—those who suffer are not excluded from the benefits of gratitude.

Gratitude enhances our character and perspective, consequently increasing our well-being. Gratitude opens us to "otherness" and in so doing counters egoism; it exposes our biases, misconceptions, and unjust practices.[16] To be receptive is not to abandon my distinct self but to let the world of another influence me, exposing my shortcomings and enriching me.

Gratitude Looks on the Bright Side

Gratitude sees and celebrates the positive. Gratitude is enhanced by our appreciation of the present moment, by social comparison (recognizing we could be worse off), by awe at natural beauty, by an appreciation for what we have, and by regular rituals that remind us to be thankful.[17] Gratitude can lessen or prevent depression through focusing on what is good rather than what is stressful or disappointing, recognizing the affirming love of others, and even through directing attention away from the self (i.e., getting out of our heads).[18] Sheldon and Lyubomirsky posit that gratitude helps us savor life experiences and thus "extract the maximum possible enjoyment,"

15. Emmons, *Thanks!*, 11–12.

16. Wadell, *Friendship and the Moral Life*, 145.

17. Wood, Froh, and Geraghty, "Gratitude and Well-Being," 892.

18. Emmons, *Thanks!*, 40–41.

counters "hedonic adaption" (the tendency to take things for granted), and helps us cope by reinterpreting "problematic life experiences."[19]

Emmons identifies several obstacles to gratitude: 1) a negativity bias, manifesting in a predilection for complaining and pessimism; 2) the failure to recognize dependency and the illusion of self-sufficiency; 3) comparison thinking that focuses on what we do not have (scarcity) rather than what we do (abundance); 4) an excessive feeling of victimhood that leads to blame and resentment (here Emmons, echoing fellow positive psychologists, critiques professional psychology's excesses in this realm); and 5) busyness.[20] Positivity, interdependence, simplicity, personal responsibility, and slowness are possible antidotes to these obstacles—all facets and/or positive outcomes of a growing virtue of gratitude.

Cultivating Gratitude

People who want to cultivate gratitude might consider what Emmons and his colleagues have identified as four facets of gratitude: *intensity* (depth of feeling), *frequency* (number of times a day), *span* (number of circumstances for which one is grateful at a particular moment), and *density* (feeling grateful for multiple persons and influences for a given event or outcome).[21] Each of these elements of gratitude could be targeted in practice.

For example, you could consciously savor a good outcome, possibly with the aid of meditation (intensity). You could set a goal of responding gratefully an arbitrary number of times each day, even increasing the number over time (frequency). You could list the presently positive features of your life with a friend, your own gratitude enriched by a second perspective that expands your list (span). You could write down the story of a positive reality, considering all the people and circumstances that preceded and made possible the present reality (density).

Further practices could grow your gratitude. Write daily in a gratitude journal, effective in its regularity. Pray more elaborate prayers of gratitude beyond "thanks God" that name with as much specificity as possible the way you are experiencing that for which you are thankful. Engage a given moment with as many senses as possible (e.g., if walking outside, what do the ground and air feel like? What do you hear? What do you see?). Smile and feign thankfulness, even if you don't feel grateful, knowing that emotion and

19. Sheldon and Lyubomirsky, "How to Increase and Sustain Positive Emotion," 75.

20. Emmons, *Thanks!*, 127–40.

21. Emmons, *Gratitude Works!*, 16.

habit can follow from behavior. Let failures and disappointments and aches and pains remind you of the countless successes and steady good health you experience to counter the tendency to take your "normal" for granted.

Such practices (among others) open us up to what is there and what could be there, cultivating our receptivity to love through developing the ability to appreciate, celebrate, and be transformed by others, God, and our valuable life experiences.

Humility

Closely related to but distinct from gratitude is the virtue of humility. As Eliot Kruse and other researchers have demonstrated, gratitude and humility are mutually reinforcing in an "upward spiral": humility recognizes the goodness and contributions of others, while gratitude recognizes how that good has benefited oneself, which facilitates humility, and so on.[22] Like its parent virtue, gratitude, humility tends to downplay the self, thus setting up a healthy tension between it and the virtue of self-care (which increases the attention and valuation of self). If self-care magnifies our own strengths, humility turns us toward the strengths of others.

Humility Is Positive

Humility, perhaps in a liberating way, shifts our focus away from ourselves. Humility is not, however, expressed through a negative view of ourselves. Given the potential pathologies that could result from a low view of self, humility can help us maintain a more positive view of ourselves combined with a strong awareness of others. And the more we see others the more we can help them, less thwarted by undue attention to ourselves. Humility facilitates our care for others.

Humility is not self-disparagement. The recognition that we are fallible, weak, and even vicious is proper, but it does not follow that the self is wretched and to be denigrated. In fact, a negative self-view is itself an obstacle to others. If I cannot recognize my goodness and potential benefit to others, I shortchange those around me. Others need for me to rightly understand my limitations; they also need for me to understand my value. The self is not a worthless entity to be discarded, but a valuable entity to be shared and used for others' good.

22. Kruse, Chancellor, Ruberton, and Lyubomirsky, "Upward Spiral," 806. Research shows that humility is predictive of "ethical business practices, helping, generosity, and cooperativeness" (806).

Humility Embraces Limitations

Humility recognizes that we are incomplete. Such an admission can make salient our dependency on others and foster a receptivity to others' contributions. Humility removes the barriers to the possible contributions others can make to our own well-being. We can better express participatory love with others by truly seeing the goodness in others and the possible gift to us they can be, if we let them.

Humility also involves transferability between persons. By letting you influence me, I receive from you and you participate in me; I, then, resourced by your loving participation, extend such love to others. The receptivity of love is not limited to dyads, but is more like a network: continual input from a variety of sources coupled with continual output to others. Furthermore, I will be less able to receive someone for whom I care if I am unreceptive to, for example, the guidance of counselors, the model of exemplary peers, or the grace of God. Our goodness, our character, our love—these all depend on our recognition of the limits of our goodness, character, and love and the willingness to receive the shaping and guidance of others.

Humility Mobilizes Us to Act

Bondi highlights the needed abandoning of the "heroic ideal" among the desert fathers and mothers for a better acceptance of weakness and a simpler view of how our actions can aid others.[23] Humility can empower churches and individuals toward action, countering the potential of being so overwhelmed by the enormity of injustice in the world that we do nothing. Taking responsibility for injustice can entail small actions toward loving others—the "specific, particular individual neighbor in need."[24] This does not mean Christians should not work for policy change or more systemic reform but that we should be wary of the potential impotency of an abstract advocacy for justice that fails to practice that justice in ways proportionate to the means of individual persons and churches.

There is also a certain anxiety some might feel about acting in the absence of perfection. We may be hesitant to share our ideas or projects with others until they have reached a certain level of polish, by our own standards. Humility can relieve us of the temptation to falsify ourselves in order to appear a certain, inauthentic way to others. It can also protect from the potential excesses of the drive to be excellent (such as never speaking out

23. Bondi, *Love as God Loves*, 47.
24. Bondi, *Love as God Loves*, 48.

or never taking action). Reception of another's goodness requires that we do not allow his or her faults to overshadow his or her potential contributions. We, in the same way, should not let our actual or perceived limitations negate our own contributions.

Humility Celebrates Others

Lisa Fullam says that humility enables us to, among other things, appreciate the "moral excellences" and "gifts of others."[25] Humility is a virtue-cultivating virtue. It turns us outward as we recognize not only that we are finite but also that our ongoing emergence (and all preceding emergence) as humans and lovers is shaped by others and will be even more fully shaped by these others the more we open ourselves to formation from without. If hope is the underlying impulse that propels us forward, implicitly challenging the pride that says we are already all we need to become, then humility demands a greater appreciation for how others are contributing and can potentially contribute to our continued growth.

Humility can also encourage in individuals and communities a "process of discovery."[26] Hope keeps us dissatisfied with our present state and opens us to the future; humility opens us to the experiences of others while challenging both our present virtue and present understanding. Humility is thus essential for our love for groups, as our capacity to receive otherness—perhaps in the form of a person of another religion, or culture, or economic status—is both others-enriching and self-expanding.

Humility Is Connective

Joan Chittister calls humility "the glue of our relationships" and a foil for narcissism.[27] Humility decenters us, maintaining the value of our own story but subordinating that story to a larger web of stories. It not only helps us receive from these others in the "web" but reveals how we are connected to others and can possibly contribute to them. It counters the anxious self-obsession of narcissism that ultimately causes us to overlook, detach from, or even abuse others. Vicki Zakrzewski argues that humility makes us less likely to act aggressively, manipulate others, be dishonest, and "destroy

25. Fullam, "Humility," 251.

26. Fullam, "Humility," 271. Humility transcends our limitations and denies "that our own experience is the final word."

27. Chittister, *Wisdom Distilled*, 65.

resources" and enables us to "withstand failure and criticism."[28] Humility makes us both gentler and tougher: more respectful and careful with others and less fragile, prone to act self-protectively and defensively. Pride severs our ties with others; humility strengthens these ties.

Humility facilitates equality and mutuality. Tongeren, Davis, and Hook posit that humble people can "overcome desires for power and authority in a relationship and, instead, strive toward building pro-relational motives."[29] Humility dismantles the closed nature of domineering, controlling individuals who cannot make space for the leadership and insight of others. It also combats a sense of entitlement in relationships that can yield unfair judgments and expectations of others who continually "disappoint" our perceived standards. When you are humble, I am more likely to trust you and feel safe, knowing I will be respected rather than exploited.

Even beyond romantic relationships alone, humility is a welcoming quality that invites others into relationship with us as equals but also contributors. Others feel loved and are allowed to love us when the excessively self-justifying tendencies that humility opposes are absent. We can train ourselves to be more open to the positive influence of others and resist the arrogance of excessive autonomy or the isolation of self-sufficiency.

As an example, the Quaker spiritual practice of clearness committee is an enactment of this kind of receptivity to others. A clearness committee—a small group convened to help an individual discern a way forward or next step in some area of life—requires the subject to depend on others to see things he or she cannot see on his or her own. We get, in a sense, "used to" ourselves and often fail to notice what may be strikingly obvious to others, who can prompt, nudge, and inquire without being imposing. Quakers expect that such receptivity will allow individuals to move past initial impulses and assumptions to determine God's call. Participants in such committees who demonstrate genuine openness are often surprised by what new directions emerge through their process, regardless of what expectations they bring to the table.

Humility can also connect us to unfamiliar individuals or groups. Suspicion and prejudice and snap judgments can thwart our receptivity to others. We will sabotage our own efforts toward benevolent, compassionate action if we are not trained to recognize quick judgments (helpful mental

28. Zakrzewski, "How Humility Will Make You." Research shows humble people to be more grateful, generous, and helpful.

29. Van Tongeren, Davis, and Hook, "Social Benefits of Humility," 313. The three studies conducted by Van Tongeren, Davis, and Hook confirmed the desirability of humility in a romantic other and the ability of humility to promote forgiveness for long-term relational health.

shortcuts but not meant to be the final word), what we feel the other threatens that raises our defenses, why we attribute ulterior or harmful motives to others, and damaging assumptions we make based on poor information or fallacious attributions.

Humility Is Unafraid

Love and fear are often juxtaposed (as in 1 John 4:18), and for good reason: the fear of change or the unknown can cause retreat. A virtue of humility welcomes mystery and novelty and also recognizes the self as a continually emerging entity, constantly in need of adjusting, adapting, and revising. We may have blind spots or problematic and ingrained ways of seeing the world. Humility helps us face the fears of being perceived as inadequate or irrelevant and welcomes whatever new information might make us better, more loving people. Humility regards the potential anxiety of being exposed or finding ourselves in uncharted waters as vastly outweighed by the possibility of learning something new and possibly transformative.

Wonder

Wonder is a feeling or emotion, characterized by amazement, reverence, admiration, awe, and appreciation. Wonder should also be considered a virtue. If gratitude is a celebration of goodness and otherness as well as a capacity to let oneself be loved, then wonder can support gratitude by magnifying what is good and beautiful in others and in the world around us.

Wonder enables us to receive the love of God (and is thus an important virtue for Christian worship). Wonder discloses not only what others *deliberately* give us but also what they *inadvertently* give us—simply by being who they are. I am not primarily grateful for or in awe of my daughters because of the favors they do for me but because of the inherent value they possess—as humans in general, as unique humans, and as *my* children. I am, however, capable of receiving their goodness to varying degrees and can cultivate a capacity to more fully receive them. Wonder, as a virtue, leads to or sustains love through enabling persons to receive what is valuable with comprehension, appreciation, and reverence.

A parallel to wonder in Peterson and Seligman's taxonomy is the strength of "appreciation of beauty and excellence."[30] I also include in the virtue of wonder two other character strengths noted by Peterson and

---

30. Peterson and Seligman, *Character Strengths*, 538.

Seligman: curiosity, which reflects our "intrinsic desire for experience and knowledge"; and love of learning, in which one is exceptionally driven to acquire skills, grow one's knowledge, or learn "something completely new."[31] Gratitude, as a love virtue of receptivity, is supported by the capacity to more deeply understand and experience what is there. While it may manifest as an active quality, one ultimately *receives* the truth, goodness, or beauty of thing—a reception that transforms us.

I prefer "wonder" to the possible synonyms for this virtue for two reasons. For one, "wonder" connotes youthfulness and enchantment; it suggests we, in part, turn our attention to childhood experience to better understand and cultivate (or perhaps rediscover) this virtue. Secondly, the word "wonder" itself is used in practice in two distinct ways that can capture a continuous movement. In one sense, we wonder *what* something is and *why* it is with an inquisitive urgency. In another sense, we wonder *at* something, having grasped it cognitively or perhaps emotionally prior to or regardless of our cognitive grasp of the thing. Wonder captures the desire to know and the awestruck response to what is known.

Wonder Receives Exemplarity

Elevation, a term psychologists Algoe and Haidt borrow from Thomas Jefferson, is the emotional response to moral exemplars that produces distinct physical feelings (especially in the throat and chest) and leads to specific action: "emulation."[32] The researchers discovered that elevation (along with admiration, the emotional response to non-moral excellence that motivates goal-oriented action) motivates people to strengthen relationships with others (especially with virtuous people). Given that frequent and deep positive emotions can lead to more enduring capacities (like virtues), a practical starting point would be exposing oneself to moral excellence. One might do this by attentive face-to-face observation, research into texts, or through visual media. In addition to moral exemplars, we can also attend to "ordinary" people—those with whom we are already in relationship.

If humility opens us to others' aid, wonder opens us to their exemplarity. Study and observation of exceptionally virtuous and loving individuals can enrich the self, clarifying the possibilities of love in one's own life and

31. Peterson and Seligman, *Character Strengths*, 125, 163.

32. Algoe and Haidt, "Witnessing Excellence in Action," 106. Algoe and Haidt's studies showed that the emotional experience of elevation (produced through viewing videos of morally exemplary behavior) motivated participants to be kind and warm toward others (118–19, 125).

encouraging the discernment needed to determine what analogical imitation of such exemplars might look like. One ought to "read" such exemplars fairly, while not glossing over shortcomings. Models should stretch us and be beyond us, but not so far beyond us that imitation of their ideal becomes an impossibility. It is not necessary to idealize individuals for their exemplarity to be clarifying and empowering.

Wonder Receives Self-Expanding Information

A virtue of wonder is deepened through increasing curiosity about all of life—asking "how?," "why?," and "what does it mean?" with regularity. Kathleen Fisher describes curiosity as a "relentless inquisitiveness," "continual scrutiny," and "vigilance and attentiveness."[33] Curiosity makes us aware of barriers to receiving others, like our own biases, tendency toward "blinding subjectivity," resistance to alternative theories, and our "entrenched opinions."[34]

The unremitting inquisition of small children ("why?") should perhaps be regulated but not stifled. Children are models for the kind of posture adults ought to take toward the world around them. Despite the potential harm to self and others of an excessive desire to "know," a proper amount of curiosity or wonder can facilitate the cultivation of love. Settling for my present knowledge can close me off to the world and others. The capacity to ask "why," tiring as it may be when spoken incessantly by a four-year-old, can enable me to be more caring and generous to others as my understanding increases.

Scholar of monasticism Jean Leclercq speaks of "admiration" as a means of learning; such admiration—a parallel to wonder—"stimulates faith" and "awaken[s] the intelligence" while also "foster[ing] charity and all the other virtues."[35] The impetus to learn and understand can be abused and shortchanged if, for example, we use our knowledge to manipulate and commodify. At its best, knowledge and understanding can grow our love for God and others.

Furthermore, love's receptivity is transferable: the more I can receive the topographical beauty of a canyon or the mathematical beauty of a particular formula, the more likely I am to receive (and actively respond to) the beauty or value of you, whatever your relationship to me. Investigations of beauty and truth through mediums like literature and art are not

33. Fisher, "Curiouser and Curiouser," 33.

34. Fisher, "Curiouser and Curiouser," 33.

35. Leclercq, Love of Learning, 226.

frivolous activities (though they could be), but are integral to receptivity to the love of God. If God's ongoing and collaborative presence with us is grace, wonder and its push toward greater learning make us aware of this grace and thus better able to participate in it. Just as we inquire into particular details about another person in the process of a developing friendship, so we inquire into the details of "being" in all its forms, thus better loving God by more fully understanding how God has revealed Godself through what God has made and is making.

Wonder Receives What We Lack

Humility works in tandem with wonder, prompting us to listen better and ask better questions. How often, for example, do our projections of how *we* would feel in a given situation cause us to misunderstand another's feelings? Similarly, how often does this cause us to give inadequate and misguided counsel to others, assuming that what was appropriate for us or another person applies to a given situation? Humility reminds us of our shortsightedness, biases, and misjudgments; wonder prompts us to inquire, probe, and savor the distinctiveness of the particular others with whom we are engaged.

Wonder and humility are mutually reinforcing: the more wonder I have, the more I recognize the limitations of my knowledge and experience. As the research of Neal Krause and R. David Hayward demonstrates, religious worship facilitates humility. An increased sense of wonder toward God effectively opens up a "vast gap" between one's "perceived and ideal self."[36] Humility raises our standards for ourselves. Self-discontent displaces self-satisfaction, motivating us (assuming we do not "overdo" humility and become self-loathing) to look to others (including God) to help us move toward our religious and moral goals.

The more I recognize my limitations, the more compelled I am to look outside myself. The more humility and wonder I possess, the more I open myself to receive what others have given me, are giving me, and can potentially give me. This "giving" may be experienced as something that others deliberately distribute to me, as in the case of advice or a meal. Yet their being-what-they-are, without benevolent activity or allocation, can be a gift to me as well.

---

36. Krause and Hayward, "Religious Involvement and Humility," 256. The authors understand their study to be the first of its kind—an empirical measure of the relationship between religious involvement and the emergence of humility (263).

Wonder Says "Wow"

People with a virtue of wonder are attuned to the sacred or sublime. They notice it and delight in it. Such wonder should be directed not only at what is obviously spectacular and grandiose but also at what is ordinary. Wonder, like gratitude, challenges the temptation to take things for granted while also not simply valuing what is there but relishing it. Wonder implicates our love for others both directly and indirectly. It might be appropriate for me, in one moment, to write down all of your excellent qualities and, in another moment, to go on a "savoring walk" through a neighborhood to heighten my receptivity to present goodness, whether the spectacle of budding flowers or the reliability of a concrete path.

Dacher Keltner identifies the two components of awe—another parallel to wonder—as vastness and accommodation. We experience vastness in what is larger than the self or transcends the "self's typical frame of reference"; accommodation, the "process by which we update and change our core beliefs," completes the experience of awe.[37] Awe, observable through gestures of smallness (e.g. kneeling, bowing), produces a modesty that places us in a larger context, history, family, or community.[38] Wonder can be pleasurable, but it is so much more than that. Wonder transforms our beliefs and attitudes and, subsequently, our actions. Wonder connects us to other people, across arbitrary lines and boundaries.

Wonder can also aid justice and hope by raising our standards of goodness. When what is before does not align with what could be—such as a park littered with plastic trash bags or a remarkably talented individual littered with self-critical doubts after a minor career setback—we reject the present reality in a way that compels us to offer a just, caring response that helps what is before us become more in line with what could be. Wonder is a decidedly optimistic virtue.

---

37. Keltner, *Born to Be Good*, 255–56. Keltner gives examples of that which inspires awe: "powerful, charismatic humans," natural experiences (e.g., mountains, oceans), "astonishing artifacts" (e.g., sculptures, novelties like "the world's longest ball of string"), and grand theories (e.g., feminism, evolutionary theory) (256).

38. Keltner, *Born to Be Good*, 258–59. In addition to these modest physical gestures, Keltner measured other accompanying responses to awe in a lab, noting common responses such as goose bumps ("piloerection") and an "expansive, warm swelling in the chest" (262–63).

An Exemplar of Gratitude: D. Elton Trueblood (1900–1994)

Quaker theologian D. Elton Trueblood demonstrated many of the qualities of the receptive virtue of gratitude. Trueblood sought feedback on his ideas from congregations (and dinner guests) before committing them to publishing.[39] Trueblood's view of Scripture reflects a middle road between traditional conservatism and liberalism that enabled a valuing of Scripture but a receptivity to new insights and interpretations (a characteristic Quaker posture).

Trueblood saw the church in a similar manner: to be a wholehearted participant in a religious tradition is to humbly recognize that one's knowledge is provisional and one's practices revisable. Trueblood's vision of the church is based on receptivity to those within and without; we ought to recognize that our "fellow members have a stake in (our) own undertakings and that the normal religious unit is the group" and also be receptive to "needy men and women," lest the church become "self-congratulatory and self-regarding."[40]

Trueblood's philosophical commitment to personalism informs his gratitude, recognizing that persons are created and shaped by others.[41] Trueblood opens his autobiography by reaffirming his "fundamental indebtedness": "There have been numerous forks in the road, but at each of these there has been someone to point the way."[42] In one of his final books, *Essays in Gratitude*, Trueblood clarifies his belief about identity formation: "It is

39. Campolo, "Quiet Revolutionary" 22.

40. Trueblood, "William Penn."

41. Personalism is an "eclectic movement" that arose in response to "impersonalist modes of thought" in the eighteenth to nineteenth centuries "that were perceived as dehumanizing" (*Stanford Encyclopedia of Philosophy*, "Personalism"). While there are various strains of personalism, all varieties tend to emphasize the dignity and value of individual humans, personal responsibility and self-determination, and the need for openness to others "as a condition for one's own realization." (*Stanford Encyclopedia of Philosophy*, "Personalism"). Personalist elements pervade this book, influenced in part by the relationality of Confucianism and care ethics, the anthropological optimism of Thomism (and Quakerism), the empowering and connective goals of positive psychology, and the personalism of another research interest—Dorothy Day. Personalism also manifests in my proposed virtues: others-dependent gratitude, self-valuing self-care, particularizing justice, dignifying kindness, and self-determining hope. Though Trueblood is not that explicit about his personalism, I would argue for its influence in his life and thought—both the more idealist American strains (which also, through Edgar Sheffield Brightman, influenced Martin Luther King Jr.) and the more phenomenological and realist European expressions.

42. Trueblood, *While It Is Day*, xi.

strange that the phrase 'self-made man' should ever have gained general acceptance, since no such creature exists. . . . Each human being is constantly
being made and remade, by outside influences."[43]

Trueblood, reflecting on the blessings of old age, acknowledges the
correlation between maturity and humility, where the "wisest people are the
most humble . . . they have discovered that advancement involves the recognition of ignorance."[44] Trueblood expresses his hopes for his own virtue:
"[The] one thing which I want to put into practice in my own life is the conscious and deliberate habit of finding somebody to thank."[45] He continues:
"The person to thank may be the driver of the bus, the teller at the bank
window, the church janitor, the policeman on the beat, the mail carrier, the
clerk in the grocery store, the telephone operator, and many more."[46]

Trueblood's expressions of gratitude to friends and acquaintances
are many. He credits his effectiveness as a speaker to Rufus Jones, who
modeled thorough preparation and adaptability to changing conditions;
his core emphasis on faith expressed in love, daily life, and work to Alfred
North Whitehead; his drive for excellence and maximization of his time
and gifts to Edith Hamilton; and his abilities as a professional fundraiser
to supervisor and academic collaborator Thomas E. Jones.[47] Trueblood
acknowledges the impact places have had on the trajectory of his life, ow-
ing his work ethic to his birthplace in Warren County, Iowa, his intellect
to London, profound relationships and creative works to Lake Paupac,
Pennsylvania, and his moral formation to living for a time with a community of Shakers in Kentucky.[48] He also cites the ways that educational
institutions have formed him, including the development of his public
speaking abilities at Simpson College, his receptivity to moral and intellectual exemplars at Harvard, his career to the collaborative and intimate
education environment at Guilford, and his academic successes to arduous and edifying advising at Hopkins University.[49]

Trueblood expresses wonder at the fact of self-consciousness—"which
we often take for granted"—and how it enables us to examine ourselves and
make changes.[50] His predilection for the language of "pilgrimage" conveys

43. Trueblood, *Essays in Gratitude*, 8.

44. Trueblood, *Essays in Gratitude*, 17.

45. Trueblood, *Essays in Gratitude*, 18.

46. Trueblood, *Essays in Gratitude*, 18.

47. Trueblood, *Essays in Gratitude*, 31, 36, 41–42, 63–64.

48. Trueblood, *Essays in Gratitude*, 79–94.

49. Trueblood, *Essays in Gratitude*, 105–24.

50. Trueblood, *While It Is Day*, 36.

his openness to others, new experiences, and new understanding: "We are always on the way."[51] Trueblood even demonstrates, by profession and character, a receptivity to being in general: "The major premise of philosophy is the conviction that ours is a sacramental universe."[52] Trueblood engaged with others as sacraments, receiving others as a way to participate in goodness. Trueblood wonders at the "Christlikeness of God", signaling his relationship to God as person (rather than idea or cause).[53] This is Trueblood's personal experience but also a theological point: by welcoming and receiving the affirming, compassionate, and courageous love of Jesus, we receive God's love, incarnated in a human life.

Trueblood models, in actions and words, the receptive virtue of gratitude.

---

51. Trueblood, *While It Is Day*, 162.

52. Trueblood, *Common Ventures of Life*, 11.

53. Trueblood, *While It Is Day*, 98–103. Trueblood credits C. S. Lewis as a theological influence.

Chapter Seven

Self–Care: Ready to Participate

So the love with which a man loves himself is the form and root of friendship.[1]

—THOMAS AQUINAS, 1225–74

Self-care is never a selfish act—it is simply good stewardship of the only gift I have, the gift I was put on earth to offer others.[2]

—PARKER PALMER, 1939–PRESENT

SELF-CARE IS THE VIRTUOUS pathway that develops our readiness to love. Because I love others with a "self"—my own self—love requires I attend to my own needs and possibilities. Our selves are gifts of which we ought to see ourselves as stewards: gifts from the gracious love of God and from the forces which have shaped us—our relationships, our genetic inheritance, our sociocultural context, etc. Though we are not isolated monads but convergences of relationships, we are nonetheless more responsible for the self—the particular convergence that constitutes "me"—than for anyone else. Self-care is a respectful concern for the self we have been given—a self-inviting care, understanding, affirmation, and actualization.

Both gratitude and self-care ought to be held in tension, two separate movements encouraging us to emphasize others' contributions as well as our own. My love for others will be limited if I cannot love myself. While

1. Aquinas, II-IIae Q 25, Art 4.
2. Palmer, *Let Your Life Speak*, 31.

loving ourselves through self-care risks leading to a kind of isolating selfishness rather than connection with others, the solution is not to neglect the self but to give it due attention—not too much but not too little.

I propose four components and sub-virtues of self-care: *self-awareness, self-sustenance, self-regulation,* and *self-appropriation.* Self-awareness is the recognition and appreciation of one's unique self in regard to things like sociocultural location or personal triggers, an understanding of how these kinds of factors impinge on the present moment or relationship, and a mindfulness of one's whole self in any given moment. Self-sustenance is the steady, therapeutic strengthening of one's holistic health through the capacity to draw on a variety of available practical resources. Self-regulation is about discipline and balance. Self-appropriation[3] is the recognition of how and for whom one's unique self, gifts, and resources can be beneficial and the subsequent "deployment" of oneself. The more pronounced any of these four components in an individual or community, the more strongly present a virtue of self-care will be.

Self-Awareness

Self-care requires self-knowledge. Without a strong understanding of ourselves—our motives, biases, fears, values, past decisions, and blind spots—we risk inflicting unnecessary harm on others. Knowing ourselves can remove the barriers to love we inherently bring to our relationships. The more I understand the complex entity that is "me," the better I will be able to enter the world of others recognizing what I can offer as well as what potential damage I can do.

Awareness of My Story

Snyder's model of hope stresses knowledge of our history as a necessary means of moving toward the future.[4] We gain a broader view of our action

3. I am indebted to Bernard Lonergan for the term (self-appropriation) and base my presentation of it on his, though have somewhat adapted the concept. See Lonergan, *Method in Theology,* especially 13–17 and 83–85. See chapter 8 of this book for more on Lonergan.

4. Hauerwas also insists on self-awareness of one's personal history and tells a particularly illuminating story that underscores the point. See Hauerwas, "Character, Narrative, and Growth." Hauerwas recalls receiving a gun from his father, a traditional white American man who did not tend to verbally or physically express love. When Hauerwas arrived at his father's doorstep, his father immediately handed him a hand-crafted gun. Hauerwas, like a good pacifist, immediately and flippantly critiqued the

(and the actions of others) when we recognize how the past impinges on the present. For example, if a member of a congregation is slow to trust a newly hired pastor, the congregant might characterize his or her actions as a healthy skepticism, appealing to a principled approach to deliberate, rightly guarded, relationship-building. Yet the fact that this person grew up with unreliable, emotionally inconsistent parents should indicate that more than principled resistance is at work.

Conversely, if the pastor cannot non-anxiously allow this person to move at his or her own speed and allows the impatient desire to "win over" the skeptical congregant to become all-consuming, the pastor's attention to his or her own relational history might reveal such reactivity to be not righteous indignation but a reflection of personal brokenness. Self-care requires that we be aware of our stories and recognize how our past shapes our present experience of others, lest we be "unready" to love.

Awareness of Privilege and Bias

Self-care, through self-knowledge, means a willingness and ability to look beyond what is obvious. Consider, for example, the subtleties of racial inequality. Many white Americans who wish to participate in the lives of systemically mistreated black Americans may feel prepared to act benevolently toward blacks while failing to recognize a pervasive but often subtle reality: their own white privilege. Learning more about the benefits one receives simply by being white—and accepting responsibility for helping redirect the future—is an important step in combating racial injustice.

An even more hidden reality implicates our ability to participate in racial justice: implicit bias. Implicit bias concerns those "thoughts and feelings outside of conscious awareness and control."[5] Our implicit biases are not deliberately hidden, though we are unaware of them; we might fight discrimination and resist stereotyping but nonetheless hold negative

---

gift and typecast his father as a "gun-lover." Hauerwas recognizes his good commitment to a reasonable social policy (fewer guns is a good thing) but complete moral failure. A more fitting response that considered his "story" or relationship with his father would have expressed gratitude, a recognition of his father's care, and a commitment to caring for the gift as an act of love for his father, regardless of Hauerwas's principles. As Hauerwas reflects, it was important to take responsibility for this action as his own, rather than as "not the real me" (248). Such honest self-assessments are crucial for moral growth and effective love.

5. Project Implicit, "About," https://implicit.harvard.edu/implicit/aboutus.html. To choose from implicit bias tests focusing on matters such as race, gender, sexuality, weapons, religion, and disabilities, see https://implicit.harvard.edu/implicit/selectatest.html.

associations unconsciously.[6] Uncovering one's racial bias is an important element of racial justice. It is not meant to invite guilt-inducing labeling (e.g., "racist") but to liberate—and liberate *everyone*.

Awareness of my bias can reveal unconscious obstacles to love. Awareness of my privilege can highlight the systemic obstacles that similarly thwart the expression of love.

Awareness of Raw Data

We ought to be acutely aware—or mindful—of the present moment, experience, time, and space. What kind of space do we take up in group settings? How do our words actually affect others' moods, regardless of what we tell ourselves about the goodness of what we are saying? Are those individuals really speaking critically of you when you are not there or do your expectations anxiously compel you to believe this is the case?

Mindfulness pushes us beyond (or to a point prior to) our interpretation of our lived experience to the basic elements of that experience. We see what is there before we judge it. Self-care is deepened with the mindful, attentive capacity to distinguish the raw data of life from the self-understanding we have formulated from such data. For example, I may have adopted a self-depreciating narrative that is then reinforced when my friend tells me she cannot meet for coffee, a seemingly clear message to me that I have done something wrong (or "am" something "wrong"). An increasingly mindful person is less bound by such scripts and can continually reassess such data, leading to other possible, more generous interpretations of events (e.g., my friend may be sick).

While it is human to categorize and expect, loving well requires the capacity not to let one's schematic interpretations of experiences and horizon of expectations blind one to what another is actually saying and doing. A virtue of self-care includes an ability to stop and smell the roses, regardless of the fact that this is the thousandth time we have strolled past them. This is a crucial skill for all relationships, whether with the people closest to us or with representatives of social groups. You can better love your partner through noticing subtle shifts that might otherwise be overlooked in cases where you are "used to" someone. Similarly, you can better love a person of another race or culture if you can quickly recognize your tendency to stereotype and instead attend to his or her particularity, allowing your

6. Roberts, "Implicit Bias and Social Justice." Research has shown how such biases affect the practices of doctors, managers, and judges and decrease the warmth and welcoming behavior of white people toward black people.

generalizing tendency to guide the interaction only insofar as it enables a more compassionate response.

Awareness of Stressors

Jon Kabat-Zinn and Thich Nhat Hanh observe that we tend to react to stressors (internal and external) through a "habitual or automatic stress reaction," which tends to lead to fight-or-flight responses, helplessness, or depression.[7] Yet we can develop a "mindfulness-meditated response" as an "adaptive" or "coping strategy" that enables us to endure a stressful situation through an extended awareness that combats the tendency to react abruptly and harmfully to the trigger.[8] Mindful people are in control, able to increase their agency by combatting a reactivity that gives undue power to momentary triggers and challenges.

The needs of others and the way they express these needs will often evoke negative impulses—impulses that can be sapped of their crippling power with greater awareness. When you accusatorily ask me, "What took you so long?" self-awareness can combat, for example, the possible defensiveness that might prohibit a gracious and straightforward response that sympathizes with you and attends to your needs in this particular moment. Self-caring individuals can overcome draining internal struggles and, in a sense, see ourselves from the outside. This does not mean we do not genuinely feel emotions but that we retain a sense of command over such emotions, lest they become depleting and debilitating.

My relationships with talented colleagues comes to mind as an example of the benefits of mindfulness. It is tempting to respond to others' successes with a despair that I allow to undermine my own successes and derail my scholarly momentum while also impairing my interested, just, kind participation in their joy and growth. Yet I could notice and accept the feelings of inadequacy and 1) not be ashamed of them, 2) allow them to appropriately reframe my perspective on how successful I am while also humbling me, that I might better celebrate my strengths but not lament my limitations, 3) recognize the possible presence of similar feelings in my colleagues, and 4)

7. Kabat-Zinn and Hanh, *Full Catastrophe Living*, 335.

8. Kabat-Zinn and Hanh, *Full Catastrophe Living*, 336. See also Kabat-Zinn, "Mindfulness-Based Interventions," 145. Kabat-Zinn traces the history of mindfulness meditation from its Buddhist roots to its increasingly prominent use in clinical settings. While the use of mindfulness in psychology is appropriated from Buddhism, the Buddhist notion of the illusory self as obstacle to be overcome is not retained; mindfulness is meant to "solidify" and "strengthen" the self (Symington and Symington, "Christian Model of Mindfulness," 72).

thoughtfully consider how I might develop a habit of self-celebration to give a more positive sense of self that is more impervious to such momentary and imagined threats from others (enabling me to also more fully celebrate my colleagues' successes).

Awareness of My Need for Grace

Self-care includes what psychologist Kristen Neff calls self-compassion—the ability to extend to the self the same kind of non-judgmental, gracious acceptance we might seek to extend to those we love. Neff offers self-compassion as a superior alternative to self-esteem, which has fallen out of favor with psychologists and more easily lends itself to narcissism and discrimination, among other negative tendencies.[9] Self-esteem runs the risk of self-deception as we convince ourselves of a narrative that, in order to boost positive feelings about ourselves, often ignores what is actually there (e.g., is it really helpful in the long run to tell a child he or she can do *anything*, is the smartest, the prettiest, etc.?).

Self-compassion, in contrast, supports self-awareness in accepting who we are, as we are, without exaggeration (but also without self-depreciation). Self-compassion is non-competitive; we can view ourselves positively without viewing others negatively. Self-compassion helps us cope with our inadequacies, freeing us to be limited. Self-compassion also weakens the power of these limitations that often lead to excessive self-criticism, such that our strengths more naturally rise to the forefront and inform our self-definition while clarifying what we can offer others.

Awareness of Opportunities

Self-awareness may also mean a recognition (and possibly an appreciation) of the possibilities and limitations of one's unique sociocultural vantage point and voice. To build upon a prior example: the economically or culturally privileged may be lulled by the comfort of their relative stability in a way that blinds them to the suffering of others and how their lifestyle as a whole might demonstrate a lack of love for less privileged persons.

Intersectionality—a theory and method whose goal is social justice and whose path is the analysis of how race, class, gender, and sexuality collaboratively shape identity—can help persons understand not only others but also themselves, whether this identity ostensibly tends toward "victim"

9. Neff, *Self-Compassion*, 8.

or "perpetrator" of injustice. Christians who seek to act benevolently on behalf of oppressed groups will shortchange their justice work without a more self-reflective approach. We ought to be "critically reflective about [our] own social location [and] about the dialectic of dominance and oppression that shapes the matrix of [our lives]."[10]

Such awareness can be empowering. While only a disrespectful and irresponsible theology would suggest that God wills the perpetual suffering of anyone, it is possible to consider our social location a "gift" and an opportunity. Discovering "who we are" extends beyond the recognition of our unique talents and desires to also include our social identity. Despite the implicit and often explicit message to the contrary of a culture privileging economically stable straight white males, one's perspective and voice as a non-rich, non-straight, non-white, non-male individual—or any combination of these identities—matters. Love has a better shot at growing when individuals understand and embrace their identities—insofar as this self-acceptance leads to greater justice for all rather than maintenance of an unjust status quo.

Self-Sustenance

Self-care requires upkeep. Vacek pragmatically notes that "we will not long be able to love others unless we get enough food, sleep, and recreation."[11] With all due respect to those in overwhelming or constant pain, we ought to, as a rule, see our bodies as gifts from God to be loved, not burdens to be endured or overcome. Those with a virtue of self-care listen to their bodies, taking seriously the subtle and overt cues our bodies give us when they have a need. Loving others requires energy. Such energy can be depleted, just as a car that does not receive regular maintenance or runs out of fuel will not get you from point A to point B.

Sustained by Practices

Self-care benefits from having a wide range of possible activities to choose from so that options are always available (e.g., having more options than outdoor jogging or watching amusing Youtube videos, in case inclement

10. Ramsay, "Intersectionality," 466.

11. Vacek, *Love, Human and Divine*, 268. "The sequence of things we do for ourselves for the sake of others can be quite long and indirect: we brush our teeth so that we will not get cavities and have to go to the dentist, which would mean a loss of money and time that could be better devoted to those who are more needy" (268).

weather or erratic internet prohibit these options, respectively). Psychologist Barbara Markway suggests seven pathways to self-care: *sensory* activities, such as attending to breathing or getting a massage; *pleasure* activities, such as gardening or art; *mental* activities, such as taking some small action on a daunting task or reading about a new topic; *spiritual* activities, like praying or spending time in nature; *emotional* activities, such as writing down feelings or laughing; *physical* activities like stretching or napping; and *social* activities, like calling a friend or joining a support group.[12]

Roy Oswald cites further examples of self-care practices, including: spiritual disciplines like journaling, spiritual direction, and meditation; "letting-go" techniques like autogenic training (attentiveness to subtleties of body) and hatha yoga (body movement); deliberate and varied forms of "breaks"; well-developed support systems; regular exercise and an informed understanding of the effects of various unhealthy foods on our bodies; therapy; "assertiveness training," which increases our valuing of and willingness to fight for our needs (without unjustly harming others); laughter; and detachment through hobbies and activities.[13] Self-caring individuals not only have regular healthy habits that endure regardless of crises, but also can discerningly choose an appropriate action from their self-care "tool belt."

Sustained by Valuing the Self

When I speak with Christians of the importance of self-care as a pathway to loving others, my words are often met with a sense of relief. Many Christians have been conditioned to have varying degrees of resistance to the concept of self-care. It is in some ways in conflict with two values many American Christians hold: self-sacrificial love and "hard work." I have already presented an alternative to love as self-sacrifice: self-*giving*.

As for hard work, one's productivity in any domain can only be aided by proper care for the self. Running yourself into the ground will make you, in a sense, useless to others. The opposite of self-care is not hard work but costly self-neglect. This is true for anyone, rich or poor, though the pressures faced by low-income individuals and families may suggest a failure of virtue, but not by these individuals and families. It may be the responsibility of the privileged to ensure self-sustenance is even an option on the table for those struggling to make ends meet. This may be a matter of justice (next chapter): ensuring that self-care is not an elitist pursuit but a practice (and virtue) accessible to all.

12. Markway, "Seven Types of Self-Care."
13. Oswald, *Clergy Self-Care*, 91–188.

Dr. Alice Domar, particularly sympathetic to the pressures and needs of women, though certainly not inattentive to those of men, maintains that self-care requires more than essential but potentially superficial techniques and exercises. Self-care demands a deeper awareness of our personal narratives, especially the presence of guilt and low self-esteem. It requires a "commitment to ourselves rooted in compassion."[14]

Self-care is an overarching posture toward the self that is gracious and nurturing. We can be nurturing toward our bodies (e.g., "progressive muscle relaxation"), our minds (e.g., "cognitive restructuring" to gain kinder and more realistic self-assessment), our emotions (including emotional awareness, expression, and communication), and our spirits (to increase one's sense of agency and peace).[15] We ought to recognize the self as sacred. We are growing, storied beings inviting nurture and development and *worthy* of nurture and development. The self-giving that ought to characterize Christian love requires a self-nurturance that affirms that God loves us not because God is ontologically bound to do so, but because humans are lovable.

Sustained by De-stressing

Stress management is a key element of good self-care. We ought to be aware of what causes us stress, symptoms of stress, and the negative consequences of being overly stressed for ourselves and others. We may have reached what Oswald calls our "stress threshold" when we demonstrate a decreased perception of what is happening around us, an inability to see options and alternatives, "regression to infantile behavior," difficulty withstanding or rectifying toxic relationships, exhaustion, irritability or even depression, and physical illness.[16] Barbara Markway notes how stress often hinders self-care before anything else; we often neglect ourselves when under pressure and overly fixate on problem-solving at the expense of our health.[17] A virtue

14. Domar, *Self-Nurture*, 6, 25. Domar is the director of the Mind/Body Center for Women's Health at Harvard Medical School. Domar utilizes "mind-body medicine"— "any method in which the mind is mobilized in the treatment of a physical order" (5). Her overarching, unifying principle is "self-nurture," which incorporates relaxation techniques, emotional expression, cognitive therapy, communication skills, and spiritual practices.

15. Domar, *Self-Nurture*, 26–27.

16. Oswald, *Clergy Self-Care*, 44–46. Oswald presents and promotes self-care particularly for clergy, though his conclusions and prescriptions extend beyond his scope and are relevant to any person in any role.

17. Markway, "Seven Types of Self-Care."

of self-care is more robust when we can endure stressful periods and resist the temptation to abandon healthy habits when crises arise.

Giving ourselves "breaks" is also crucial to self-care. Our routines are important and can ensure we are highly productive, yet those routines should occasionally be broken. Whether through the practice of Sabbath or the commitment to taking walk breaks after hours of looking at a computer screen, the ability to step out of "work mode" and slow one's mind is an important element of self-care.

Sustained through Relationships and Boundaries

Limiting our availability to others is also crucial. This can be a self-protective act that brings more good to others in the long run. Saying "no" from time to time is not a selfish act of neglecting our responsibility but a way of increasing the likelihood we are our best selves, prepared to fulfill our responsibilities well.

Those with a virtue of self-care strike the right balance between independence and dependence. Just as it as crucial to set relational boundaries, so our path to love is aided by the presence of a supportive network. Self-caring individuals are good at enlisting others, discerning who to reach out to and when to reach out to them for guidance, whether mentors or friends or acquaintances prepared to offer assistance in some particular way. This includes the presence of a spiritual director or trusted friend who can allow space for us to vent so as to relieve distress and address our obstacles in an honest, non-judgmental way. Thus, self-care may be a self-prioritizing pathway but it is not a constant and perpetual retreat into isolation.

Self-Regulation

A strong virtue of self-care includes command of one's emotions and desires. Self-caring individuals can self-regulate: they can follow the mean (not too much, not too little) in various practices while avoiding the extremes of self-indulgence or self-denial. They are balanced.

Between Present and Future

Self-regulation can be future-oriented, as Mischel's studies in delayed gratification and children show (i.e., the "marshmallow experiment").[18]

18. See Mischel, *Marshmallow Test*. Mischel argues that self-control not only aids

Self-regulation takes a long view of the self, considering how our present actions will impact our future. In ethical terms, this is one of the rare
consequentialist elements of virtue ethics: what effect will this have on the
future of this virtue and thus, my capacity to love? If I become sloppy and
neglect to put my things fully away in their proper drawers, closets, and
nightstands at home, how might this lead—regardless of seemingly momentary triviality—to a more substantial habit of negligence (not return-
ing calls, not listening to details, not paying bills on time)? Virtue ethics is a
comprehensive ethic; it considers even the most basic experiences of daily
life as potential shapers of my developing self and thus the extent to which
I can lovingly participate in others.

Between Too Much and Too Little

Self-regulation is the "sweet spot" between self-indulgence and self-neglect.
Self-indulgence might lead me, for example, to eat excessively or to take
excessive credit for a friend's success. In this case, my gluttony may cause
physical discomfort (and show a lack of appreciation for the food). My need
to be appreciated may cause obsession and negatively shape my behavior
toward others. At the other extreme, self-neglect would be damaging, as I
deserve and need food and also ought to value the contributions I make to
others. Self-care is a kind of mean, where we recognize that we ought to eat
and enjoy what we eat (with the rare but occasional splurge) and ought to
value our contributions to others.

   Self-regulation and the classic cardinal virtue of temperance are related. Thomas Aquinas's temperance moderates, restrains, and enables one
to act reasonably. It primarily concerns matters of food, drink, and sexuality but also can regulate "movements" that could be self-destructive, such
as excess passion, ill-founded hope, or anger.[19] While Thomas may have a
general reticence about sexual pleasures and passion, the spirit of temperance endures in its relevance: to be temperate is to be able to do the good
one wants to do without getting in one's own way. It is to *not* be one's worst
enemy. The person who is temperate or self-controlled may be highly affective and passionate and yet possess perspective.

---

the pursuit of long-term goals but is also "equally essential for developing the self-
restraint and empathy needed to build caring and mutually supportive relationships"
(6). Mischel's test, the first serious scientific study of self-control, entailed offering child
participants a choice between one marshmallow (or other appealing reward) immediately or two marshmallows after a brief period.

   19. Aquinas, II-IIae, Q 142, Art 1.

In this way, temperance is closely related to hope and its integration of reason and emotion: hope takes a long view and sees momentary activities and feelings in light of a compelling, energizing, and emotive goal. My anger about an injustice done to me might be fundamentally valid (a sensitivity to injustice anywhere is a valuable instinct). Yet without the moderating aid of self-control, I risk harming myself and others, undermining my larger goals of justice, and limiting subsequent potential for goodness.

Self-regulation warrants moderation in all facets of our lives. Even our seemingly trite "sins"—whether an inability to properly regulate our sugar intake or an unreasonable, spiraling irritation at the refrigerator door not closing properly—impact our character and readiness to love.

Between Holding Back and Diving In

Self-regulation requires an awareness of which possibly opposite responses are most fitting. Do we bite our tongue or speak out? Do we abstain from unhealthy food or reward ourselves with comfort food? Self-regulation is both restraint and assertion: one might need to override an initial response or push oneself toward a response.[20]

Keenan cites sexuality as an example of the need for people to discern for themselves what constitutes appropriate self-regulation. While self-care might call some to sexual restraint, others might need to "seek sexual love" that has been denied out of inhibitions or fear of intimacy.[21] The right expression of sexuality is thus determined, in part, by looking at our own life stories. We may be too passionate but it is possible we are not passionate enough. Anger, for example, can be consuming, debilitating to us and destructive to others. At other times, our love might be hindered because we are not angry enough, perhaps in response to an abuse or injustice. To borrow from C. S. Lewis, self-caring individuals know when their desires are too strong but also when their desires are too weak.[22]

Regulation Is About Mastery Not Restraint

Self-regulation does not see passions and emotions as enemies but as fundamentally good forces to be mastered rather than mastered by. It is about shaping ourselves and our emotions, not stifling them. We demonstrate

20. Peterson and Seligman, *Character Strengths*, 500.
21. Keenan, "Virtue Ethics," 132.
22. Lewis, "Weight of Glory," 26.

self-care when we non-judgmentally accept but subdue disruptive emotions, such as fear or anger that thwart our ability to love. We demonstrate self-care when we can cognitively reappraise emotional situations, like laughing off an insult instead of being emotionally crippled by it.

Our passions and desires *can* exceed what we can handle such that we demonstrate a lack of virtue. For example, our good desire to fittingly meet another's needs could morph into a controlling pattern that squelches the autonomy of others or becomes abusive. Our passion for a hobby could become an obsession that no longer invigorates our care for others but isolates us from others. Yet we ought to listen to such desires with welcome rather than suspicion, in order to decrease the potential dismissiveness that may come from even the most well-meaning persons in our lives (e.g., "That's not what a man is supposed to feel" or "You'll lose donors if you say that" or more simply "I don't understand you").

A human is not a composite of reckless desires, disorders, and passions that, once stifled or under control, will indicate positive health or normalcy. Rather, our desires and passions are fundamentally good allies, part of our unique gift to the world.

Self–Appropriation

Self-care recognizes the self as a gift to be stewarded and shared. Self-appropriation is to own oneself: to take responsibility for who we are and to act upon the implications of who we are for our relationships. If we are to love others in a self-giving manner, a knowledge of what constitutes our unique skill set and personality will help us recognize what we can give to others. This means valuing who we are and what we contribute to each of our relationships. Lovers are not pushovers, but possess the self-respect needed to retain a sense of self with others (a unity-in-difference) while generously sharing this self with others. Further, we share with others a *good* self—a self that is both fundamentally good and continually growing in goodness (i.e., love).

Strengths, Styles, and Gifts

A self-caring person is habitually engaged in self-discovery and acting upon such discovery. There are many great resources to aid this process. Peterson and Seligman offer an imperfect but useful method of virtuous self-assessment in the form of the "VIA Survey."[23] The Gallup Organization's "Strengthsfinder" inventory, which measures one's "greatest potential for a strength" among thirty-four possible "signature themes," can clarify how particular inclinations and abilities in ourselves can be affirmed, embraced, and utilized.[24]

Spiritual gift assessment tools are a mixed bag. They can be limited by an unfitting separation between "spiritual" and "natural" or an overly literal reading of Scripture that misunderstands Paul's lists (Rom 12 and 1 Cor 12) as timeless and comprehensive. Despite these limitations, spiritual gifts assessments can be useful if the results are held loosely and intended to stimulate conversation. A better way to maintain continuity with but expand upon the tradition of spiritual gifts might be for individual churches to create a dialogue between their own sense of God's call, their expressed goals, and the virtues, abilities, and resources of their own members. Out of this conversation may come a sense of which "spiritual gifts" exist within a congregation.

In terms of personality typologies, the Enneagram and the Myers-Briggs Type Indicator are popular in religious contexts as tools of self-understanding.[25] While the scientific community generally views these as ultimately pseudoscientific and unreliable, such typologies are easily accessible and can facilitate self-discovery, provided the results are used with caution and not allowed to be overly restrictive. The "Big Five" taxonomy, while still bound to the limitations of simplified groupings of traits, is the most widely accepted personality assessment of its kind, useful in its integration of other taxonomies and as a springboard for further self-discovery.[26]

23. While the twenty-four "character strengths" are outlined in the CSV, the VIA online test provides a quick assessment (the result of which should be used with discretion, not as binding but as a guide). See "Via Survey," from the VIA Institute on Character, http://www.viacharacter.org/www/Character-Strengths-Survey. I offer an alternative virtuous self-assessment in chapter 10 in the form of "questions of examen" or "queries"—the Ignatian and Quaker ways, respectively, of asking self-reflective questions intended to lead to greater understanding of self and God.

24. Buckingham and Clifton, *Now, Discover Your Strengths*, 78. The strengths approach is guided by a preference toward understanding strengths over limitations (though it does not claim the strengths to be moral qualities but talents). The authors audaciously but aptly inquire: "What one, two, or three things can you do better than ten thousand people?" (10).

25. See "Learn the Enneagram," https://www.enneagraminstitute.com/how-the-enneagram-system-works/ and "MBTI Basics," http://www.myersbriggs.org/my-mbti-personality-type/mbti-basics/.

26. John, Naumann, and Soto, "Paradigm Shift," 116. The five dimensions of personality are extraversion (versus introversion), agreeableness (versus antagonism), conscientiousness (versus lack of direction), neuroticism (versus emotional stability),

Awareness of one's "emotional style" can facilitate self-appropriation.[27] One premise of this approach that starkly contrasts with personality typologies is the emphasis on malleability: we are not bound to a "type" by genetics or any other shackle. This is the premise of neuroplasticity: the brain's ability to change throughout the entire lifespan. While discovery of our unique self may reveal a fairly stable, consistent entity, self-stewardship is not the discovery of a static self; it is the responsibility for a self that is always changing and can often be deliberately changed to fit the needs of new contexts, situations, and relationships.

Living Authentically

Writer and Presbyterian minister Fredrick Buechner eloquently captures self-appropriation: "What we hunger for perhaps more than anything else is to be known in our full humanness, and yet that is often just what we also fear more than anything else."[28] The potential burden of modified, crafted self-presentation saps emotional and mental resources as well as our availability to others. Hiding truths creates anxiety and fear—both obstacles to love. Making known our uniqueness and resisting the pressure to conform to types (e.g., what a man or woman should be, what a pastor should be, what a Democrat should be, what a career should entail, etc.) is a means to more fully appropriating God's gift of ourselves.

We are responsible for a self for which we may not be fully *causally* responsible but for which we are *practically* responsible. Self-care considers others' opinions to an extent (as both gratitude and justice require). Yet self-care recognizes that others' actual or perceived desires for us may be barriers to recognizing what gifts God has given us—even the potential gift to others of past sufferings, insecurities, or presently shameful elements of our lives. Assuming the movement toward authenticity does not

---

and openness to experience (versus closedness) (John, Naumann, and Soto, "Paradigm Shift," 138). See also "The Big Five Project," http://www.outofservice.com/bigfive/.

27. Davidson and Begley, *Emotional Life*, xii. The six dimensions of emotional style are resilience, outlook, social intuition, self-awareness, sensitivity to context, and attention. These dimensions are value-neutral. For example, one might be crippled by excessive self-awareness such that it becomes pathological; yet one might also be ignorant of the ways one is harming others through a lack of self-awareness.

28. Buechner, *Telling Secrets*, 2–3. We ought to share "the secret of who we truly and fully are . . . because otherwise we run the risk of losing track of who we truly and fully are and little by little come to accept instead the highly edited version which we put forth in hope that the world will find it more acceptable than the real thing" (3).

foster a cheap, lazy self-acceptance, self-care invites this movement as a pathway to loving others.

This raises a theological issue. God loves us, but Christians ought to be hesitant to say "God *accepts* us as we are." In terms of affection, receptivity, or valuation, God *does* accept us. In fact, God has never *not* accepted us. The language of "acceptance" may be especially helpful as a presentation of God toward persons who have experienced real, traumatic incidents of rejection—those who pathologically struggle with self-acceptance.

But "acceptance," if it must be used and exhorted, is not a license to abandon efforts toward spiritual growth. I adore my three children, but I do not "accept" as a permanent reality their present inability to write complete sentences, understand where the "sun goes" at night, or safely and effectively use a toaster. If I did not desire more for them and assist them—in dialogue with their developmental readiness—in cultivating their various capacities, I would be a bad parent and severely shortchange their human experience. God accepts us but knows what we can become. Grace should not stifle but energize.

Living Out Your Calling

Self-appropriating persons experience what Csikszentmihalyi calls "flow"—where one's "skills match the opportunities for action."[29] As Buechner puts it: "The place God calls you to is where your deep gladness and the world's deep hunger meet."[30] Those who have so aligned their talents with opportunities for expression are not only potentially loving others in a profoundly self-giving way but are also likely to be happy. Self-appropriating persons recognize the self they have been given but also recognize how and to whom to give it.

Educator and Quaker Parker Palmer notes that the word "vocation" is rooted in the Latin "voice."[31] Discovery of my voice entails that I discover my talents, passions, and distinctives, and disallow external pressures to shape my vocational path (though I should be hesitant to critique a person who, for the sake of supporting his or her family, abandons this path). Self-appropriation encourages the integrity of living "divided no more"— refusing "to act on the outside in a way that contradicts some truth [we] hold deeply on the inside."[32] Negatively, this could be simply an act of self-

29. Csikszentmihalyi, *Flow*, 6.

30. Buechner, *Wishful Thinking*, 119.

31. Palmer, *Let Your Life Speak*, 4.

32. Palmer, *Let Your Life Speak*, 32. Palmer calls this the "Rosa Parks decision," as

expression that tends toward narcissism. But positively, this is the kind of acting-upon-conviction that leads people to oppose corrupt leadership and pervasive marginalizing attitudes through prophetic critique; to embrace a non-normative gender identity rather than conceal oneself on a likely path toward depression and isolation; to risk financial instability for the sake of pursuing a more satisfying job; to share a talent with others with a willingness to endure the potential but likely imagined repercussions of a poor reception of such talents.

Self-care entails listening to what God calls us to and assuming that God calls us to particular ways of participating in the world because God believes we are capable of such participation. While persons may share a general call that works itself out in various ways (be mindful of water usage, do not text while driving, say "thank you" to parents often), the discovery of our specific call reveals the creative particularity and diversity of God and humans that allow each of us to contribute to others in distinct ways.

Self-appropriation also means we value ourselves enough to believe that we are worthy of good things. Consider the way a person may downplay or dismiss the generosity of others. Even if a strong concern for the other informs the moment, there may often be a devaluing or neglect of ourselves at play that provokes our dismissiveness. A dramatic example of this might be the slothful, spoiled child who squanders the opportunities provided for him or her, an endowment birthed from decades of parental toil and care. A subtle form might be the potentially feigned humility or unhealthy self-degradation implied in the words "You didn't have to do that!" Gratitude needs self-care to ensure that we are not only willing to receive gifts but that we can also recognize what kind of gifts we deserve. We not only shortchange ourselves by not counting ourselves worthy of others' gifts to us. By not welcoming others' generosity, we potentially thwart their expression of and dynamic movement toward love. Our ability to receive love—strengthened by self-affirmation—can aid or stifle growth in others.

Exemplar of Self-Care: Cameron Partridge (1973-present)

Cameron Partridge, now the rector at St. Aidan's Episcopal Church in San Francisco, was one of the first transgender chaplains at a major university (Boston University). He is one of a small number of trans clergy in the Episcopal Church and the first openly transgender priest to preach at the

---

her subversive act on a Montgomery, Alabama bus is "emblematic of what the undivided life can mean." (32).

Washington National Cathedral.[33] Partridge is emblematic of the journey of a community of people who have sought to live authentically, joyfully, and safely and demonstrates a strong virtue of self-care.

Media portrayals of trans persons tend to, understandably and deservedly, emphasize the liberation for the transitioning individual. Yet transitioning can also be a loving means of liberating others: from transphobia, from stubborn resistance to what is conceptually foreign, and from oppressive insistence on right ways to be men and women—socially constructed categories that often dismiss lived experience and can harm trans and non-trans persons alike. Given the discrimination and resistance faced by transgender persons, their courage can inspire others to pursue good goals at a potential harmful cost to oneself.

Partridge affirms the benefits for others of his own courageous journey: "I seemed to need to pass through a certain kind of fear before I could embrace a fuller vocation to contribute to conversations on trans and wider LGBT equality."[34] Partridge also recognizes the need for self-appropriation, which for him means affirming and promoting the whole of his identity rather than simply his gender transition, including prioritizing his family (an act of care for them but also a means of self-sustenance).[35] In an eloquent sermon, Partridge's experience as an "other" becomes a lens through which we can understand not just his identity but Christian identity as a whole, demonstrating his self-caring ownership of his identity: "As we take up [our] agency, we must remember from whence we came, must remember our otherness—ancient and contemporary—and in so remembering rediscover our border location as Christians."[36]

Partridge's self-care has enhanced his spirituality and increased his love through clarifying his own agency. Partridge recently spoke at Boston University on the topic, "Coming Out as Spiritual Practice"; he expressed that the experience of coming out "can be a profoundly spiritual process of confronting our fear, letting it go, and claiming afresh the lifelong process of becoming who we are."[37] Partridge certainly speaks out of his own ex-

33. Hafiz, "Rev. Cameron Partridge."

34. Garrison, "Crossing Boundaries."

35. Garrison, "Crossing Boundaries." Partridge shares, "When it comes to my family, it's one thing for me to be openly trans, and even to be open about being a husband and dad, but my family members need space to be who they are. . . . The public pieces of my vocation are not necessarily theirs" (Garrison, "Crossing Boundaries.").

36. Partridge, "Other Sheep." Partridge continues, "We remember the process of our incorporation into the wider flock, we remember that we are 'Other Sheep,' a people oriented to the margin, inviting 'other others' into this holy terrain, this sacred journey."

37. Ledtke, "Boston U Encourages Students."

perience, acknowledging the care for self expressed through moving past crippling fears and allowing one's interconnected but unique identity to emerge.

Becky Garrison highlights how Partridge's transgender status has helped him lovingly participate in the lives of college students as a chaplain. Partridge suggests that, in some ways, being trans is a non-issue, but "in another way, I'm able to have certain conversations about the complexities of human identity with college students, who are figuring out their own identities."[38] Cindy Jacobson (a former chaplain at BU) affirms this availability to others: "A unique gift (Partridge) brings is himself. Because he is a trans man, perhaps this gives permission for students who are trans or are questioning to seek him out."[39] Partridge exemplifies the importance of self-giving love and enhances others' giftedness through modeling and encouraging others to become self-aware and self-valuing. Partridge's expected concern for transgender justice extends not only to all LGBTQ+ injustices but also to a wide range of social justice issues.[40]

Partridge practices self-care by resisting the potential imposition of "before-and-after" narratives: "'Before-after' narratives can have a way of boxing people in. Plenty of trans people don't medically transition, and those who do transition do so in various ways."[41] While narrativity may be an ally to identity formation, we ought to take care not to undermine our lived experience. Self-care affirms the nuanced, non-generic quality of one's story. Partridge describes his understanding of his relationship to his body: "I'm not a huge fan of the trapped-in-the-wrong-body-narrative" of some transgender people; "I never felt like God made a mistake. . . . I just had sense of growing discomfort [and] disjunction. . . . [By transitioning], I felt like I was able to kind of reclaim the body God had given me."[42] By valuing and caring for themselves, transgender persons can value and care for others. Partridge exemplifies what it means to ready oneself to love through discovering, nurturing, protecting, and sharing the gift of self.

38. Garrison, "Crossing Boundaries."

39. Garrison, "Crossing Boundaries."

40. Garrison, "Crossing Boundaries."

41. Markoe, "Five Questions." Partridge elaborates: "So 'before-after' questions can sometime feel invasive . . . because they may unwittingly carry assumptions about how binary or not binary our identities may be."

42. Barlow, "New Episcopal Chaplain."

Chapter Eight

Justice: Taking Care of Others

The greatest radiance anyone can have on earth is truth in works of justice performed in imitation of the Son.[1]

—HADEWIJCH, THIRTEENTH CENTURY

A religion that professes a concern for the souls of men and is not equally concerned about the slums that damn them, the economic conditions that strangle them, and the social conditions that cripple them is a spiritually moribund religion.[2]

—MARTIN LUTHER KING JR., 1929–68

THE PREVIOUS TWO CHAPTERS ("Gratitude" and "Self-Care") and the subsequent two ("Kindness" and "Hope") are structured in roughly the same manner, parsing the primary virtue into multiple sub-virtues. I take an alternative, narrative approach in this chapter and do so for two reasons. First, it better enables me to tell the "story" of justice, presenting the history of understandings of justice and how I am building upon this tradition.

Secondly, the sub-virtues of the virtues of gratitude, self-care, kindness, and hope are more naturally conceived of individually and are easily identifiable with their parent virtue (e.g., self-sustenance and self-regulation have different concerns but are always virtues of self-care; the

1. Hadewijch, *Hadewijch*, 47.
2. King, *Strength to Love*, 159.

same is true of, for example, courage and discernment as parts of hope). However, the "parts" of justice are more interdependent; it is difficult to say a person is just or practicing justice if any of justice's four components (or sub-virtues) are absent. Furthermore, the terms for these components themselves risk becoming too vague when extracted from the context of the movement of justice (e.g., see "competence" below) and thus their collaboration is significant.

I begin with a comparison of justice as a principle versus justice as a virtue, followed by a reframing of justice in light of the work of care ethicists. I ultimately propose a four-part definition of the virtue of justice that is operationalized not in terms of asynchronous sub-virtues (though I do not object to them being read in that way) but as a progressive movement through stages. Given my clear appreciation for care ethics and the work of Carol Gilligan, "care" rather than "justice" would arguably be more suitable as a virtuous pathway that fits our love to others, especially evident in the following treatment. Nonetheless, justice has a long, rich tradition; while it is a loaded (and for some, negative) word that I could discard, I prefer to retain it while updating it in light of my overall project here.

As a starting point, I define justice as *the virtue that enables us to actively fulfill our natural and social obligations to others.* It is a matter of giving to each his or her due, as determined by our relationship to them and by their discerned, particular needs. Justice is thus relationally guided and context-specific. It is neither blind and universal nor something that can be enacted in isolation from others. Justice respects the dignity of every individual.

And justice can only be practiced by participating in the goodness of others. Justice is concerned with what is real and so, while hopeful, is not idealistic. For example, despite the positive contributions of John Rawls's theory and the value of his method (including thought experiments such as the "veil of ignorance"[3]), his rationalistic approach is inadequate. Even if logical and benevolent laws and structures could be conceived and subsequent effort made to implement such laws and structures, persons—who are not isolated individuals as Rawls seemingly presumes—would still be "stuck" in their social and physical reality, inextricable from their community, personal history, and bodies. Justice can be aided by a degree of idealism

---

3. See Rawls, *Theory of Justice*, 118. Rawls, for all the importance of his work on justice, seemingly loses a degree of relevance to a conversation about a virtue of justice that considers "where to go from here" in the context of our varied commitments to those whom we love "unfairly"—preferring some over others. Rawls is self-admittedly taking justice to a "higher level of abstraction" than many, including his philosophical predecessors Locke, Rousseau, and Kant (10).

but is primarily guided by the situation "on the ground"—the particular needs of the other.

Conceptions of Justice

The *principle* of justice and the *virtue* of justice are intertwined but distinct. Justice, as a principle, can guide the practice of the virtue of justice. Herein lies the relevance of various theories and forms of justice, whether distributive justice (the fair and equal allocation of resources), retributive justice (concerned with punishment either as a deserved response or as a safeguard for others), procedural justice (fair, consistent processes), or restorative justice (actions to heal, reform, and reconcile victim[s] and offender[s]).

A virtue of justice can be informed by the four abovementioned forms of justice. Consider as an example my relationship to black American women and men as a group and my relationship with my spouse as a close individual. Distributive justice might consider where black Americans are disproportionally paid, educated, targeted by law enforcement, or incarcerated and what steps could be taken to improve this situation to make it more equitable (racially transcendent or indifferent). Distributive justice could also reveal disproportionate responsibility, power, or voice in my relationship with my spouse and guide the creation of a more balanced, shared agency.

Procedural justice might distinguish between the severity of low-level misdemeanors and violent crimes, push back on "fair" processes that are "blind" to allow for more nuanced attention to the person, their life situation, and the particular pressures that led to the crime, and recognize implicit or overt racism at work in such processes and participants. Procedural justice can facilitate good listening, decision-making, and conflict resolution with my spouse to ensure no one person dominates or manipulates the conversation or process.

Retributive justice, applied with compassion, ought to recognize the long-term consequences of non-rehabilitative forms of punishment while also opting for an anthropological optimism that emphasizes personal responsibility but magnifies the contexts and pressures informing particular crimes. Similarly, while I should not "punish" or be punished by my spouse, it is important for the "offender" to show remorse beyond a spoken "sorry" or apologetic flowers. The offender should convincingly demonstrate both self-scrutiny and a willingness to grow, to reduce the likelihood of repeat offenses.

Finally, a concern for restorative justice can encourage honest, open conversations between black and white Americans that lead to greater understanding between both parties and greater self-awareness and repentance among whites. Restorative justice with my spouse, as between racial groups, is a misnomer. Justice, if substantial, will not actually *restore* anything (as the sought-after harmony may never have existed) but create something new and better. Good marriages ought to grow, moving not backward toward an illusory past goodness or equilibrium but forward toward stronger, more intimate bonds. True justice does not empower us to make our marriages or country "great again" but to participate in their becoming something greater than they have ever been—and greater for *all*.

Just people possess vision, responsibility, respect, skill, compassion, and flexibility. They are profoundly attuned to your particular struggle yet can follow the causal chain to determine the structural inequities that have contributed to your struggle. They care for you as an individual and care for the world that shapes your opportunities and limitations. They are aware of the ways in which they are related to others and habitually take responsibility for these others.

Just people "respect, empower, promote, uphold, [and] care for [others]."[4] They set others free from "the slavery of social and personal relations patterned by gender or class or race of any other category that divides people and allows one group to keep another from full self-determination, from full participation as subjects in history, from full liberation."[5] Just people recognize not only institutional injustices but also how our own character and actions, in our closest relationships, are prohibiting those we allegedly "love" from self-determination, participation, and liberation. Justice—if we are living it rightly—is an expression of care.

Justice and Care

Care ethics emphasizes the "maintaining and enhancing [of] caring relations—attending to those we encounter, listening to their expressed needs, and responding positively if possible."[6] Relationality takes primacy over

---

4. Isasi-Diaz, "Spirituality and the Common Good," 253.

5. Cleaver, *Know My Name*, 27.

6. Noddings, *Caring*, xvi. Thomas Aquinas's distinction between general and particular justice reinforces the continuity of all forms of justice and invites an ethic of care. Thomas posits that general or legal justice concerns the common good and respect for laws, while particular justice enables us to act rightly toward others, not "withholding" what is due nor "injuring another person" (Aquinas, IIa–IIae Q 58, Art 7, 11).

autonomy in an ethic of care. Care ethics can thus remind us of the proper focus of virtues: not simply my own personal betterment, but the improvement of caring, mutual relationships. Self-cultivation is a relational process in an ethic of care: my goodness grows not in a vacuum but in the context of my relationships, affected not only by the care I give but the way in which that care is received. Our virtues depend on others for their growth and full expression.

Carol Gilligan initially admired Lawrence Kohlberg's theory of moral development, especially the primacy of justice in his model. Justice, understood as fairness and the transcending of "self-interest and societal conventions," reflected the spirit of the 1960s and provided a "justification for civil disobedience."[7] Yet Gilligan noted in the early 1980s that Kohlberg's stages of moral development implied moral "deficiency" in women's prioritization of care and sensitivity to others' needs.[8] Kohlberg's stages insinuated that relational obligations ultimately ought to be subordinated to a commitment to rules and universal principles.

Gilligan responded through the development of her own theory. She critiqued the predominantly masculine voice of Kohlberg's theory, in which "autonomy and rationality . . . were the markers of maturity."[9] The silenced feminine voice on morality, as she observed it in the lived experience of women, emphasized attentive, responsive care to expressed needs. In her care-based approach, the highest moral responsibilities are "seeing and responding to need" and "sustaining the web of connection."[10]

While Gilligan may have initially intended to amplify underrepresented voices and to hold in tension these two approaches—justice and care—I think that she has, in reality, called justice to become what it can be. Her "care" is a better kind of justice, freed from the trappings of a principle-based ethics and the false simplicity of rule-based decision-making. What began as a statement about women's experience is relevant to all persons and a better way to understand both morality and our relationships. Participatory, compassionate lovers are not impartial, outside observers but participants immersed in, attentive to, and emotionally affected by others. Humans are not primarily aggressive, competitive, and self-interested but are more fundamentally "empathic and cooperative."[11]

7. Gilligan, *Joining the Resistance*, 2.

8. Gilligan, *In a Different Voice*, 18.

9. Gilligan, *Joining the Resistance*, 16.

10. Gilligan, *In a Different Voice*, 59, 62.

11. Gilligan, *Joining the Resistance*, 32.

Yet an ethic of care is not a gentle ethic but an ethic of "resistance to in-justice" and to "self-silencing."[12] A virtue of justice should compel the marginalized to voice their needs and reprimand the powerful. Yet the blindness of power and privilege often yields willed ignorance or hopeless shrugs. A virtue of justice should compel the privileged to magnify the voices of the underprivileged, sacrifice for them, and tell the truth about past and present wrongdoing.

Joan Tronto, a care ethicist, has handily (but of course unintentionally) provided a guide for the cultivation of justice that fits the vision of spiritual growth this book proposes. Tronto identifies four components of the process of caring: *attentiveness, responsibility, competence, and responsiveness.*[13] Care is attentive, recognizing where needs exist. It is responsible, driven to act upon those needs. It is competent, acting *effectively* in caregiving. And it is responsive, listening to (rather than presuming) others' expressed needs and adapting one's care as necessary.

The virtue of justice should reflect these four elements of care. A just person is *attentive*, noticing the people, close or distant, individuals or groups, who need us in some way. A just person is *responsible*, recognizing and acting upon our varied obligations to others, whether we ought to help because to assist is humane or because we have directly or complicitly caused their suffering. A just person is *competent*, not citing good intentions or listless effort as sufficient but capable of and willing to meet needs well (or at least prepared to learn how to meet such needs). Finally, a just person is *responsive*, not dismissive of his or her own natural way of helping but also not so overly reliant upon it that he or she fails to help others in the way they need to be helped, especially as such needs evolve over time.

I will let these four elements of justice guide the subsequent. How can we express love through justice? Be attentive; be responsible; be competent; be responsive.[14]

12. Gilligan, *Joining the Resistance*, 175.

13. Tronto, *Moral Boundaries*, 126–135.

14. I allude to Bernard Lonergan's transcendental method partly because it offers a useful heuristic for justice as I articulate it here but also because I am struck by the parallels between Tronto's four-part definition of care (the four parts functioning not only as components but steps in a process) and Lonergan's four transcendental precepts: "Be attentive, be intelligent, be reasonable, be responsible" (Lonergan, *Method in Theology*, 20). The two methods do overlap to a degree. Lonergan is describing the process of knowing and learning that transcends any one discipline or subject matter (14). Full realization of our capacity to know and act well on that knowledge involves four operations: *attention* to the fullness of our experience, *intelligent* investigation of that experience, *reasonable* judgments and forming of opinions, and *responsible* action (14–15). As with justice, the transcendental method opens us to more—more

Attentiveness

To fittingly participate in others through the virtue of justice, we have to pay attention. We have to notice and see what's really there. When we pay attention, we begin to see the presence of oppression as it affects both individuals and groups. But for what do we look?

Justice Pays Attention to Oppression

Iris Marion Young differentiates five modes or "faces" of oppression: exploitation (unfairly benefiting from others' labor), marginalization (dismissing and ignoring people's contributions), powerlessness (no space for self-definition or self-assertion), cultural imperialism (the collective voice of the oppressed are not heard amidst the cultural imposition of the dominant culture), and violence (systemic victimization and susceptibility to violation simply for being a member of the oppressed group).[15] These five faces are, of course, not only pertinent to society at large but can manifest in our most intimate relationships. Just persons are attentive to how they or others directly or indirectly exploit, marginalize, overpower, impose, and violate. They recognize

perspectives, more voices, and more data. In this way it is relevant to the receptive virtue of gratitude (particularly wonder). It also reinforces the necessity of praxis—mutually informing knowledge and action. Where justice goes in a different direction than the transcendental method may be due to where the weight of the process lies, or because the transcendental method is more like practical wisdom than justice. Justice draws on the analytical tools prudence provides but prioritizes the actual delivery of love. A comparison of Lonergan's method and justice (informed by Tronto) can further clarify. The primacy of attentiveness is shared. Tronto's "responsibility" probably contains Lonergan's "intelligence" and "reason" as the point of analysis of the situation. Lonergan's "responsibility" parallels Tronto's "competence," though Tronto may more strongly emphasize actual skill than Lonergan (i.e., if Lonergan's "responsibility," which seems to emphasize the "will" to do good, can translate into effort toward improving one's capacity to act for the good of others, then the two are more closely related; though it may simply be that Lonergan's method is too rational for justice as described here—too Kohlbergian). Finally, Tronto's "responsiveness" can be seen as employing the entire transcendental method in its willingness to continually analyze our experience with others for the sake of improved justice. Lonergan's method can enhance justice, but does not (nor does it claim to) place the same weight on our sustained, ongoing activity with and for others as justice does.

15. Young, *Justice and the Politics of Difference*, 48–63. Young challenges conceptions of justice based on fair distribution, preferring to define justice in terms of dismantling of both oppression and domination. Her proposed "politics of difference" echoes Vacek, Gilligan, and others' explicit and implicit support of a justice that values particularity and appreciation of difference. She also emphasizes that combatting oppression requires looking beyond ineffective policies to the failure of individuals to recognize personal prejudices and appreciate otherness.

manifestations of oppression and can articulate the nature of this oppression with enough specificity and nuance to fruitfully guide the discernment of appropriate strategies for confronting such oppression.

Justice Pays Attention to Real People

The attentiveness of justice demands a readiness to reinterpret data, revise perspectives, and challenge myths in light of our encounters with real people. So we scrutinize the hope of "upward mobility" and admit that the system is biased toward children from affluent and well-educated families.[16] We consider how fearmongering has created unfounded prejudices toward people who, when we actually get to know them, do not fit our narratives of suspicion. We consider what our national budget reveals about how lightly we prioritize equal, easy access to quality education, despite the lip service we give it.

We pause before barreling forward with our default conclusions to notice how this situation is and is not like other somewhat comparable situations. When our logic and beliefs do not adequately explain the situation of the person or people before us, we choose persons over dogma. We look more closely at the reality of power, recognizing the actual ease or difficulty with which individuals or groups can attain their goals.

Attentiveness includes differentiating which needs are universal and which are not. In some cases, others' needs *are* the same as our own. I think of the Black Lives Matter protestor who responded to the insensitive middle-class white person's question, "What do they want?," with a reasonable request: "A family, an education, and a job."[17] Yet presumption can be damaging, doing violence to others or simply prohibiting us from coming through for others.

Attentiveness, as a starting point, means affirming others' humanity while recognizing what Paulo Freire identifies as our central human problem: dehumanization.[18] To humanize the oppressed, Freire affirms that justice requires not a "paternalistic treatment of the oppressed" that keeps them dependent but the commitment of just persons to "enter into [their]

---

16. See DeParle, "Harder for Americans."

17. Wallis, *America's Original Sin*, xxi.

18. Freire, *Pedagogy of the Oppressed*, 43. For Freire, dehumanization occurs when one person or group hinders the "self-affirmation" of another person or group; the oppressed remain "things" without their own reflective participation in their emergence and growth (55).

situation" and "fight at their side."[19] Men ought to listen to women's voices to facilitate gender equality. White people ought to support black leadership of movements like Black Lives Matter. Volunteers ought to scrutinize their own well-intended charity and ask homeless people what they actually need. Justice opposes presumption and makes us better allies.

Justice Pays Attention to My Own Oppressive Inclinations

Attentiveness means recognizing when we overpower, steamroll, control, or act dismissively toward others. Growth in justice means increasingly making space for others to be, think, feel, and act on their own volition, without our interference. Attentiveness recognizes objectification and commodification and admits where we have been complicit in the reduction of others to "things." We should also attend to where some enjoy privileges or acceptance that others do not, such as in cases of exclusion based on gender or sex, and attend to how our own thoughts, words, and actions reinforce this exclusion. Justice starts from being able to say to another: "I am glad you exist."[20]

John Milbank writes that "justice should mean not punishment, but voluntary expiation, and social participation in the process of atonement."[21] We live justice when we atone not merely through saying "sorry" but through participating in the increasing health, wholeness, and capacity for self-shaping of historically oppressed communities and of those individuals closest to us. Participating in a fitting way requires we listen to these persons.

Justice Pays Attention to Others' Values

A fundamental valuing of the other is essential to justice. Justice is motivated not by pity but by respect. This kind of dignifying respect also puts the lover and loved on equal terms, such that we do not act justly toward others out of a "delusion of superiority" but out of a more egalitarian (or possibly supportive) role. Being "supportive," in this case, has nothing to do with a hierarchical or complementarian view of gender roles but signifies that an

19. Freire, *Pedagogy of the Oppressed*, 49.

20. Hauerwas and Vanier, *Living Gently*, 69. Vanier uses this phrase to describe "the heart of L'Arche" (L'Arche is a network of communities in which people with and without disabilities live together for the sake of community and mutual care).

21. Milbank, *Theology and Social Theory*, 73. Milbank, discussing nineteenth century French philosopher Pierre-Simon Ballanche, goes on: "Charity and co-responsibility redefine expiation and make a society without sacrifice possible" (73).

empowering kind of justice may mean allowing the other to lead in his, her, or their liberation or fulfillment of needs.

Justice personalizes. It treats people as persons rather than "cases" or "types" on which to employ patterned strategies.[22] Many who have called customer service for assistance with a particular product have undoubtedly seen the best and worst of this phenomenon. It is possible to be treated by a representative with attention, sympathy, and constructive guidance, such that one feels one's problem has been understood and resolved. It is also possible to be interrupted and patronized and thus misheard and incorrectly diagnosed. One's individuality has been squeezed into an inflexible protocol, often leaving both representative and customer exasperated.

While our human tendency to categorize and simplify is an essential psychological function for our survival and normal functioning, it is also an ever-present threat to a just recognition of needs. We must attend to what people are actually saying and what is actually happening. What we expect to hear and see can prevent us from truly hearing and seeing.

To be just, one needs to be attentive, thus requiring the presence of previously discussed virtues: a gratitude that receives, appreciates, and inquires; and a self-care that effectively manages stress, emotions, and general health so as to prepare one to attend to injustice.

Responsibility

Justice responds to the general value and dignity of others, whom we ought to respect simply for being human. Justice secondly responds to the uniqueness of others. To "fit" love responsibly, we must recognize that every person and every need is unique. Fitted love typically arises from our relationships with others more than our preconceptions about what others need.

Justice Is Particularized Responsibility

Walter Burghardt argues that sin is a rejection of our responsibility to others.[23] One can *deliberately* reject a responsibility: I could choose not to say "thank you" to someone who holds open a door for me, an arguably socially obligatory response to this above-and-beyond courtesy. Perhaps I choose this because I know the person and am upset with him or her about a past wrong. On the other hand, I may *not* know the person but be pompously

---

22. Noddings, *Caring*, 66.
23. Burghardt, "Spirituality and Justice," 199.

irritated that someone would assume I need such assistance. One can also *inadvertently* reject a responsibility, which is more likely in the example at hand. I may be absorbed on my smart phone, anxious about the demands of an errand that has led me to this place, or possess a sense of entitlement that takes for granted such kindness. In any of these cases, I am unable to fulfill what this moment demands of me. I have rejected my responsibility to others and have thus, arguably, acted sinfully, against love.

A virtue of justice has a broad scope, from a more involved care of family to the momentary but not inconsequential social courtesy of a "thank you" for a kindness extended. Whatever the level of involvement, justice is not blind but strikingly aware of others' claims on us. This is true at a neurological level, as research has shown that the relationship and situation affect the extent to which our brain (specifically the orbital-frontal cortex) is engaged and the consequent experience of positive emotions.[24] Our brains are more responsive to intimate others, which does not indicate a biological justification for preferential treatment but does underscore the wide range of claims people do have on us and the urgency of discerning and acting upon these claims. By admitting these varying degrees of responsibility, we *take* responsibility.

Justice Is Sustained Responsibility

As our relationships typically demand a certain consistency and reliability, justice is faithful, committed, and trusting. On a personal level, our faithfulness to spouses, children, friends, and associates creates a regularity and sense of expectation that gives us consistent opportunity to participate in love. Keenan's argued-for virtue of fidelity challenges a more individualist reading of our human situation, emphasizing the loyal and covenantal nature of these close, particular bonds.[25] The binding nature of such covenants invites the expression of hopeful virtues, in which the motivation to overcome obstacles to justice is stronger where we are both willfully and ontologically linked to others: integrated by choice and integrated by the transformative nature of relationships.

On a social level, our faithfulness to the common good takes the form of citizenship and is built on a kind of trust. Eric Uslaner argues that trust—which we learn from our parents—is an optimistic quality; trusting people believe the world is good and can be improved through their active

24. Underwood, "Compassionate Love," 12.
25. Keenan, "Proposing Cardinal Virtues," 725–26.

participation and are thus more likely to be socially engaged.[26] Trust allows us to "cooperate with strangers" for the sake of common values and expects that others will fulfill promises; it "presumes others are trustworthy."[27] This is not necessarily a trust based on our experience with others who have proven themselves trustworthy but more of a leap of faith: we trust others because this is a better, albeit risky, way to live. Trust assumes the best in others and enables us to collaborate for common ends.

Justice Is Practiced Responsibility

Christian development ought to consider our participation in the present and potential goodness of our nation and local communities. Peterson and Seligman identify the character strength of "citizenship," which deepens and expresses justice through loyalty, generativity (concern for future generations), and active involvement in civic affairs.[28] Civic involvement may be enacted through various modes, all potentially valid and integral. Joel Westheimer and Joseph Kahne identify three modes of civic involvement: the "personally responsible citizen" (emphasizes individual virtue and small actions), the "participatory citizen" (is involved in collective, community-based efforts), and the "justice-oriented citizen" (critically addresses root causes).[29] Each mode is essential to the work of social justice. To ensure balanced social engagement, churches setting justice goals for themselves ought to consider each mode.

Justice might lead to volunteering. Regardless of the strong possibility that institutional evils will counter small-scale just efforts, Paul Loeb suggests we ought to nonetheless engage on an individual level.[30] He calls for an "ethic of witness" that balances the two: we stay grounded in real relationships with individuals while also seeking to address the roots of their situations.[31] Such interaction with real people can minimize the abstract nature of our pronouncements about injustice. By listening to real people and their real struggles, our ability to act in a relevant and fitting way is increased. In acting for justice, logic and imagination should be a second-

---

26. See Uslaner, *Moral Foundations of Trust*. Uslaner argues that increasing equality correlates with increasing trust and that, as the income gap has increased in the US, Americans have become less trusting (3).

27. Uslaner, *Moral Foundations of Trust*, 1–3.

28. Peterson and Seligman, *Character Strengths*, 370.

29. Westheimer and Kahne, "What Kind of Citizen?" 240–42.

30. Loeb, "Soul of a Citizen," 1.

31. Loeb, "Soul of a Citizen," 2.

ary authority to the authority of our lived experience in relationships with oppressed persons.

Cultivating justice through the pathway of citizenship could take many forms, including contacting government officials, community collaboration to address an issue, signing a petition, joining a protest, or volunteer work.[32] While these examples are arguably demonstrations of kindness, due to the above-and-beyond nature of each, we are responsible to those whose lives are impacted by these acts. Social responsibility tells us we are obligated to the whole, even if we are not directly responsible for the sufferings of individuals we have never met.

Justice Is Expanded and Shared Responsibility

Just people act upon a sense of co-responsibility. A just driver is mindful of traffic patterns such that her on-ramp merging is a seamless integration exempting her from excessively contributing to the congestion (knowing her inattentiveness or ineffectiveness would cause problematic ripples). A just driver may also be compelled by a sense of co-responsibility to pull over to remove a large piece of debris blocking the road (assuming this action is nearly certain not to harm the driver).

On a larger scale, justice prompts me, as a somewhat arbitrary beneficiary of my nation's economy, to participate in the alleviation of others' suffering though paying taxes or voting for just politicians and programs. More intimately, a large family gathering gone awry by decades-long tensions might invite my participation, not through dramatic therapeutic intervention but through tactful and timely redirections (e.g., "Dessert is ready!" or "How are the Seahawks doing this year?"). Justice affirms our particular responsibility to groups, even if our participation is limited (though kindness can expand the intensity and duration of this participation).

Justice reveals our responsibility for strangers. The anonymity and enormity of those who suffer can leave us feeling helpless. What can I or we actually do? Just people overcome such barriers of physical, cognitive, and emotional distance. A just person reframes strangers as neighbors. A just person selects persons to help and ways to help, rather than offering no help at all. A just person recognizes the potential value of offering oneself, rather than assuming more available or capable others will do the work of justice. A just person is comfortable entering the worlds of others, unafraid of the ways his or her way of life will be confronted and challenged. Biblically speaking, we welcome the stranger, recognizing Christ in all (Matt 25:35).

32. Peterson and Seligman, *Character Strengths*, 376.

Justice Is Responsibility to Victims and Wrongdoers

Love's favor should tend toward the victim, as we have a special responsibility—certainly modeled by Jesus!—to care for those who have been physically and emotionally hurt by abusive individuals or an oppressive system. Just people protect, shelter, advocate for, and defend those whose voices have been silenced, whose bodies have been mistreated, whose contributions have been ignored, whose livelihood and health have been made subordinate priorities.

Yet we are also responsible to wrongdoers. Whether it is a friend who has slighted us or a convicted murderer, a just attitude toward others is hopeful, affirming, and dignifying. People are treated as presently good and capable of becoming better, their offensive actions—no matter the degree of severity—seen as defining in a secondary but not fundamental sense. Nobody is to be tossed aside, scapegoated to assuage the grief of others. While oppressor and oppressed hardly deserve equivalent sympathy—there are no "two sides" when one side habitually spews hate or enacts abuse—just people recognize that offenders are also victims of whatever pressures and circumstances led to their unfortunate and horrific actions.

As an example, the Insight Prison Project helps those who have committed crimes take responsibility for the harm they have caused while making amends with their community and the families of their victims.[33] The victimized are given opportunities for self-care and a generally more effective healing experience. The offenders are viewed through a hopeful lens, recognized as socially formed, innately good, and capable of moral growth. This restorative process aids offender and victim but also indicts the systemic issues that give rise to such reconciliatory conversations in the first place. Prisoners make connections between their own childhood trauma and their subsequently stifled emotional processing abilities (which generally have played a role in substance abuse and criminal behavior).[34] This approach emphasizes the potential transformation of everyone over the finality and resignation of punitive action and affirms that the identity of those in prison extends beyond their crimes alone.

---

33. Suttie, "Can Restorative Justice Help?" Victim Offender Education Groups (VOEG) teach emotional skills, violence prevention, mindfulness, and yoga, and unite victims and survivors with prisoners to elucidate the consequences of crimes (Suttie, "Can Restorative Justice Help?"). Such restorative justice models have emerged in response to the disproportionate number of African Americans, Hispanics, and poor housed in prisons and how this trend makes communities less stable and more dangerous (Suttie, "Can Restorative Justice Help?").

34. Suttie, "Can Restorative Justice Help?"

John Woolman, an eighteenth century Quaker minister and abolition-
ist, highlights the effects of slavery on slaveholders: "[Holding slaves], tho'
done in calmness without any show of disorder, do yet deprive the mind. . . .
These steps taken by masters, and their conduct striking the minds of their
children whilst young, leave less room for that which is good to work upon
them."[35] Oppression of others, as Woolman points out, has a destructive effect on oneself and one's family. Justice should not let anyone "off the hook"
if this means condoning oppression and perpetuating it. Yet the scope of
justice extends to bullies and oppressors, who are themselves captive to their
own deformed perspective, attitude, set of assumptions, habits, and lifestyle.
We should love oppressors and oppressed differently because each needs
something different to facilitate their growth in goodness. Yet we ought to
love them both, nonetheless.

Justice Is *Our* Responsibility

The responsibility component of justice condemns a spirituality that seeks
God's intervention in place of our own. It moves us beyond love for all to
love for actual people. Noddings offers a spirited but pointed critique of
religiosity: "Under the illusion [of universal love], some young people retreat to the church to worship that which they cannot actualize."[36] Noddings
highlights a potential danger of Christian worship: its susceptibility to letting us off the moral hook under the guise of "humility." If worship widens
the moral gap between God and us such that only God is good, we not only
shortchange ourselves but also shortchange those we care about.

Worship can be transformative, putting us in touch with God and
our ultimate goals and energizing us toward incremental realization of
these goals. Devotion to God can act not as a retreat from the troubling
elements of reality but as an energizing source that clarifies how we ought
to act in the world and in our relationships. But if worship reinforces the
status quo of our spirituality and does not deepen our loving participation in others, it is hollow and meaningless noise. God is, if anything, not
worshipped but irritated.

35. Woolman, "Considerations on Keeping Negros," 236–37.
36. Noddings, *Caring*, 90.

Competence

To be just you have to know *how* to be just. Justice requires competence. A just person does not shrug in resignation upon realizing he or she does not know how to address a particular injustice. Nor does a just person rest on the laurels of sincere effort, saying "well, I tried" as though the outcome of one's efforts were negligible. Rather, a just person is teachable, willing to learn how to meet the needs of others and then live out one's learning. Justice is not sloppy or half-hearted but seeks to be thorough and complete.

Competence Grows Through Solidarity

Isasi-Diaz cites four elements that must be present if justice is to be realized: the oppressed must be allowed to contribute to alleviating their oppression; difference must be embraced; power dynamics must be recognized; and there must be the possibility for a radically different future.[37] How then do individuals live out justice as a virtue that reflects these considerations? Isasi-Diaz's answer is "solidarity," which enables us to support the oppressed as change agents, overcome the fear of difference, share or sacrifice power, and work toward creating a radically different reality.[38] Justice guides us not simply to act on behalf of the oppressed, risking patronization or ill-advised action, but to make space for their voices and take a supporting role in their liberation. Competence in justice requires the ability to appreciate difference, be secure in ourselves (but adaptable), not be threatened by what we do not understand, keep our labels and definitions fluid and revisable, and share power.

Competence Grows Through Vision

To be competent in justice, one ought to possess vision: the prophetic ability to imagine and articulate a different, more just reality; to "nurture, nourish, and evoke a consciousness and perception alternative to the consciousness and perception of the dominant culture around us."[39] Justice thus guides our relationship with the future, reminding us that while the past informs and in some ways binds the present and thus cannot be ignored, the possibility of a reimagined future remains. While change may occur sluggishly, the visions

37. Isasi-Diaz, "Spirituality and the Common Good," 256.

38. Isasi-Diaz, "Spirituality and the Common Good," 257.

39. Brueggemann, *Prophetic Imagination*, 3.

and plans we devise for the future—whether on a national, relational, or personal scale—need not be bound by inertia but can reflect a drastically different possible future, attainable but stretching as well as confrontational toward present reality. Hope facilitates justice by challenging our resignation and numbness to the oppressive, shackled present.

Competence Grows Through Concretization

While intimacy with those for whom we act justly will wane as the nature of our relationship moves from close to distant or from small group to larger group, the efficacy of our justice can be aided by deliberate concretization of such distant others. Studies have shown an increase in charitable donations and action on behalf of suffering others when potential donors encounter individual cases rather than general statistics. Tehila Kogut and Ilana Ritov studied the "identified victim effect" and demonstrated how our "affective process" often trumps the "principle of economic rationality" when faced with the possibility of giving to others or taking action to alleviate their suffering.[40]

To energize our social justice efforts, we might try to replicate the kind of emotional response we have to close, present others as we consider oppressed groups and the suffering individuals within these groups. Finding ways to personalize members of other groups—going beyond the more abstract "poor" or "minority" or "abused"—is an essential part of growing a virtue of justice. Attentiveness to these individual cases—perhaps facilitated through meditative visualization, reading articles about individual cases, or, when possible, face-to-face conversation—can strengthen our sense of responsibility to take action. Just people particularize others to awaken their caregiving instincts and enhance personal, compassionate participation in groups.

Competence Grows Through a Willingness to Learn

The efficacy of just, fitting, loving participation depends on competent delivery but also on the willingness to *become* competent, where possible. Once I have recognized the presence of homeless persons in my city and

---

40. Kogut and Ritov, "'Identified Victim' Effect," 157, 164. The researchers showed that individuals were more likely to donate to a sick child—named or anonymous—when the solicitation was accompanied by a photo; and that benefactors gave more when presented with one child rather than eight (photos included in each case). For a related study, see Small, Loewenstein, and Slovic, "Sympathy and Callousness," 143–53.

determined my responsibility to act on their behalf, competence requires that I understand the causes of homelessness, can conversationally engage with a homeless person, and can effectively give them whatever it is that combines their need with my resources (good listening, a bottle of water, directions to a shelter, my coat).

Once I have recognized my wife's ongoing or momentary needs, competence enables me to learn and administer appropriate massage techniques, fix the garbage disposal, inquire into new parenting discoveries so as to be on the same page in our shared child care, notice and adapt quickly to patterns so that I can anticipate requests rather than wait for them, or skillfully prepare her favorite cocktail.

Once I understand the people to whom my job obligates me and what constitutes excellent service or duty to such persons, competence requires the commitment to the kind of research, professional development, and reflective practice that will help me realize my work-related goals and fulfill my obligations well.

Competence in justice may mean learning the cooking skills and repertoire needed to provide healthy meals that accommodate for the allergies of family members. Competence may mean embracing rather than dismissing social media as a means of strengthening relational bonds. Conversely, competence may require the ability to communicate well in person lest social media become an obstacle to relationships.

Competence might require a middle-class person to understand the causes of poverty so as to better engage the poor (or be cognizant of local, community resources for such engagement). Competence might mean the ability to differentiate between various forms of "waste" and their appropriate bins so as to fulfill our social responsibility to one another as stewards of the earth (not to mention our responsibility *to* the earth). Competence might mean hanging up the dish towel properly to expedite the drying process, out of courtesy for roommates. Competence may involve the skill of translation, both literally (the ability to speak and move between multiple languages) and conceptually (able to explain, for example, Christian theological concepts in a relatively jargon-free and audience-appropriate way to non-Christians).

Competence plays the role of ensuring that our just action is not impotent and shoddy but excellent—not for the sake of bragging rights but for effectiveness. Quality unquestionably matters if we are to claim what we are experiencing or doing is, in fact, love.

Responsiveness

Justice requires a readiness to adjust, whether because people or circumstances change or because becoming just is often a process of trial-and-error. The need to be competent should not mean we ought to be perfectionistic about our justice, too timid to act or take risks. We ought to act, but with a continual readiness to adjust our actions as needs emerge and evolve.

Responsive to Experience

Justice follows the logic of Underwood's "feedback loops"—a "process of action, internal feedback, inner correction, and action."[41] Justice listens and grows. Justice fits our love to others but becomes continually "refitted" through ongoing, responsive, relational participation in others. Justice draws on gratitude to receive others—their particularities, their feedback, their praise and critique—and then responds with ever-more fitting love and suitable meeting of needs.

Responsive to Others as They Are

Borrowing from Noddings's characterization of care, the responsive nature of justice involves both engrossment and motivational displacement. Engrossment is the capacity to receive others as they are, free from our impositions and projections. Motivational displacement involves the outward flow of our "motive energy" toward the other and, possibly, his or her goals.[42] Just people give others, in addition to physical resources or verbal encouragement, emotional energy. The sharing of motive energy as a component of justice may even lead us to advocate for causes we care little about, simply because they are important to others.

When we are responsive, we get angry at what angers others; we are saddened by what saddens others; we feel others' concerns as if they were our own. This means momentarily setting aside one's own biases and judgments and valuing the concerns of others, perhaps even assisting others in acting on these concerns—not because we share their values but because we value the individuals. While we should prudently guard against abandoning our principles for others, we should also be wary of opposite dangers, like

---

41. Underwood, "Compassionate Love," 17.

42. Noddings, *Caring*, 33. That is, we put ourselves, often vulnerably, at the service of others.

dismissiveness and downplaying, or even making idols of our own principles. Justice takes others seriously.

Responsive to the Whole

Just persons recognize their relationships with all living things. Just people adapt to the needs of others but also to the world as a whole. The just person knows the ways in which he or she is complicit in various systems of oppression. Simultaneously, he or she is perpetually ready to take and is actively taking small steps (if not big ones) to remedy this.

The Confucian concept of *ren*—the highest Confucian virtue—emphasizes the responsiveness of justice. When Confucians talk about *ren* they speak of a multivalent concept that functions as both an overarching reality and a concrete virtue. *Ren* decenters us. It prioritizes the whole over the individual while encouraging me to integrate myself with others and with the world. A person expressing *ren* does not simply impose his or her will on others or the world but responds to the cues of others—individuals, groups, and the natural world.

Ren counters one extreme of egoism and another extreme of withdrawal, neither of which lead to *ren*—the "ways and procedures of integrating oneself with others."[43] *Ren's* universality does not neglect family but uses family as a starting point, turning familial love into a training ground for empathy and compassion. *Ren* is also the ideal quality of rulers, as a government of *ren* persons would, theoretically, reduce crime and poverty and lead to economic flourishing.[44]

This more collectivist dimension of justice, intimated by the Confucian tradition, can expand a more individualistic conception of justice (where I "do something" for you) and support a participatory conception of justice. We do more than act on others' behalf (though justice *is* active); we responsively integrate ourselves with others. The highly relational, responsive person affirms and respects others while avoiding excessive and insufficient self-expression. He or she also recognizes his or her part in the whole.

Emotional Responsiveness

The responsiveness of justice is deepened through empathy and compassion. Empathy is the emotional experience of another's emotional experience that

43. Yao, "Jen, Love, and Universality," 182, 184.
44. Li, "Confucian Concept of Jen," 73.

can motivate us to act for their good. While the risk of over-identification with others' suffering looms, the consequences of under-identification may be greater. For example, I may cry in response to another's distress and thus sacrifice the therapeutic advantages of being a calm, detached outsider. Yet such tears may reflect my attentive engagement and facilitate my ability to actively and faithfully assist the person in healing. Similarly, we might avoid images of suffering in the media because of the crippling distress and helplessness it may cause. Yet ignoring such suffering can insulate us and prohibit the living out of justice.

Empathy, while perhaps destructive in excess, is good. We are "hard-wired" for empathy, displayed, for example, in aptly named "mirror neurons"—"nerve cells that allow humans to understand one another's experiences by undergoing a kind of involuntary 'neurological echo' while observing one another's behavior."[45] Our neurological and practical responses to others are in harmony: the capacity to mirror another and thus demonstrate a fitting emotional and cognitive grasp of another's needs is key to the full expression of justice.

Compassion is another responsive emotion. Goetz, Keltner, and Simon-Thomas define compassion as "the feeling that arises in witnessing another's suffering" that "motivates a subsequent desire to help."[46] Compassion is more than pity; it compels us to participate in the suffering of others. Compassion, as a more instinctive response to suffering, is not love or justice; it lacks, among other things, a strong awareness of the goodness of the other and a propensity toward more sustained involvement (even if brief). Yet compassion can lead to justice and also emerge in the process of justice and strengthen justice's expression.

Compassion can incorporate our emotional response not only to others' suffering but also to their not-yet-actualized good. My compassion for my child's "owie" awakens and enlists my virtue of justice as I become engrossed in alleviating her suffering and ushering her toward tranquility. My compassion for her age-appropriate inability to read or make an omelet similarly evokes a loving response that compels me to participate in these "deficiencies"—shortcomings only in the sense that they indicate unfulfilled goals or undeveloped capacities. Compassion facilitates our responsiveness to others' suffering and unfulfilled potential while ultimately resulting in benevolent action and adjustments to our own lifestyle.[47] Unlike the po-

45. Gerdes, Segal, Jackson, and Mullins, "Teaching Empathy," 114.

46. Goetz, Keltner, and Simon-Thomas, "Compassion," 351. Compassion has evolutionary roots, historically playing a role in protecting "vulnerable offspring," informing "mate selection," and promoting "cooperative relations with non-kin" (354).

47. Nolan, "Spiritual Growth," 45.

tentially isolating emotions of distress, sadness, or anger, compassion is connective, aiding our self-giving participation in others.

Empathy and compassion act as sparks of a kind of justice that *fits* our love through attentive, responsible, competent, and responsive action toward our "neighbor," whomever he or she may be.

Exemplar of Justice: Alice Walker (1944–present)

Alice Walker, an activist and author best known for *The Color Purple* and her womanist (her terminological creation) writings, has demonstrated a strong virtue of justice. Walker's childhood experiences in the rural South informed her connection to the earth, her valuing of community (sharecropping forced people of color toward economic and social interdependence), her interest in writing (her family prioritized education) and her resilience (notably as a result of being shot in the eye by her brother).[48] While Walker's social activism and apt care for others express her virtue of justice, her writing is her primary tool for just action in the world.

Walker has displayed justice by highlighting the voices and experiences of black female contemporaries and ancestors. In such activity Walker demonstrates attentiveness to others, responsibility for her felt obligation to these others, and competent communicative abilities to magnify otherwise underappreciated voices. Walker laments the responsibility placed on black women to "carry the burdens everyone else . . . refused to carry" and the subsequent neglect of these women's gifts.[49] Walker justly raises up these voices, seeking also to liberate her readers to "identify the living creativity some of our great-grandmothers were not allowed to know."[50]

Walker's virtue of justice highlights the importance, particularly for black women, of naming oneself. Self-naming strengthens one's sense of "personal power, freedom, worth, and value."[51] Her exhortation of others to self-naming comes from her own profound experience of learning to value herself, particularly through an epiphany related to her shame about her own physical appearance in light of her damaged eye. Upon her daughter's affirmation of the beauty of her mother's eye, Walker realizes that "it was possible to love [my eye] . . . in fact, I did love it, for all it had taught me of shame and anger and inner vision, I *did* love it."[52] Walker

---

48. Harris, *Gifts of Virtue*, 16–25.

49. Walker, "In Search of Our Mothers' Gardens," 237.

50. Walker, "In Search of Our Mothers' Gardens," 237.

51. Harris, *Gifts of Virtue*, 85.

52. Walker, "Beauty," 384–94, 390.

makes her love "fitting" by recognizing the non-categorical uniqueness of those before her, expressed and named by these others. She also demonstrates justice through her lived and exhorted freedom from oppressive gender norms. Walker notes the potential liberating quality of lesbian relationships without the threat of male oppression while, in fairness, recognizing the still-present threat of "invisible, internalized forms of oppression" even within such relationships.[53]

Walker has demonstrated justice through activism. While she had experiences with physical activism—she disquietingly sat in the white section of a bus on her way to begin her studies at Spelman College—her experiences as a poor, black woman raised in the South informed her literary voice.[54] Walker's literature is an expression of justice, reflecting attention to oppression, responsibility for the oppressed, competence to alleviate this oppression through literary craft, and responsiveness to continually discovered marginalization.

Yet Walker's gaze has extended beyond literature. She has "protested the South African apartheid, the Iraq War, the Israeli occupation of Palestine, and female genital mutilation."[55] Walker participated in civil rights demonstrations and voter registration campaigns, married interracially when it was taboo, and visited Fidel Castro in an attempt to create amicable relations between Cuba and the US.[56] Pamela Smith suggests that "raising her voice and using loving weapons of resistance are Walker's ways to Earth-saving and people-saving."[57]

Walker has demonstrated justice through her commitment to community. Her writings reflect a value of wholeness, including a reconciled global community that affords "unity, equality, freedom, and basic rights" to "every person and every part of creation."[58] Walker's "commitment to maintaining wholeness in community . . . pushes her onward to uncover injustice and reveal places where the community is fractured and in need of healing."[59]

Walker's practice of justice is particularly supported by her sense of loving participation in and relationship with all creation: "I have a deep sense of oneness with the planet, the cosmos [which] seems perfect in every

53. Harris, *Gifts of Virtue*, 84–85.
54. Harris, *Gifts of Virtue*, 29–34.
55. Mack, "Biography."
56. Smith, "Green Lap, Brown Embrace, Blue Body," 476.
57. Smith, "Green Lap, Brown Embrace, Blue Body," 478.
58. Harris, *Gifts of Virtue*, 66–67.
59. Harris, *Gifts of Virtue*, 123.

way.[60] Walker personalizes this oneness, acknowledging the claims that not only her own children but Palestinian children as well have on her: "Children are the responsibility of all adults. . . . To turn away from them is impossible for me."[61] Walker, compelled by justice, loves the whole and affirms the relevance of each part to the whole.

Walker's attentive, responsible, competent, and responsive participation in the goodness of others provides an exemplary model of how love can be expressed through justice.

---

60. Walker, "Recently I Wrote a Letter." Walker laments: "It is tragic that our focus on harming others is fatally distracting humans from this invigorating reality."

61. Walker, "Recently I Wrote a Letter."

Chapter Nine

Kindness: Extravagance

Miss no single opportunity of making some small sacrifice, here by a smiling look, there by a kindly word; always doing the smallest right and doing it all for love.[1]

—THÉRÈSE OF LISIEUX, 1873–97

It is quite incredible the capacity people have shown to be magnanimous.[2]

—DESMOND TUTU, 1931–PRESENT

KINDNESS IS EXCESSIVE AND extravagant. It is often spontaneous, surprising, and comforting. If justice is the virtuous pathway that enables us to fulfill our relationship-dictated obligations to others, the virtue of kindness transcends obligations. Kindness occasionally "breaks the rules" and surpasses the expectations of our natural and social bonds.

Kindness is exemplified in Jesus's feeding of the five thousand (Matt 14:13–21). In this instance, Jesus produces an excess of food that would have little use for already satisfied stomachs but would benefit many with whom he might not be in contact beyond this event; it might also "wow" people in such a manner that inspires them or even literally equips them to meet the needs of others.

---

1. Thérèse of Lisieux, *Sermon in a Sentence*, 1:79.
2. Tutu, *No Future Without Forgiveness*, 160.

My distinction between justice and kindness receives a compelling vote of confidence from David Heyd's philosophical investigation of "supererogation," which, most basically, refers to doing more than is required. Heroic acts, acts of beneficence, kindness and consideration, forgiveness and mercy, and volunteering are examples of supererogation.[3]

What I "owe" you, in most cases, is not a fact but more of an agreement—personally, socially, or religiously—and often a provisional one. This also means that what constitutes an excess of what I owe you is not fixed, inviting an ongoing dialogue about how we are obligated to others and what it looks like to go beyond this obligation. This ambiguity is hardly a problem and actually a benefit: it can stimulate the kinds of discussions that, while potentially futile, can at best reveal the possibilities in our relationships. A congregation that wrestles with what they owe a particular population in their city and what constitutes supererogatory action may become more mindful of their Christian call, their local call, an awareness of their resources (people, financial, material, etc.), and clarity about how to lovingly participate in their community.

Heyd argues that acts are supererogatory if they are "neither obligatory nor forbidden," their "omission is not wrong," they are morally good in terms of consequence and intrinsic value, and they are "done voluntarily for the sake of someone else's good."[4] Consider the recent story of District Court Judge Lou Olivera. After sentencing a war veteran to prison for twenty-four hours for a DUI, Olivera chose to spend the entire sentence with this man who suffered from PTSD. Olivera knew, as a fellow war veteran, that the sentenced man would likely suffer more excessively than the typical inmate.[5]

This act was unquestionably supererogatory—or *kind*. Olivera was not bound by his role or relationship to the sentenced man to offer such companionship, nor was it in conflict with his role. No one would have found moral fault in Olivera had he not joined the sentenced man. The anticipated effect of the action would have been positive, and the action itself—taken at face value and not scrutinized for ulterior motives such as public recognition or a guilt-ridden response to his sentence—was intrinsically valuable as an affirming, caring action. Finally, Olivera freely acted out of compassion

---

3. Heyd, *Supererogation*, 2. Rawls also speaks to supererogatory acts such as "benevolence and mercy . . . heroism and self-sacrifice" (Rawls, *Theory of Justice*, 100). Like Heyd, Rawls notes that these acts are good but not "one's duty or obligation" and are "not required" (in the context of the social contract that delineates such requirements) (Rawls, *Theory of Justice*, 100).

4. Heyd, *Supererogation*, 115.

5. Wang, "Compassionate Judge."

for this man. Though one could argue that all God's creatures deserve to be treated as more than obligations, a more realistic response to this situation is, "No, the judge need not have done that."

Furthermore, this action is inspiring and flashy in a way that most expressions of quotidian justice are not. While we often praise people for their day-in-and-day-out care for others, such activities may not inspire the same degree of creative imitation that supererogatory kindness does. My attentiveness to the movement of the drive-through line at Starbucks is expected by other drivers; only when my absorption in my phone distracts me from aiding the flow of traffic do others become mindful of my actions (or inactions) and subsequently honk at me. If I am doing what I should be doing, no one will notice. But if I pay for the order of the person behind me, the beneficiary may feel gratitude, surprise, conviction, and a call to imitate my supererogatory act. Kindness is contagious.

Violations of duty are often legally punishable offenses while the failure to act supererogatorily is either unnoticed or merely met with wistful disappointment. Yet in the context of spiritual formation, both justice and kindness ought to be given equal emphasis. Kindness is neither a luxury nor the culmination of the journey from love novice to love expert. In fact, some people may often appear more kind than just, even if justice is arguably *conceptually* prior. The friend who generously pays the bill on your lunch date but is a poor listener displays kindness but lacks the attentive, responsive qualities of justice. Kindness may be supererogatory but should not be considered optional.

Kindness acknowledges our natural responsibilities but often takes on non-obligatory responsibilities, usually for a short period of time. There are no fixed "rules" to kindness; its practice is often unsustainable and spontaneous. If my child drops a Kind bar wrapper on the ground, it is my responsibility to ensure that it is picked up. While I have no such responsibility for others' litter on the sidewalk, kindness might compel me to pick it up anyway (although few would reprimand me if I ignored it as "not my problem"). We may not know how to get to the post office when asked on the street and do not owe the inquirer more than a clearly spoken "I don't know." Kindness may compel us to take a minute to look up directions on our smart phone.

To echo Aristotle, kindness is often "the right way" of being virtuous, where *how* we do something—not just that we do it—is crucial. William Hamrick, in his comprehensive philosophical treatment of kindness, notes that a virtue of kindness is demonstrated through actions, omissions (not acting when one could), and the way in which one acts.[6] These three forms

6. Hamrick, *Kindness and the Good Society*, 29.

of kindness will be expressed in the virtues that follow, as some expressions of kindness concern acting beyond what a baseline action would be (e.g., volunteering), withholding an action toward which we are naturally inclined (e.g., not criticizing someone's mistake in a possible shame-inducing context), or "delivering" an action in the right way (e.g., greeting another with a warm rather than cold tone of voice).

The vices of kindness take many forms. An excess—too much kindness—could look like injustice or self-neglect, if our kindness toward some causes us to abandon our crucial care for others or self. Too little kindness, as an active deficiency, could look like rudeness or cruelty (the rarer deficiency). As an *inactive* deficiency, too little kindness could take the form of isolating monotony, in which we shortchange ourselves, our own happiness, and others by failing to ever live beyond duty and routine (a more common deficiency). To not be kind is to cut ourselves off from significant opportunities to delight others and delight ourselves (as kindness is personally rewarding), just as the opposite of loving participation in others is nonparticipation.

Kindness expands our vision and increases our sensitivity to the subtle, unexpressed needs of others. Kindness turns ordinary others into celebrities and saints, a cognitive reappraisal that can inspire more extravagant activity. We courteously hold a door open for another. We listen well enough to remember details of another's story and experience because it is uplifting to know you have been heard. We do not separate people into us and them, good and evil, or right and wrong, but more charitably recognize that the views of our opponents are not "stupid" but emerge from a unique set of concerns and pressures. We deal truthfully and non-manipulatively with people because we believe they are not means but ends. Kindness elevates its beneficiaries.

I will subsequently examine five supporting virtues of kindness: *generosity* (abundant giving), *consideration* (thoughtfulness and courtesy), *hospitality* (making others comfortable), *magnanimity* (great actions, heroic or subtle), and *forgiveness* (transcending justified retribution).

Generosity

Generosity is a "deep willingness to give help, assistance, time, and money freely with no ulterior motive."[7] Greed, in contrast, is the "overwhelming

---

7. Harris, *Gifts of Virtue*, 114.

desire to have more than one actually needs."[8] Generosity enhances loving participation; greed withdraws from such participation.

Generous in Small Ways

Kindness virtues act as the finessing or fine-tuning of love in any kind of relationship. We need to show or remind those we love that we love them in ways they will experience as loving. Small acts of abundant giving, to be truly loving, may necessitate extra creativity and attention to those to whom love obligates us.

So we deliberately express affection rather than rely solely on unspoken understandings ("Of course I love you, why do I need to say it?") or the regularity of justice (e.g., paying the bills, cooking dinner, etc.) in our intimate relationships. We tell our children the specific ways we appreciate them rather than fall back on good but generic affirmations. We occasionally redirect our finances budgeted for eating out toward a disaster relief effort. We spend ten minutes talking with someone who we would otherwise avoid because it would benefit the other. Love gives, regardless of the extent to which this giving benefits us. But such giving can often be expressed in small ways that require "extra" effort and sacrifice—but often not that much.

Generous With What Is "Mine"

Gregory Spencer describes generosity with the image of open hands as opposed to clenched fists. This juxtaposition emphasizes how we might view our possessions and talents in relationship to others. This might entail a willingness to say "yes" to requests for our assistance, a capacity to be joyfully interrupted, a detachment toward one's possessions, the welcoming of others into our home and experience, and a balanced blend of frugality and liberality that enables us to give from our financial resources.[9] We ought to love with open hands and without fear because, rather than depleting our love, generosity *grows* love.

We can be generous with our time through volunteering, which is a giving of our time and self to a collaborative effort. Heyd cites the donation of blood—at least in societies where it is voluntary—as a paradigmatic example of generosity.[10] In this case, the anonymity of giving ensures no

8. Harris, *Gifts of Virtue*, 115.

9. Spencer, *Awaking the Quieter Virtues*, 166–75.

10. Heyd, *Supererogation*, 148.

reciprocal reward for the giver, other than the intrinsic (and not valueless) reward. This example also highlights the possibility of anonymous participatory love; others need not necessarily know we have acted on their behalf to be loved, nor do we always need to know whom our love directly benefits (though structures should be in place to ensure that such love is still fitting). Generosity can contribute to real (but for us unknown) others while growing a virtue of generosity in us that will ultimately manifest in our regular relationships.

Generous in Assessments

We can also be generous in our assessments of others. Generosity helps us go beyond quick judgments and first impressions. We listen critically and carefully. Where possible, we attribute positive motives to others and trust them, giving them the benefit of the doubt. Since our assessment about the goodness or badness of someone can be a somewhat arbitrary, subjective interpretation of the data of his or her life, generosity may call us to adopt an optimistic narrative about another. Generosity allows us to assume the best, even against evidence to the contrary, as long as our "reading" does not cause us to overlook or condone harmful behavior.

Being Generous Makes Us Happy

Two related studies demonstrated that the more money individuals spent on others, the happier they were. The first study, by focusing on prosocial giving rather than income, may have also revealed the value of intentionality and the benefits of deliberate, effortful engagement (in addition to the value of generous giving).[11] Generosity unites us with others by matching our resources with others' needs while also allowing us to consciously and actively participate in something greater than ourselves.

The second study demonstrated a "positive feedback loop": the positive emotions experienced by those in this study who spent money on others (rather than on themselves) increased the likelihood of future giving.[12] The study revealed two additional sustainers of future giving: one, later reflection upon such giving is likely to also produce the kind of happiness that leads to more giving (as opposed to remembering something that made one momentarily happy that one now regrets in retrospect); two,

---

11. Dunn, Akin, and Norton, "Spending Money on Others," 1687–88.
12. Akin, Dunn, and Norton, "Happiness Runs in a Circular Motion," 347–55.

the amount of money given seems not to affect happiness as much as the "positive social contact" gained by the giving.[13] We are satisfied by our generosity because it increases our participation in others. We are more likely to continue being generous when we can recall positive experiences of such connective participation.

What Motivates Generosity?

A recurring philosophical question in positive psychology comes to mind: is giving altruistically or egoistically motivated? That is, do we give to others for their sakes or for our own? Fortunately, this is an unnecessary dichotomy for Christian spiritual development. If humans are oriented toward love, wired to be relational and others-centered, then generosity is a matter of self-fulfillment. While unloving motivation is possible, love of self is not suspect by default.

Generosity means giving not only resources but also ourselves; if possible, we ought to offer "happy" or "fulfilled" selves. Our giving may be a response to an eros-based need for self-fulfillment, an agapic self-forgetfulness, or a philia-driven desire for strong relationships (or all three). Generosity—assuming it truly honors the beneficiary and is not manipulative, qualified, conditional, with "strings attached"—ought to more deeply unite us with others rather than distance us from them.

Considerateness

Considerateness is a subtle kindness virtue. When we are considerate, we treat others "with deference and respect because they are the image and likeness of God."[14] Considerateness is often effective when is not noticeable. We choose not to correct someone's error in speech when their intended words are obvious. We pretend not to have been bumped by someone in line rather than offering a knowing glare. Being on time, doing small favors, or remembering a birthday are the expressions of someone who can look outside of their own concerns and self-centered needs and consider simple ways to honor and affirm others.

Considerateness is primarily about respect and meticulous care, not submission or silencing: considerateness is no longer a pathway to love

13. Akin, Dunn, and Norton, "Happiness Runs in a Circular Motion," 352-53.
14. Lovasik, *Hidden Power of Kindness*, 13.

when it becomes a sedative to righteous anger or a "polite" upholding of oppressive relationships or structures.

Considerateness is of course subject to cultural variation; what is appropriate in one culture might not be in another. Mutual graciousness is warranted. Yet the supererogatory nature of kindness might compel one toward competence in intercultural discourse and richer understanding of particular cultures to increase culturally relevant considerateness.

Considerate of Others' Voices

Considerateness entails "creating room for others to come into their own voice" through careful listening and tactful speaking.[15] It is often more kind (and courageous) to be direct with those we love, as beating around the bush can indicate cowardice and create insecurity in our relationships. On the other hand, an ability to indirectly communicate truth, through creating opportunities for others to come to discoveries and insights on their own, can be a form of extravagant love.

The manner in which I often feign ignorance when teaching my child age-appropriate lessons as a pedagogical strategy ("gosh sweetie, I don't know how ketchup will taste on your chocolate ice cream; why don't you try it and see?") might be a model for how considerateness plays out in our relationships. It can often be considerate (and loving) to let others be their own primary teachers, even when we have legitimate and relevant knowledge.

Considerate Words

The *way* we say things—not just that we say them—matters. It might be a fulfillment of my responsibility to you to confront you about how your actions are harming yourself, me, or another person. But to be effective, the words used in my confrontation should reflect that I understand you—your needs, desires, triggers, and anxieties—and can discern which words will most effectively assist you. A person who is inconsiderate cannot communicate with that right balance of clarity and delicacy.

Considerateness recognizes the perils of non-humorous exaggeration, misrepresentation, criticizing others (where our critiques may contain truth but are presented more for self-advancement than from a concern for factual accuracy), or participating as a listener in slanderous

15. Harris, *Gifts of Virtue*, 117.

conversations.[16] Considerateness may often mean saying nothing rather than something. Speech will often magnify the problem or continue a perpetual back-and-forth that silence can halt. Silence is an improvement upon defensiveness, when defending one's position takes one away from loving participation and becomes isolating.

Praising others is a kindness. We may not owe people compliments, yet praise helps others grow, improve, and move toward goals. Like many acts of consideration, praising others is easy to practice as there are numerous positive and constructive things we could say to others throughout the day, assuming we are attentive.

Considerate Awareness

A lack of considerateness is often experienced as a lack of sensitivity or awareness. Coldness, rudeness, and thoughtlessness stand in opposition to considerateness. On a global scale, it may be incumbent upon us not to mindlessly purchase that product from the grocery store as though it miraculously appeared on the shelf and had no backstory. In fact, our purchases do affect other people.

On a smaller scale, I might give my friend a ride home but lack warmth, speak offensively, or fail to warn her that we will be making a "brief" stop at the supermarket before I drop her off at home. I may have acted justly, if one thinks friends "owe" friends the occasional ride. Yet I have not acted kindly, foregoing words of welcome and reassurance ("It's my pleasure to give you a ride"), making quick, ill-founded judgments ("Didn't plan very well, did you?"), and foregoing full disclosure ("I can give you a ride, if you don't mind a quick stop.") Such oversights and shortcomings are the kinds of simple but collectively impactful actions a virtue of considerateness can counter.

The more aware we become of how our actions affect others, the more considerate we are likely to become. We do not live our lives in a vacuum. Whether talking boisterously in a quiet restaurant or eating this restaurant's food, the production of which depends on environmentally harmful methods, attempting to become more considerate may call us to personal change.

Considerateness is more than small favors; it is a way of illuminating more fully the opportunities for extravagant love in the relational obligations that justice reveals.

16. Lovasik, *Hidden Power of Kindness*, 137–57.

Hospitality

Hospitable Space

Hospitality is both receptive and outgoing. What we give is a spaciousness that allows others to feel at home. Henri Nouwen describes hospitality as "the creation of a free space where the stranger can enter and become a friend instead of enemy."[17] Hospitable people create comfortable, inviting, and safe environments for others. Hospitality is more than an articulated stance ("You are welcome here"); it is a welcoming presence and posture lived out in practices, gestures, and details.

Hospitable Gestures

Smiling is an important act of hospitality, as is humor, which helps us cope with the "contrasts and inconsistencies in life."[18] Using a person's name, possibly multiple times, throughout an encounter with them can be hospitable. Educator John Yeager notes the positive and connective effects of using names in conversation, observing that such salutations involve three elements of PERMA (the acronymic summary of the core concerns of positive psychology): we tend to enjoy hearing our name (positive emotions); we respond viscerally to our name, especially when paired with some form of touch such as a handshake, creating a multifaceted experience that is at once auditory, visual, and kinesthetic (engagement); and the use of our name communicates the message "you matter" (meaning).[19]

However, as with considerateness, hospitable persons do not thoughtlessly use their own preferred gestures (eye contact, hugs, etc.) but discern—as much as is possible—personal and cultural differences. We might forgive someone for (and possibly even laugh about) a culturally inappropriate gesture, keeping reasonable expectations about another's aptness in cross-cultural exchange. Yet hospitality, as a supererogatory virtue, encourages both savvy delivery and above-and-beyond awareness of what will actually increase the comfort of another.

---

17. Nouwen, *Reaching Out*, 71. Nouwen elaborates: "Hospitality is not a subtle invitation to adopt the lifestyle of the host, but the gift of a chance for the guest to find his own" (72).

18. Lovasik, *Hidden Power of Kindness*, 44–45.

19. Yeager, "'I've Got a Name.'"

Hospitable Preparedness

There is a regularity to hospitality, despite its exceptionality: while we need not (and cannot) be perpetually supererogatory through successive hospitable acts, we ought to be hospitably prepared for unexpected needs and opportunities. This could mean habitually keeping one's home clean rather than enacting a more dramatic cleaning the day before a guest arrives. It could mean keeping a couple of dollars or a couple of bottles of water in one's car, should we encounter another in need of such resources. It could mean practicing good hygiene so as to not thwart a potentially meaningful conversation with something as seemingly inconsequential as bad breath. It could mean keeping our friend's favorite tea on hand in case he or she should drop by. Hospitality is inclusive and comforting, often highly attentive to detail so as to maximize our ability to lovingly participate in others.

Hospitable Ownership and Boundaries

Hospitality challenges my sense of what's "mine." While ownership of anything can lead to possessiveness and entitlement, it can also allow for good stewardship. Hospitality puts what is "ours" in a new light, revealing how our possessions can be used in service of others. But a lack of hospitality should not necessarily be faulted, as this might not indicate rudeness as much as unexceptionality. If my friend gives me a standing invitation to enter his home without knocking, I experience his hospitality; I would not think twice if the offer had never been made and I had been expected to knock upon arrival. My friend has welcomed, even if only marginally, my greater participation in his life and possessions through transcending the socially expected rules of privacy and property.

Hospitality can transcend natural boundaries. Psychologist Richard Beck explores the psychology of disgust—our natural, positive visceral resistance to possible contaminants—and its relationship to hospitality. This protective emotion can extend to how Christian churches function socially—"always tempted to separate, withdraw, quarantine."[20] Disgust can create "sociological barriers and motivate acts of exclusion."[21] Hospitality, while often expressed in simple, thoughtful gestures that make others comfortable, in some cases means overcoming an instinctive response to what we do not understand or what seemingly threatens us.

---

20. Beck, *Unclean*, 30. Beck is also a lay theologian and popular Christian blogger.
21. Beck, *Unclean*, 9.

A virtue of hospitality allows us to share space comfortably with what is different or possibly revolting. Hospitality could allow those of opposing political parties—convinced as they are of the destructiveness or "evil" of their opponent's stances and compelled by justice to resist the other—to receive one another. It could also allow a host to easily receive a guest despite his or her context-inappropriate loud chomping of food, able to forgive the "offense" and see the entirety of the person rather than reductively defining them by one behavior.

The Bible exhorts us to "welcome the stranger" (e.g., Lev 19:34, Rom 12:13). It is more natural and possibly more immediately rewarding to care for those who are already an integral part of our lives. Hospitality can make us aware of those who are outside our sphere of concern and may have very little to offer us, at least at first glance. Hospitality helps us participate in others' goodness—a goodness that may not be immediately obvious to us.

Magnanimity

While kindness is by definition extravagant, it can be magnanimous—going the *third* mile on occasion. Thomas Aquinas describes magnanimity as the "stretching forth of the mind to great things."[22] Such greatness could be displayed in acts of great size and scope but also in the "good use of" a thing.[23] This "thing" could include oneself, as a self-caring individual may be compelled to share oneself with others in an extraordinary manner. Magnanimity pushes us to do great things for others. A virtue of magnanimity can enable individuals and congregations to take creative action to supplement

---

22. Aquinas, II-IIae Q 129, Art 1. Thomas annexes magnanimity to the virtue of fortitude, classified as such because it helps the mind "stand firm" in a manner similar to and supportive of the obstacle-overcoming virtue of fortitude (Q 129, Art 4). While this works for Thomas (and could work for me, as I could similarly make a case for magnanimity as a virtue of hope in my scheme), this placement is not necessary. Thomas does not give as much weight as I do to a virtue of kindness. "Friendliness," a part of justice, is too insignificant in his scheme; charity, which is in some ways an above-and-beyond virtue for Thomas, becomes difficult to treat alongside kindness since it is also the greatest virtue. By annexing magnanimity to kindness here, I hope to draw attention to how kindness can be lived out in ways both small and simple and large and complex.

23. Aquinas, II-IIae Q 129, Art 1. A related virtue is that of "magnificence," which Thomas refers to as the "doing of something great" (great in quantity, value, or dignity) and more concretely, for Thomas, indicates substantial public expenditures (Aquinas, II-IIae, Q 134). I am admittedly conflating magnanimity and magnificence, arguably about becoming great and doing great, respectively.

their regular, consistent kindnesses with occasional projects or collaborative actions that are possibly more demanding but more impactful.

Magnanimous Cultivation of Love

Magnanimity pushes us to become more loving (and thus shares the self-cultivating qualities of gratitude, self-care, and hope). Herdt contends that magnanimity can avoid a self-preoccupied, self-congratulatory quality by maintaining a communal understanding of the way in which character is formed.[24] Thus, magnanimity and humility can coexist by recognizing our successes not as personal achievements as much as responses to what we have been given—by God, by others, by indiscriminate luck.

Magnanimity, self-appropriation, and hope collaboratively guide persons toward growth in our loving capacities. Edward Sri writes, "The person who daily endeavors to be a better spouse, parent, friend or child of God is truly seeking 'greatness of soul.'"[25] While self-care reminds us to set limits and not overburden ourselves, magnanimity pushes us. It encourages an already loving individual to go even further. A magnanimous person might "defer to others' preferences . . . endure criticism with patience . . . respond gently to his [or her] child's temper tantrum . . . avoid defending his [or her] opinion in non-essential matters."[26]

Thomas clarifies the function of magnanimity by highlighting an opposite: "pusillanimity," essentially a kind of resignation to the status quo, the easier path, or perhaps, a dramatic failure of self-appropriation.[27] Magnanimity stirs our creativity and deepens our enthusiasm for unlocking the possibilities in others and in our relationships. While gratitude, as the virtue of receptivity, might be characterized as the virtue of interfaith dialogue for its openness to new experience and new wisdom, magnanimity also challenges the security of present knowledge and encourages us to step into new ways of seeing, even when there is seemingly no urgent pressure to do so.

Magnanimity—Kindness Writ Large

Small acts of considerateness are not inferior to the grandeur of magnanimity; they simply play different roles. Most people have the capacity for

24. Herdt, *Putting on Virtue*, 43.
25. Sri, "Called to Greatness."
26. Sri, "Called to Greatness."
27. Aquinas, II-IIae Q 133, Art 1.

a greater number of considerate acts in a given window than they do for acts of magnanimity. We would not expect the person who can forgive their toddler five times in a month for spilling milk on the carpet to forgive with comparable ease someone who physically harmed said toddler in the same time span. Considerateness is often subtle yet essential; magnanimity is "louder" though not ostentatious.

John Timmerman observes that the power of magnanimity lies in its apparent difficulty: "It is easy to be tolerant about what means little to us."[28] This raises the issue of actual virtue versus semblances of virtue: what truly constitutes a good kindness goal or an authentic demonstration of kindness? My wife might watch a baseball game with me on one night, following which I might watch a movie of her choice the next night. But given our similar cinematic tastes and her general indifference to baseball, these are not equivalent acts of kindness. In fact, our system is not really all that sacrificial but a matter of simply taking turns, with her turn requiring more personal sacrifice.

While small, unflashy, and unnoticed kindnesses are essential, magnanimity calls us to grander and possibly more orchestrated forms of kindness. A Christian congregation might enhance the lives of others through simple gestures like smiles, warm greetings, or words of affirmation. Yet a congregation might also collaboratively address a felt need in a manner that is novel, inspiring, and greater than the sum of its parts. This action may be a creative expansion on present ministry efforts, observable in a way that provokes other churches to participate or replicate the ministry, and dependent on orchestrated effort (as opposed to the "holy" living of individuals). Thus, magnanimity is especially a virtue of communities. It pushes persons-in-community to imaginatively consider what could be and to address particular needs (which could inspire larger social reform), perhaps at a personal cost.

Magnanimity also reinforces the interchangeability of justice and kindness in terms of starting points. Justice is often a foundation upon which kindness builds, expanding on the basics much as a jazz soloist riffs on an established chord progression. Here, adeptness at identifying and meeting needs is expanded upon by the creative and surprising virtue of kindness. Yet at times, kindness precedes justice, initiating a relationship on which justice can build. The gratuitous giving of one's coat to someone who is cold could ultimately lead to better understanding, new relationships, and organized action to alleviate or eradicate homelessness.

---

28. Timmerman, "Some Notes on Magnanimity," 4.

Magnanimity—Heroic Kindness

Magnanimity aids generous giving by strengthening our resolve in the face of ungrateful recipients. Timmerman writes that "to retain a generous disposition toward one who seems like a termite gnawing successfully at the pillars of your temple requires grace as well as largeness of mind."[29] Kindness is fundamentally gracious, giving others something to which they are not entitled—especially when the beneficiaries are rude or dismissive. Magnanimity, however, keeps our kindness focused on those who might not return such kindness.

Heyd's closest parallel to magnanimity is "moral heroism"—displayed in acts that are rare, extraordinary, and of greater risk to the agent than other expressions of kindness (and thus requiring a collaborative virtue of courage).[30] Magnanimity may or may not threaten one's life, but it could threaten reputation, schedule, or other time or relational commitments, among other things. Magnanimity may thus be the costliest of the kindness virtues.

Forgiveness

Forgiveness underscores the amorphous boundaries of my proposed virtues, as it could easily be discussed in the context of every other virtuous pathway. Forgiveness receives, welcoming rather than resisting (gratitude). Forgiveness prepares, caring for oneself by abandoning life-depleting resentment (self-care).[31] Forgiveness actualizes, overcoming painful obstacles to relationships (hope). Given the sheer frequency with which others do not live up to our expectations or thwart our plans, steady, "quiet" forgiveness maintains caring, just relations with others (justice). While all of these approaches are valid (and supported by scientific and theological literature), we often experience forgiveness as freely chosen, profound, and impressive. We may sympathize with those who choose not to forgive but admire those who do. Forgiveness is extravagant.

29. Timmerman, "Some Notes on Magnanimity," 4.

30. Heyd, *Supererogation*, 144.

31. Everett L. Worthington Jr.'s work on forgiveness has focused on the personal health benefits of forgiveness. He argues for forgiveness as a coping strategy and stress reducer. See Worthington and Scherer, "Forgiveness," 385–405.

Forgiveness Reframes

Forgiveness is exceptional in part because it reflects an agent's capacity to transcend the potentially painful reality of the situation or the relationship. If I forgive you, you are no longer a "wrongdoer," identified solely by the harm you have caused me or others. You may have spoken or acted offensively because of pressures of which I am unaware, some past trauma impinging on the present, as a consequence of your social or communal identity, or because of an injustice being done to you. Forgiveness looks beyond the surface reality to grasp the story behind the action.

Such a perspective is fundamental to restorative justice and its impetus to repair relationships and aid the growth and flourishing of offenders. Yet forgiveness goes beyond justice on an intuitive level: we recognize the reasonableness of simply cutting offenders out of our lives (or world) and yet choose to take a hopeful, optimistic view of their potential for greater goodness. We also recognize the benefits to those outside of the offender-offended relationship of a reconciled rather than discordant relationship, as in the case of a conflict between two persons that places a burden on the community in which these two participate.

Forgiveness Grieves but Accepts

Fred Luskin, director of the Stanford University Forgiveness Project, emphasizes that forgiveness means acceptance (but not condoning) of what has happened for the sake of our present relationships.[32] Forgiveness is extravagant in part because it requires that a person choose grief rather than, understandably, avoid it. To note the extravagance of this grieving process, consider the degree of confidence or reticence we might feel in exhorting another person toward virtuous behavior. Saying "you ought to support your family" or "you should educate yourself on poverty" appeals to a person's sense of responsibility for others and is a justifiable, unimposing suggestion. Saying "you ought to forgive that person for assaulting you" risks dismissing and demeaning another's experience, even if we are convinced they would benefit from forgiveness. A person who forgives, especially in cases of severely felt injustice, has to overcome his or her intuitive sense of what another deserves and possibly confront serious personal trauma—no easy tasks.

Yet Christians ought to be liberal forgivers, assuming our forgiveness does not put our or others' safety at risk. But just as we should not expect to

32. Luskin, "What is Forgiveness?"

lift three hundred pounds before we can lift two hundred, so the ability to forgive must be cultivated by starting small. We forgive the slow person in the checkout line. We forgive our internet connection for being slow or too expensive. We forgive the homeless person for making us feel uncomfortable. We forgive people for forgetting our names. Such small steps of forgiveness build the kind of resilience, perspective, and compassion needed to address more substantial or legitimate wrongs.

Forgiveness Spreads

Forgiveness toward an offender ripples out to and implicates our other relationships. Some research has demonstrated that forgiveness extended toward an offending individual is associated with a greater "general prosocial orientation" and with greater likelihood of making charitable donations or volunteering.[33] Forgiveness seems to have an opening affect, in contrast to unforgiveness, which can have an opposite, "closing" effect. This openness transcends any one relationship; forgiveness of one can facilitate our love for many.

This is, of course, what an ethic of virtue proposes—continuity between our relationships linked by the presence or absence of virtue in us. My unforgiveness toward another limits our mutual participation, in terms of both the incoming and outgoing movements of love. In addition, one might overreact with accusatory suspicion of well-intentioned present others whose behavior seemingly echoes past ill-intentioned others. Our forgiveness of one can liberate many.

Forgiveness Transforms

Forgiveness alters our relationships. Forgiving people make generous appraisals and attributions about both transgressors—they give others the benefit of the doubt or reduce blame for the negative behavior of others. Whether one is alone in one's claims to victimhood or has the concurrence of others, forgiveness changes the relationship from offender and victim to something more like equals collaborating toward a just resolution. This is an impressive act (more impressive as the severity of the wrongdoing increases); the cognitive and emotional work needed to achieve this feat is not negligible.

33. Karremans, Van Lange, and Holland, "Forgiveness and Its Associations," 1315–26.

Forgiveness may require something like a "divine perspective" on others that can see from above, so to speak: understand the motivations and causes of wrongful behavior, recognize the good in the offender, and have the magnanimous capacity not to expend emotional resources brooding on an offense. Easier said than done, of course. But not impossible.

Exemplar of Kindness: Desmond Tutu (1931–present)

Desmond Tutu, "the prophet of South African apartheid" and Archbishop Emeritus of Cape Town, has loved extravagantly.[34] Tutu forcefully and publicly fought against apartheid—the white-maintained systemic segregation of blacks and whites in South Africa—from 1975 until its demise in 1994. He was subsequently appointed by then-president Nelson Mandela to chair the Truth and Reconciliation Commission, which sought a "'third way,' a compromise between the extreme of Nuremberg trials and blanket amnesty or national amnesia."[35]

Howard Anderson describes the kindness of Tutu: his ability to "wait with a smile on his face"; his generous displays of pastoral care amid overwhelming responsibilities; his inclusivity and quest to eradicate sexism and homophobia; and his frequent risking of his life "to save those who were against the cause of freedom."[36] Tutu's kindness is displayed in the courtesy of warm gestures and in the willingness to risk his own well-being for his enemies. Tutu even expresses kindness in his soteriology, thwarting any Christian attempts to draw boundaries or deduce the scope of redemption by affirming the inclusivity of God's love and future: "None of us could in my theology ever consign anyone to hell as being ultimately irredeemable."[37]

Tutu's sense of human connectedness enables his generosity toward others. He recognizes, in the context of his consternation at the national blindness in his country, the "power of conditioning" and his own susceptibility to being on the wrong side of history.[38] His generosity manifests not by condoning wrongdoing but in a sympathetic willingness to slow his judgments of others and give others the space to forgive themselves.

---

34. Haws, "Suffering, Hope, and Forgiveness," 477.

35. Tutu, *No Future Without Forgiveness*, 30.

36. Anderson, "Moral Example of Desmond Tutu." Anderson, an Anglican like Tutu, was the warden and president of the Cathedral College at the Washington National Cathedral.

37. Tutu, *No Future Without Forgiveness*, 84.

38. Tutu, *No Future Without Forgiveness*, 254–55.

Michael Battle contrasts Tutu's approach to liberation with those of other black leaders, noting Tutu's emphasis not only on black liberation but on the liberation of whites as well.[39] Tutu's affirmation of the dignity of all widens the circle of those who deserve and need liberation.

Tutu frequently emphasizes the concept of "ubuntu" (a Nguni term) as his and others' goal and motivation in the South African quest for reconciling, restorative justice. Ubuntu is a virtue of kindness emphasizing commonality and interdependence. People with ubuntu are "generous," "hospitable," "friendly," "caring," and "compassionate."[40] Tutu's tireless efforts for reconciliation in South Africa reveal ubuntu to be characteristic of Tutu himself.

Tutu also emphasizes the virtue of magnanimity, which he sees embodied in Nelson Mandela, who broke the retributive cycle and responded to his own suffering with extravagant efforts toward forgiveness and reconciliation.[41] Haws describes Tutu's vision of forgiveness and ability to forgive as magnanimous, as it is an "unmerited" gift, given by a gracious victim, breaking rather than sustaining "the cycle of bondage."[42]

Tutu notes the risks of forgiveness: those we want to forgive might be "arrogant, obdurate, or blind; not ready or willing to apologize"; "such rejection can jeopardize the whole enterprise" of personal and national forgiveness.[43] Forgiveness "is not easy.... In almost every language the hardest words are 'I am sorry'"; culprits often forgo forgiveness, either denying their wrongdoing or "feign[ing] ignorance."[44] Forgiveness does not condone but "draws out the sting . . . that threatens to poison our entire existence."[45] Tutu's kindness shapes a generous view of those with whom he disagrees—a vision of others essential to true forgiveness.

Amina Chaudary, a Muslim scholar who interviewed Tutu, was struck by Tutu's warmth and hospitality.[46] Tutu, a Nobel Peace Prize winner, continued to be socially active following his formal retirement from ministry, going beyond what is expected of a retired person out of compassion for persons suffering from various forms of oppression.[47]

39. Battle, "Liberation," 520–21.

40. Tutu, *No Future Without Forgiveness*, 31.

41. Tutu, *No Future Without Forgiveness*, 38–39.

42. Haws, "Suffering, Hope, and Forgiveness," 486.

43. Tutu, *No Future Without Forgiveness*, 269.

44. Tutu, *No Future Without Forgiveness*, 269.

45. Tutu, *No Future Without Forgiveness*, 271.

46. Chaudary, "Interview with Desmond Tutu," 117.

47. CNN Wire Staff, "South Africa's Tutu."

Tutu once described his fellow anti-apartheid collaborators—and by association himself—as "peace-loving to a fault," listing the heroic actions of many involved in this struggle.[48]

Tutu affirms the biblical basis for his activism: "[I]t is the whole nature of God. . . . Grace means [God] acts on behalf of those who do not deserve it, those who have no claim on [God]."[49] It is easy to acknowledge the claims that parents, spouses, children, friends, coworkers, fellow citizens, or oppressed groups have on us. But for those we identify as oppressors or those who are close to us but have temporarily wronged us, the ability to lovingly participate requires something "extra." Tutu demonstrates this extravagance, tirelessly devoting himself to people with arguably no claim on his love. Though Tutu, mindful of "ubuntu" and our mutual indebtedness, might disagree.

Christians ought to look to Tutu's extravagant love as a guide for becoming more generous, considerate, hospitable, magnanimous, and forgiving.

48. Tutu, "Christian Witness in South Africa," 17. The phrase should not be taken literally, of course; there is no moral "fault" in these extraordinary efforts.

49. Tutu, "Prisoner of Hope," 40.

Chapter Ten

Hope: Making the Possible, Actual

> Because of our Mother called hope, we human beings are not
> prisoners of the past; our time extends to eternity. . . . Hope is
> then the womb in which we live, struggle, travail, dream. In it
> we are in touch with the source of life, in communication with
> all that was, is, and shall be, and in communion with that power
> of love called God.[1]
>
> —C. S. SONG, 1929–PRESENT

> We certainly must have the long view into the future to see and
> realize the awakening of the masses of people throughout the
> world and the growth of a new vision among them.[2]
>
> —DOROTHY DAY, 1897–1980

The Power of Hope

IN CHAPTER 2 I articulated a multilayered concept of hope. Hope is the
narrative momentum of Christian spiritual development, moving lovers
toward love. Hope is a three-part structure for the basic components of
spiritual growth—agency, pathways, and goal—that invites enfleshment

1. Song, *Jesus*, 55.
2. Day, "On Pilgrimage–February 1969."

and provides a hermeneutic for assessing present practices. Hope is an intentional and creative method of spiritual growth.

Here, I define hope as the virtuous pathway that actualizes love. Hope reveals the possibilities in situations, relationships, and individuals, motivates us to develop these possibilities, and assists us in realizing them. Hope helps us grow and helps us help others grow. Love acts as a meta-goal for spiritual development, and our diverse relationships invite clarity and pursuit of goals; we may have "hopes" for our relationships but do well to identify them. A commitment not only to strategic plans but also to a life-long project of virtue cultivation shifts the more cognitive element of Snyder's model (pathways) to the dispositional.

Hopeful people can more easily cultivate virtues than unhopeful people. They can better participate in the present and potential goodness of others because they are better equipped to overcome obstacles to love, whether such obstacles come from the one loved (e.g., our friend is too proud to accept advice), from ourselves (e.g., we fear the repercussions of upsetting our friend), or from somewhere in between (e.g., we cannot seem to coordinate schedules to find time for unhurried face-to-face communication). Hope overcomes all kinds of threats to love.

Hope Actualizes Gratitude

Receptive participation in others is threatened by the delusion of self-sufficiency, the inability to appreciate others' strengths and successes, and resistance to or indifference toward discovering the true, the beautiful, and the good. Hope invites others to participate in our movement toward our ultimate goals, combatting our rugged individualism. Hope instills a more interdependent vision of personal agency. Hope allows others to influence our goals and expand our vision of what is worth pursuing. Hope allows others' examples to elevate and empower us.

Hope looks forward by looking backward, recognizing how others have already participated in us and sensing what is possible for us given the resources at hand. Hope is not afraid that you will threaten, disrupt, or irreparably alter my identity but welcomes the enhancing and expansion of self that comes from your participation in me.

Hope Actualizes Self-Care

Ready participation in others is threatened by a lack of self-understanding, neglect of emotional, physical, and mental health, an inability to regulate our emotions, and the ongoing failure to express our unique abilities in concrete, others-benefitting ways. Hope makes sense of our actions in the context of a unified whole—agents shaped by the past and compelled by the future.

Hope guides meticulous goal-setting in various domains of health, recognizing strategy as an aid to self-discipline. Hope places ultimate values at the forefront as we face momentary challenges, allowing us to gain increasing regulatory power over ourselves. Hope affirms God's desire to collaborate with humans in their particularity and takes on the project of self-development of talents, recognizing that personal fulfillment and love of others go hand in hand.

Hope takes seriously the call to all to contribute to the increasing presence of love in the world and takes on this burden oneself, believing that change comes not primarily through optimism and counting on external forces but through personal participation.

Hope Actualizes Justice

Fitting participation in others is threatened by a failure to understand our responsibility for others and how to act on this responsibility. Hope imagines a better future for others, in dialogue with the expressed needs of individuals and communities. Hope guides the concrete steps and setting of provisional goals on the way toward this future.

The goals I have for (or have been given by) others guide the attentive-responsible-competent-responsive process of justice toward others. Hope overcomes the obstacles of inattention, neglected responsibility, incompetence, and unresponsiveness that threaten my loving participation in others.

Hope gives justice a future, so to speak; it sustains and invigorates lovers amid the often unspectacular and underappreciated work of long-term care for others by situating our present activity in the context of a larger narrative. Hope recognizes that self-fashioning is often a privilege and thus acts, non-patronizingly, to increase the agency of the underprivileged that they too may engage in hopeful goal-pursuit.

Hope Actualizes Kindness

Extravagant participation in others is threatened by over-commitment, lack of creativity, the perceived absence of shareable resources, and an unpleasant disposition, among other obstacles. Hope can balance my life so as to allow space for spontaneous altruism. Hope can imagine varied, enjoyable, and meaningful ways to delight others. Hope can reframe my understanding of what I have so that I do not hoard my finances, time, and other resources but recognizes possessions as "mine" in a chastened sense.

Hope can aid goal setting in the area of personal demeanor and conduct so as to smooth out my rough, inhospitable, and inconsiderate edges. Hope may make supererogatory behavior an ideal starting point for the cultivation of love virtues, as doing simple kindnesses might be easier and more personally and immediately rewarding than other virtues (e.g., the steady care of justice may often lack the positive reinforcement that the gift of a dollar to a person in need might immediately grant). Hope breeds positivity, and positive people may more easily overcome the cynicism that questions the value of small kindnesses.

The Supporting Virtues of Hope

Hope is the power to overcome obstacles to love. In what follows, I will examine five supporting virtues of hope: *faith, discernment, courage, presence,* and *grit.* Each of these corresponds with and addresses an obstacle to love.

A lack of commitment to our goals, values, a sustaining narrative, other people, and to living with mystery are obstacles to love. *Faith* is the commitment to a worthwhile story, to others, and the ability to live at ease with a chastened epistemology.

Bewilderment is an obstacle to love, stifling our ability to enact a plan, choose between competing goods, make sense of something in front of us, or discern God's call. *Discernment* is the hopeful virtue of practical wisdom, creativity, empathic vision, perspective-taking, and nonbinary or outside-the-box thinking.

Fear is an obstacle to love, hindering our ability to be and do. *Courage* is the virtue that overcomes fears for the sake of the good.

Over-commitment, distraction, and repulsion are obstacles to love. *Presence* is the virtue of being with others and refusing to withdraw emotionally, physically, or mentally from challenging persons, places, and situations.

Resignation, acceptance of the status quo, and unwarranted or premature abandonment of goals are obstacles to love. *Grit* is the virtue of

goal-oriented passion and determination and the patient endurance of challenges that would tempt one to abandon goals and relationships.

Faith

Faith is the commitment to a worthwhile story and to worthwhile relationships. It is "an orientation of the total person, giving purpose and goal to
one's hopes and strivings, thoughts, and actions."[3] What does faith do?

Faith Commits to a Story

A developing virtue of faith enables increasing commitment to an overarching, future-oriented narrative. Faith also grows a persistent trust in
the goodness of this narrative. Faith energizes the other virtues by giving
the virtues a context—a story worth living. Faith enables us to commit to
becoming the person we feel called to become, as envisioned and guided by
this overarching story.

Faith should lead the Christian to reject the inadequate stories of
consumption, oppression, dehumanization, egocentrism, and so on, and
commit to actively hoping for a more just future—a commitment clarifying
the "pathways" we ought to be travelling. Those with faith "enter a different
world than the one revealed by human discovery. They receive from God an
invitation to a new way of seeing and a new way of living."[4]

Despite the variety of ways to make meaning of what humans discover,
Christian faith means habitually choosing to "read" human experience
through the eyes of the love-centric narrative God has revealed through
Jesus. Commitment to this reading sustains and validates our efforts to love,
even when the rewards are not obvious or immediate. Our actualization
of love might be threatened by a sense of futility or meaninglessness; our
loving efforts might be poorly received, dismissed, or seemingly fail in their
intended effect. Faith reminds us that such efforts our worthwhile. Faith is
our continued "assent" or commitment to what we believe God has told us
about the future and about the significance of love.

3. Fowler, *Stages of Faith*, 14.
4. Brown, "Theological Virtue of Faith," 228.

Faith Takes a Thoughtful Leap

Faith helps us envision and articulate the goals we are pursuing. If I believe that love is a worthy goal, faith compels me to define love in a way that will be motivating and compelling. Faith clarifies the future we pursue, even if only partially and provisionally. We ought to have an idea of what it is we are putting our faith in.

Faith is therefore a highly thoughtful virtue; it does not trust lightly and is not blind. It is, however, not based on a false sense of security, and it invites mystery. To say, in any context, "I have faith it will be okay" should not be wishful thinking. It should be a conclusion based on good intel either about a likely (but not guaranteed) outcome or about the ability of this conclusion to effectively and compellingly guide my next steps. Faith is an educated (even if also emotional) choice, not one made willy-nilly.

Faith is tenacious but not stubborn; it is open to revision, knowing we make our commitments with provisional knowledge but are constantly learning as we go. A person with faith cannot be closed-minded, which can create an overconfidence that masks our anxieties about the unknown. Faith does not demand proof, partly because "proof" is often relative, forced, angled, and perspective-laden. Faith inquires, discerns, makes a choice, and acts, knowing there is both more to know and much that is unknowable. Faith allows us to act despite our epistemological limitations; it frees us to be honest with ourselves about what we do not know and yet be wholeheartedly committed amid such ambiguity.

Faith Does Not Become Defensive

Faith enables us to function in a world of competing narratives without feeling threatened yet without being unreceptive. Faith invites interfaith dialogue because it helps us be grounded enough to not be threatened by religious others yet welcome the pushback, enhancement, and expansion that engagement with other religions can provide. Faith demands we commit to something but welcome assistance as to how to live out this commitment.

Faith is a personal commitment to what we have experienced as God's truth, yet it is not to be equated with our stances, beliefs, and opinions. Faith is thus not defensive about what constitutes orthodoxy, yet also compels us to commit to something, rather than nothing at all, even if we can't say we are "certain" of what we believe. Christian faith should lead to trust primarily *in* Jesus and only secondarily and provisionally in my beliefs *about* Jesus. This is an important distinction that reminds us that our highest commitment is to a person, not our beliefs (even if beliefs matter and implicate the way we live out that ultimate commitment).

The virtue of faith calls Christians to make apologetics—the rational defending of faith—not a primary focus but an occasional explanatory tool. Nor should Christians expend energy on self-legitimization in combat with other faith traditions (or against the perceived "threat" of agnosticism or atheism). Christians should not hesitate to proclaim the metanarrative that undergirds their practices but must consider two things: how to hospitably and humbly articulate this story in ways that allow other competing stories to be heard and learned from; and how to avoid dichotomizing belief and practice and, instead, look to one's lived beliefs—what one practices—as the most reliable indicator of one's true faith. For Christians, faith is the commitment to the truth as told and lived by Jesus about what God is like, what God values, what it means to become fully human, and what things are worth caring about.

Faith Trusts Others

Finally, faith can entail a belief in others and energizes our participation in others' possible goodness. Faith is often needed to actualize other virtues. Gratitude may require that I have faith in you and the value of what you are contributing or can potentially contribute to me. Justice may call me to demonstrate faith in you, combatting my attempt to control the outcomes of my participation in you or imposingly dictate your next steps. Faith in this case is still about commitment, but particularly my commitment to your dignity and freedom rather than to my possibly flawed determination of what is best for you. Lack of faith makes us controlling and anxious; faith helps us let go.

Discernment

Discernment is a virtue of decision-making that includes creativity, imagination, outside-the-box thinking, and good application of our reservoir of experience-based knowledge. In relation to love, discernment attends to: the balance of self-care versus care for others; the short-term versus long-term effects of our choices on another's actual and potential flourishing; the negotiating between caring for those close to or distant from us; and the importance not only of giving but of receptivity.[5] To hope well, we need a strong ability to choose.

5. Underwood, "Compassionate Love," 14–15.

Discernment Is Wise and Creative

The virtue of discernment draws on practical wisdom, or prudence, one of the classic cardinal virtues. Practical wisdom depends not only on past experience but is also partly determined by our experiences with others and by nuanced contexts. It entails not just reliance on one's present storehouse of memories but also the capacity to think creatively about possibilities and is thus, like its parent virtue hope, future-oriented. It requires moral imagination, "the ability to see how various options will play themselves out and the ability to evaluate them."[6] We face obstacles like the potentially crippling choice between competing goods, lack of understanding and empathy, and habitual, default responses to situations. Practical wisdom clarifies choices, grows understanding and empathy, and helps us see the uniqueness of the situation and person before us.

Barry Schwartz and Kenneth Sharpe postulate that wise people know the goals of the activity at hand and the needs of those in question; wise people are emotionally aware and can improvise, intuit, think in gray rather than black-and-white, take on another's perspective, think contextually, and appreciate similarity and difference.[7] Peterson and Seligman similarly speak of ingenuity—the ability of persons to "generate creative solutions to the various problems they encounter."[8] Discerning people know the music but are adept at improvisation, so to speak.

Discernment may follow the pattern of Thomas's outline of prudence: "counsel," the process of inquiry; "judgment," an act of speculation and choice to take concrete action; and "command," or taking action.[9] Cultivating discernment could target these three moments. We can study existing wisdom, especially reflection upon the virtues. We can increase our ability to notice particularity, through everything from learning to differentiate varieties of coffee or wine to the preferences of one's children. We can practice making small, basic, quick decisions to prepare ourselves for future, larger decisions.

Discernment, while more than a purely cognitive exercise, requires the complex thinking and imagination of practical wisdom. Practical wisdom should not be associated with the image of the elderly sage; it is a habit that supports the demands that all the virtues place on us but perhaps the responsibility-clarifying virtue of justice most of all. Prudent

6. Schwartz and Sharpe, *Practical Wisdom*, 22.

7. Schwartz and Sharpe, *Practical Wisdom*, 25–26, 52. There is "evidence from psychology that humans are born with the capacity to be wise."

8. Peterson and Seligman, *Character Strengths*, 110.

9. Aquinas, II-IIae Q 47, Art 8.

discernment clarifies which actions will aid or detract from our hopeful movement toward love.

Discernment Listens

Elizabeth Liebert describes discernment as a matter of "seeking and responding to God's call in the midst of all the forces, options, and decisions that mark our lives."[10] Liebert's choice of "call" over "will" here is deliberate and coheres with a fundamental theological claim of this book: God does not intend to override our agency but energize it. I am concerned that the quest for the "will of God" too easily lends itself to neglected responsibility and epistemological overconfidence. We can ignore the call to grow in love when we invoke God's will. We can fail to help those in need by being fatalistic or passing the buck to God. We can also convince ourselves that our choices are foolproof and even wholly good while villainizing those who choose oppositely. "Call" is more spacious, open, and perhaps honest.

God does not primarily command but invites and nudges. God welcomes our collaboration, graciously calling us to be "partially responsible for the shape and direction of both evolution and history."[11] Discernment encourages our participation in and co-creation with God and others. Discernment overcomes the obstacles of cognitive impotence or indecisiveness on the one hand and rash or blind action on the other. It values our contributions to others but listens attentively to others' expressed needs; it helps us strike that right balance between taking too much responsibility for others and taking too little.

Discernment helps us distinguish between a leading from God and "less worthy" impulses like the "desire to feel important or look clever."[12] A failure to recognize my hidden motives and influences can thwart my loving participation in others; discernment draws attention to these forces so as to weaken their efficacy. Discerning people know themselves. They also know the voice of God, which may be synonymous with the voice of Love. The call of this voice will often meet our expectations and fit our rules and norms but will often supersede them.

10. Liebert, *Soul of Discernment*, 19.

11. Vacek, "Discernment in a Mutual Love Relationship," 689.

12. Birkel, *Silence and Witness*, 55.

Discernment Intuits

Discerning people can intuit the unspoken fears, anxieties, and agendas impinging on the moment and graciously respond amid these forces. People often resist embracing an idea or plan not because the idea or plan are bad in themselves but because something is at stake—perhaps the potential loss of something precious or seemingly essential. Discerning people recognize the deeper story behind the plain, immediate facts of a situation.

Discernment does not rest solely on prior experience (as "wisdom" might connote). A recurring obstacle to love is the often-subtle divergence in patterns. My wife typically welcomes hugs and is reticent to "end" our hugs despite my attempts to escape from her embrace. During an extreme heat wave, however, a "fitting" or "good" hug is short or perhaps supplanted by a quick kiss. To make good decisions, we "need cognitive and perceptual machinery that picks up on similarities without being blind to differences."[13] Discernment overcomes the obstacle of unfamiliarity by, on one hand, revealing how the present situation is analogous to other situations and, on the other hand, highlighting the situational factors that make this moment distinct.

In my experience, many Christians often assume a level of comfort with other Christians and use religious language they assume will evoke affirming nods from their listeners. The discerning Christian, however, recognizes the diversity of perspectives on matters such as biblical interpretation, morality, and the nature of God's involvement in human affairs and speaks authentically but with as much awareness as possible of the theology and values of the hearer so as to be both fitting and hospitable in what he or she chooses to say.

Discernment Transcends Rules

Discernment prioritizes relationships and views rules as *aids* to love but not as static, context-free idols. Consider Claire, a participant in one of Gilligan's studies. In response to the oft-cited "Heinz dilemma" used by Kohlberg (among others) in which one must choose whether or not a man ought to rob a druggist to save his dying wife, Claire supports the theft not by an appeal to a hierarchy of rights but because nothing is more important than "seeing and responding to need" and "sustaining the web of connection."[14]

13. Schwartz and Sharpe, *Practical Wisdom*, 85.
14. Gilligan, *In a Different Voice*, 62.

Whether or not this justifies her choice (Heinz is, after all, obligated to the druggist), the example emphasizes how discernment supports love. Justice is threatened by failing to understand our responsibility for others; discernment highlights our inextricability with others and the opportunities that come from our relational and social location. A virtue of discernment also guides our navigation between the various virtues. Discernment guides the choice to step back from our care for others to care for self; it also clarifies when those we love should be given similar space for self-care. Discernment guides the choice of for whose good we act in a given moment, determines what amount of something ought to be given, and clarifies time constraints.

Discernment is also essential as a means of ensuring that our love is not located in good intentions alone, but is fulfilled in action. While those we love may be forgiving to us, we should not expect to receive the grace that might be extended to a child for sweetly thinking he or she is helping to clean the house by dumping shampoo all over the carpet. Love requires intelligent deliberation to ensure we are not harming those we love out of ignorance or cognitive laziness.

Courage

Courage is a prominent virtue in classical virtue lists. It was highly valued in ancient warrior cultures, an essential quality for combating the dangers one might encounter, most notably in battle but also in a world marked by scarcity of resources and uncertainty of survival. To downplay the importance of courage before I subsequently amplify it: in the context of the modern world and in light of the goal of love, hope is more suitable as the primary obstacle-overcoming or actualizing virtue.

Consider the kinds of obstacles people face on a daily basis. The obstacle of lack of focus, given the numerous and frenetic demands for our attention, can be met with the hope's attentiveness and specificity. The obstacle of choosing between clashing goods requires the creativity and future-orientation of hope. The obstacle of vagueness and stifling generalizations can be overcome by hope's attention to the particular and concrete. The obstacle of indifference can be overcome by cultivating a concern for creating a better future. The obstacle of having one's "life-situation" determined by often corrupt or indifferent others or even by simple bad luck can be overcome by hope's creative, collaborative efforts to make a more just world. The obstacle of "enemies" can be overcome not by battling one's enemies but by reframing such dichotomies, recognizing that "the line dividing good and evil cuts through the heart of every human being"[15] and that sometimes an empathetic, deconstructive reversal of such a binary can do more to resolve a conflict than courage. Hope includes courage, but sees more obstacles to goodness and love than fear alone.

That said, courage is essential to ensuring hope's efficacy. Whether courage is physical (dealing with threats to our bodies), intellectual (responding to self-doubt and criticism from others), social (enduring real or imagined threats from others) or psychological (overcoming fear and anxiety), courage helps us overcome the fears we face on the way to love.[16]

Courageous Faith

If faith helps us imagine and commit to a worthwhile goal or story, courage is the capacity to act upon that goal and live that story "despite the presence of risk, uncertainty, and fear."[17] Courage aids faith in helping us endure our epistemological limitations so that our inability to know some things "for sure"—if we are honest without ourselves—does not cripple us and prevent us from acting. Such uncertainty could be construed as an act of cowardice by those who feel they are "courageously" adhering to their beliefs, enduring the threats posed by relativism and shifting cultural norms. But such a tight grip on one's stance is not really courage at all but rashness or possibly hubris, an overestimation of one's abilities. Courage allows for beliefs—just chastened ones. Courage helps us act on our knowledge, even as it allows us to risk unknowing and unlearning.

---

15. Solzhenitsyn, *Gulag Archipelago Abridged*, 75.

16. Martin, *Happiness and the Good Life*, 39.

17. Biswas-Diener, *Courage Quotient*, 10. Biswas-Diener identifies the neurological basis of courage in two motivational systems: the "behavioral inhibition system" (the activation of the hippocampus, which encourages caution) and the "behavioral activation system" (located in the pleasure centers of the brain and facilitating goal pursuit) (12). This echoes Aristotle's description of courage as the mean between cowardice and rashness (Aristotle, *Nicomachean Ethics*, 41–42). Speaking of Aristotle, Daniel Putman's examination of a range of historic conceptions of courage is helpful. Putman's survey includes Aristotelian courageous action in the face of danger, Stoic endurance of and management of daily challenges, existentialist willingness to be one's authentic self, and the Zen readiness to be present to the moment and give up the "comfortable and routine" (Putman, "Philosophical Roots," 10–21).

Courageous Authenticity

Courage enables us to live the calls of self-care to accept and appropriate oneself. Consider the example of same-sex attraction and marriage. Kristen Aune observes that some evangelicals, who tend to have fairly rigid notions of what constitutes true masculinity (and femininity), recognize and tolerate non-heterosexual orientation but push for repentance and for change from an inferior form of masculinity to "hegemonic masculinity."[18] In this case, resistance to same-sex marriage is not simply a problem of morality but of gender. Given the pressure to conform (from preachers or religious peers, for example), advocating for same-sex marriage in a way that affirms the beauty (not just the tolerability) of same-sex attraction and non-hegemonic conceptions of gender can also call for courage to face oneself.

To be authentically oneself and acknowledge with confidence one's desires and/or behaviors that do not appear traditionally masculine or feminine is an act of courage in its divergence from social pressure. By embracing the nuances of one's personality and eschewing restrictive "types," one may gain more sympathy for difference and for LGBTQ+ identity. Consequently, one might also more clearly see the injustice at work in prohibitions—official or sentimental—of the right of same-sex couples to marry, a right we may be rejecting not out of fidelity to "God's commands" but simply because we do not like how it makes us feel.

Furthermore, the more we can accept the nuances of our own gender identity, the more we can lovingly participate in others without the barrier of preconceptions of what a man or woman "should" be that often cause us to unfairly pressure others or simply misunderstand who others are—what is important to them, what they need, what they have to offer. Self-affirming authenticity requires what Paul Tillich calls the "courage to be."[19] Tillich's ontological courage—strengthening persons to overcome angst in the face of potential non-being—speaks especially to the need for a virtue of self-care that values one's experience, uniqueness, inherent value, and actual or potential value to others.

Authenticity in sexuality and gender is of course just one dimension of being who we are rather than what we have been told we should be. It often requires courage to pursue our own vocations, develop our talents, and express our dissatisfaction with injustice, whether in our most intimate relationships or society at large.

---

18. Aune, "Between Subordination and Sympathy," 49.

19. Tillich, *Courage to Be*, 3.

Courageous (but Nonviolent) Fighting for Good

Courage calls me not simply to *feel* something but to *do* something, at a potential cost to myself. We might be called to "fight" for others' good with confidence, an eye toward accomplishing something significant, tenacity when confronted by obstacles, and faithfulness to goals, the attainment of which may take time.

Courage also overcomes the fears of loss and change. Churches and individual Christians might find themselves risking their status, approval, and financial support as they seek to love individuals or groups in unpopular ways. Yet courage calls the church to celebrate its tradition as a *living* tradition, not a stubborn, unchanging fidelity to the past. Traditions evolve, reinterpreting and reapplying foundational truths as understanding grows and as the character of social and cultural brokenness changes.

Churches might feel an impulse toward maintenance, as if making changes signifies betrayal of the tradition or betrayal of God in favor of cultural acceptance and accommodation. But often our fight for what is good will not mean abandonment of Christian truth but fidelity to it. Christian truth is discovered in the celebration and imitation of a loving, justice-seeking God more than in doctrines and affirmations that may have outlived their usefulness in pointing us toward the heart of God (if they ever pointed to this God in the first place). Courage invites us to take risks where justice and human flourishing are at stake, perhaps trusting our deeper sense of who God is and what God cares about more than our articulated teaching.

Courage also overcomes the laziness and lack of integrity of words without actions. It is easy and in some cases lazy to be dogmatic. It is more difficult to cultivate the virtues that give visibility and tangibility to these beliefs. Courage helps us practice what we preach, which will often feel much riskier, more challenging, and possibly more terrifying. It is easy to sing "I will follow Jesus" with sincere conviction; it takes something extra to actualize this conviction in a way that ensures we are not just voicing a palatable idea but are willing to *really* follow Jesus to the places he went—which undoubtedly required immense courage.

Courageous Movement Toward Goals

Lee Yearley speaks of courage in terms of its three goals: the external goal of a "hoped-for state of affairs" that "animates" courageous action; the internal goal of the value of both the goal and actions toward the goal; and the "countergoal" or possible negative outcomes of the action.[20]

This might be a helpful way of thinking through what courage entails in order to muster the needed courage to act. Courage actualizes love by targeting a meaningful desired outcome, such as correcting a social inequity; rashness may result from vague or absent goals (we want to do *something* and so act haphazardly without clarity of ends). Courage actualizes love because of its internal goal, such as the recognition that vocally combating social ills is an inherent good and a better moral alternative to silent complicity. Courage is, to an extent, its own reward. Courage also helps us act despite the threat of countergoals, the presence of which might indicate that we are doing something worthwhile. The abandonment or scorn we may experience for condemning an injustice may come from those who stand to lose something should our hoped-for justice become a reality.

Sharing Courage

As we can hope for others, participating in their growth, so we can instill courage in others. This is well-illustrated by Jesus's interaction at the pool of Beth-zatha (John 5:1–9), in which a man is arguably not simply physically crippled but also crippled by fear and resignation. Jesus's provocative question ("Do you want to be well?") is followed by a jolting command to "stand up and walk." Jesus, through justice (recognizing what this man needed to hear) and discernment (guiding his choice of words), transfers his own courage (certainly on display as Jesus entered Jerusalem, not naïve about the danger awaiting him) to this man, shaking him out of his "stuck" state.

Similarly, Christians ought to consider where the circumstances of others have weakened their capacity to overcome their fears and anxieties. While the risk of patronizing, misguided care is present when the privileged attempt to help the oppressed, it is possible that many are too "stuck" to act self-determinedly. We can love by strengthening others' agency (rather than supplanting their agency with our own, with the exception of young children and the extremely ill, among other unique cases) through helping cultivate courage in others.

20. Yearley, *Mencius and Aquinas*, 114.

Presence

Presence overcomes the obstacle of non-participation or relational absence. We are tempted to withdraw and not truly "be with" the people before us. The actualization of love requires overcoming the noise of our own internal dialogue, the noise of technology, and the noise of other commitments that are valuable but not contextually pressing. It also requires that we overcome the obstacles of our biases, visceral recoiling, and judgments.

James William McClendon suggests presence means "refusing the temptation to withdraw mentally and emotionally" (and I would add physically).[21] Presence can be a welcomed act of love, as in the case of sitting with someone too distraught to be alone. It can also be a subversive way of demonstrating opposition to injustice.

Listening Presence

Presence can overcome the potential barriers of modern communication, where texts and emails may offer expediency but carry the potential to cause misunderstanding and to isolate. We are "sensory creatures" and the more sense we lose, the greater the likelihood of misunderstanding.[22] Face-to-face communication can increase the likelihood of clear communication. We can read people right in front of us in ways we cannot through electronic communication. We are also forced to be authentic in ways that can be lost with the inherent selectivity of our self-presentation through social media.

Presence helps us overcome the obstacles to good listening, such as our constant "moving and shaking," our commitment to our routine (generally a good thing but a potential obstacle), and our often excessive need for self-expression.[23] Presence stills us, prepares us to occasionally break our routine for others, and lessens the interruptions and rambling that often make others feel like we are not truly hearing them. Presence may guide us to say nothing at all, simply supporting those we love by doing literally nothing more than putting our bodies near theirs.

Furthermore, the way we judge, evaluate, and make sense of what others are saying to us can potentially hinder our presence to others. Present people ward off the temptation to draw premature conclusions and can wait patiently, difficult as this can be, to ensure a fuller understanding of those with whom we are present.

21. McClendon, *Systematic Theology*, 106.

22. Spencer, *Awakening the Quieter Virtues*, 85.

23. Johnson, "Being Present to Others," 27.

Aware Presence

The need for presence extends beyond conversations with individual others to the hierarchies at work in the world. Jan Johnson explains: "Men's eyes wander when women talk. Employers shuffle papers as employees answer questions. Well-to-do people evaluate the appearance of the poor as they pass on the street. Parents wonder how children could drag out a story any longer."[24] A virtue of presence can combat a natural tendency to neglect others, especially those with less privilege, power, or voice. Presence is connective and thwarts hierarchies and privilege. Present people do not cut themselves off from the harsh realities of the world or the ways their actions have consequences for others. Presence saves us from isolation and insulation.

Presence, like self-care, is aided by mindfulness, helping us keep our "mind in the present moment, while staying nonjudgmentally detached from potentially destructive thoughts and feelings."[25] Mindfulness makes us more cognizant of our surroundings, enhances our perspective-taking ability, and helps us "relate to our emotions in a healthy way" so that our own negative emotions do not "hijack" us as we respond to others.[26] When any number of distractions pull us away from the hopeful movement toward love, the virtue of presence brings us back.

Humanizing Presence

Presence is dignifying, helping us take others seriously by allowing us to see the distinct person before us. Presence thus saves us from a potentially dehumanizing collectivism or a self-exaggerating individualism: it helps us see how a person's experience is unique and yet how it is universal. To be present to others, we have to loosen our expectations of others, remove the "distorting lenses of convention, self-interest, and routine," take the risk of intimacy while remaining critically distant, and give our full attention to what is before us.[27] Our love is threatened by imposed expectations, self-seeking motives, potentially tedious regularity, resistance to intimacy, and multiple demands on our attention. Presence guides us to be fully with what is before us, overcoming its opposite vice—absence.

Presence strengthens gratitude, opening us to the transformative and enriching benefits of others and deepening our receptivity to self-enhancing,

24. Johnson, "Being Present to Others," 27.

25. Symington and Symington, "Christian Model of Mindfulness," 71.

26. Simon-Thomas, "Meditation Makes Us Act."

27. Newman, "Person to Person," 108

informative experiences. Presence strengthens self-care, revealing the subtleties of our needs, our temptations, and our potential offerings to others.
Presence strengthens justice, equipping us to remain with others despite
various forms of resistance or recoiling we might experience, attuning us
to the subtle needs of others, and keeping us focused amid distractions.
Presence strengthens kindness, revealing otherwise missed opportunities to
delight and inspire others with acts deemed extravagant only in relationship
to a more normative level of responsibility for others.

Grit

Love requires not only a determination to remain present to the people
we love but also a virtue that can help us remain tenaciously connected to
the overarching pursuit of love, informing our participation. We need the
passion and perseverance of grit: the "tendency to pursue long-term goals
with sustained zeal and hard work."[28] We need the emotional toughness and
mental focus in response to the temptation to quit. Grit is a virtue of resilience and determination.

Gritty through Setbacks

Psychologist Angela Duckworth observed in her study of West Point cadets
that the best predictor of success in the programs was neither intelligence,
athleticism, nor leadership experience, but grit—a combination of passion
(knowing what you want) and perseverance (including resilience and hard
work).[29] Grit compensates for lack of skill, as the intense determination
and focus of grit can lead to goal attainment. Gritty people are emotionally
aware, able to withstand challenging emotions that would otherwise derail
us in our goals pursuits.

Grit sustains love by pushing us through the pain of setbacks and let-
downs. It ensures that our ever-increasing love for others is not deflated
or dampened by unappreciated gestures (e.g., the gift we gave our loved
one didn't produce the reaction we hoped it would) or perceived method-
ological failures (e.g., our protest against the construction of a pipeline with
potentially devastating consequences did not *seem* to have the impact we
had anticipated).

28. Von Culin, Tsukayama, and Duckworth, "Unpacking Grit," 1.

29. Duckworth, *Grit*, 10. Duckworth studied spelling bee contestants in a similar
manner, noting the correlation between high grit scores, practice, preparation (regardless of talent and ability), and success.

Efforts to love are threatened not simply by failure, which should be expected, but also by exaggerating the meaning of failure. People with grit do not anxiously attempt to avoid failure, but recognize its inevitability, sapping such failures of power. My failed attempt to address a social injustice becomes an opportunity to find alternate routes and gain a deeper grasp on the nature of the problem. My friend's defensive reaction to my advice does not cause me to resign in quiet frustration but to persist, seeking other ways—verbally or not—to be supportive. Failures are unavoidable; grit recognizes such setbacks as potential educational and formative steps toward greater participation in others' present goodness and—should grit and presence keep us "with" others—their future goodness.

Grit and Goals

When we believe in our goals and enjoy their pursuit, grit comes more naturally. Grit may also be reflected in "coherent goal structures," for in "very gritty people, most mid-level and low-level goals are, in some way or another, related to that ultimate goal."[30] For example, a gritty individual or congregation might allow the ultimate goal (love) to guide the formation of sub-goals (through cultivating love virtues or through setting love goals in particular relationships). All of one's activities, commitments, and obligations are then seen as connected to this larger goal of love, clarifying and enhancing each of these domains.

My grit as an individual pushes me to play harder (self-sustenance leads to love) and endure criticism more easily (humility leads to love). Our grit as a congregation pushes us to sustain our good ongoing ministries despite their potential repetitiveness, the waxing and waning of volunteer interest, or the ambiguity of long-term impact on the people we serve. Our increasing and loving participation in the lives of others energizes these ministries.

Gritty in the Right Way

What are the vices opposed to grit? A person with too little grit might be considered halfhearted, weak, lacking backbone, lazy, or wasteful of talent (as grit can build on talent or compensate for a lack of it). The greatest risk for a person with too much grit might be fixation: a solitary focus that harms our other commitments, or perhaps the direction of energy toward

30. Duckworth, *Grit*, 64.

poor goals. Grit thus works in tandem with other hope virtues. A virtue of faith can guide the setting of worthwhile goals. A virtue of presence can help one remain with people and avoid becoming disengaged, occupied by other goal-pursuits. A virtue of discernment can clarify how to give energy to something while balancing our commitments and also clarify when the problem is not our lack of grit but a misunderstanding of the need.

Grit and Self-Doubt

Grit perseveres not only through setbacks but also through self-doubts. Grit enhances and is enhanced by self-efficacy—an increasing sense of mastery that comes by persisting in challenging situations.[31] When we are effective at persisting or coping in one instance, we perceive ourselves as equipped to similarly persist and cope in future situations. The opposite is also true: our perceived failures will have a debilitating effect, weakening our ability to be gritty in the future. Self-efficacy can also decrease the likelihood of futile applications of grit that might occur when we demonstrate passions and persistence for goals we are not capable of attaining. Grit facilitates the formulation of realistic (though stretching) goals. Yet self-efficacy does not dampen our movement toward goals but energizes them, increasing our aspirations and strengthening our commitments to our goals.

Grit and Growth

Our grit—and our ability to grow—is influenced by our beliefs about our ability to succeed and about to whom or what we should attribute blame in a perceived failure.[32] Gritty people tend to be optimistic and opportunistic, not debilitated by challenges and obstacles but energized by them. Gritty lovers do not rest on their laurels but allow their resolve to love and get better at loving, creating a kind of mental guide that constantly challenges their present capacity for love. This cannot mean that grit becomes manic and obsessive, as this would likely thwart our ability to love well. The energy of grit should connect us to others rather than separate us from them. Christian communities can cultivate and sustain grit. They can remind

31. Bandura, "Self-Efficacy," 191.

32. Zakrzewski, "Two Ways to Foster Grit." Zakrzewski cites the work of Carol Dweck and her delineation between a "fixed mindset" and a "growth mindset," in which the former is more debilitated by failures and assumes a more static view of one's traits while the latter (Dweck's suggested aspired-to mind-set) sees failures as opportunities and assumes traits are not given but can be developed. See Dweck, *Mindset*.

individuals of why the ultimate goal of love deserves our passion while also magnifying relational opportunities that might call on the actualizing and hopeful qualities of grit.

An Exemplar of Hope: Dorothy Day (1897–1980)

Dorothy Day possessed a strong virtue of hope, largely resulting from her continued exposure to people in need of hope. Day was active in the relief efforts for those affected by the San Francisco earthquake in 1906 and lived for a time in the Chicago slums, discovering that people were not necessarily the cause of their own poverty.[33] She was cognizant of the systemic flaws creating unjust hardships for laborers and starkly encountered suffering while working as a nurse during World War I.[34] Day eventually joined revolutionary intellectual circles, wrote for social newspapers, and participated in protests that often led to prison time before ultimately turning to Christianity in part because of the *potential* of religion, if more bent on social change.[35]

The spirituality that ultimately emerged linked her social radicalism to the love and mercy of Christianity and found expression in the Catholic Worker (CW) Movement (1933), which aimed, through the publication of one-cent newspapers and through houses of hospitality, to "change the hearts and minds of (people) . . . to give them . . . the vision of a society where it is easier for (people) to be good."[36] Day was eager to energize all people, but particularly Catholics, to realize these goals primarily through her ubiquitously proclaimed pathway: the practice of the works of mercy, a striking display of compassionate, participatory love.[37]

Day demonstrated hope in giving weight to small acts and linking them to her goals and the goals of the CW: "Doing a week's wash for a sick mother is no small work of mercy!"[38] Day's hope raised her expectations about the quality of her efforts; for example, she occasionally lamented the sporadic, shoddy cooking at the CW, suggesting that the call to "feed the

33. Forest, *All is Grace*, 11, 20.

34. Day, *Long Loneliness*, 41–50; and Forest, *All is Grace*, 49.

35. Day, *From Union Square to Rome*, 48, 102.

36. Day, *Long Loneliness*, 206.

37. "The spiritual works of mercy are: to admonish the sinner, to instruct the ignorant, to counsel the doubtful, to comfort the sorrowful, to bear wrongs patiently, to forgive all injuries, and to pray for the living and the dead. The corporal works are to feed the hungry, to give drink to the thirsty, to clothe the naked, to ransom the captive, to harbor the harborless, to visit the sick, and to bury the dead" (Day, "Scandal of the Works of Mercy," 103).

38. Day, "Poverty Without Tears."

hungry" be done with care and respect for the food and those eating it.[39] Day's love went beyond intentions to effective actions, a move sustained particularly by hopeful virtues.

Day had faith. Not only was Day highly engaged in religious rituals and practices, she had a strong commitment to her social and religious vision, believing firmly in God's call as expressed in Matt 25—the key scripture for the CW and the one from which many of the works of mercy are derived. Day stated that "the immediate solution will always be the works of mercy," yet countered this by emphasizing the necessity for study and vision in order to gain a "long-range view" and "understand how far-reaching the works of mercy can be."[40] Faith provided this vision for Day, manifesting in a trust that her small-scale efforts had long-term value. Her participation in individual strikes seemed to yield little immediate gain but "in the long view . . . [had] achieved much."[41] Her faith connected such isolated incidents into a unified, hopeful narrative.

Day was discerning. Day was apt at making decisions that attend to the individual and defy convention, as the famous "diamond ring" story illustrates.[42] Day's political ideals evolved over time from passionate rigidity to a more spacious and personal approach, in dialogue with lived experience and real people. Day was once asked what she would do if her own daughter were threatened: "How many times have I heard this? Restrain him, of course, but do not kill him. Confine him, if necessary. But perfect love casts out fear and overcomes hatred. All this sounds trite, I know, but experience is not trite."[43] Day's response is nuanced, nonviolent, and creative, neither diminishing the integrity of her pacifism nor her love for her child. Day's discernment was demonstrated in her ousting of "squatters" taking advantage of the CW's hospitality and refusing to vacate a building; rather than involving police because of her compassion for the pseudo-residents, Day

39. Forest, *All is Grace*, 294.

40. Day, "On Pilgrimage–March 1959."

41. Day, *Long Loneliness*, 217.

42. Day received a diamond ring from a donor and then quickly gave the ring away to "the Weasel," a particularly difficult client of the *Catholic Worker*. Jim Forest recalls: "Later, someone asked if it wouldn't have been better to sell the ring and pay the Weasel's rent for some time in advance. Dorothy said, 'She has her dignity. If she wants to sell the ring, she is free to do so and pay her rent'" (Forest in Riegle, *Dorothy Day*, 145–46). Day continues: "But if she wants to take a cruise to Bermuda, she can do that, too. . . . Or she can wear the ring, just like the woman who gave it to us. Do you suppose God made diamonds just for the rich?" Day, channeling Jesus and his often-confounding responses to the Pharisees, displays not only a discerning choice but extravagant kindness.

43. Forest, *All is Grace*, 162.

sold "out the place from under them."[44] Recognizing the difficulty of "visiting the prisoner" (for security reasons), in 1954 she implored the Commissioner of Prisons James Bennet to transfer Morton Sobell (a Soviet spy) from Alcatraz to "a penitentiary in the East where he can be visited by his wife and children as well as by his lawyer."[45] Day aptly juggled multiple loyalties and values to find ways to honor these commitments.

Day was courageous. She was constantly in the position of taking unpopular stances at odds with both her Christian and radical circles; courage enabled her to take those unpopular stances and persist at them. Day writes in her journal in 1935, early in the CW Movement's existence: "We are criticized . . . for the very works of mercy we are doing. Outside criticism is not so bad, but the criticism from within (the church), the grumbling, the complaints, the insidious discontent spread around—these things are hard to bear."[46] Yet she finds resolve: "The thing is to bear it patiently, to take it lightly, not to let it interfere with one's own work."[47] Day had the courage to be vulnerable, recognizing that halfhearted efforts to address poverty are "not enough. . . . One must live with (the poor), share with them in their sufferings too. Give up one's privacy, and mental and spiritual comforts as well as physical."[48] A virtue of courage also enabled her confrontational letters to acquaintances and frequent indictments of authorities.[49]

Day was present. Day acknowledged how much easier it was to "throw people the clothes" than to "sit down with them and listen patiently," especially when such presence affected other work.[50] Day continually wrestled with this tension, typically tending toward personal, intimate contact with individuals. Day notes in her journal in 1950 the need to "cultivate the austerity, the detachment, the self-discipline, and the interior poverty we so lack" for the sake of being "poor with the poor."[51] One of Day's patients during the flu pandemic was a woman with "filthy habits" who caused Day

44. Forest, *All is Grace*, 241. A recollection from Tom Cornell.

45. Day, *All the Way to Heaven*, 297–98.

46. Day, *Duty of Delight*, 15.

47. Day, *Duty of Delight*, 15.

48. Day, *Long Loneliness*, 214.

49. In 1947, Day wrote to Gerry Griffin, a fellow worker who later left the CW: "I want to accuse you of being anti-female and anti-clerical" and "I could curse and tear my heart out whenever I read one of your letters" (Day, *All the Way to Heaven*, 210). Day later wrote to President Kennedy in 1963: "In love we ask you to show the world Christ's new commandment and accompany Negro students to enroll for Alabama University. This may seem a foolish gesture, but the foolish confound the wise" (378).

50. Forest, *All is Grace*, 132.

51. Day, *Duty of Delight*, 159.

visceral discomfort; Day tended her daily, "gritting her teeth and hold-ing her breath."[52] Day consoled herself in the midst of such situations by remembering the dignity of her profession and the "sacrament of duty."[53] Day's personalism also increased her capacity for a virtue of presence.[54]

Day was gritty. Day writes: "Compassion makes them think there must be some quicker way . . . (but) perseverance, endurance, faithfulness to the poor . . . these are the things to stress.[55] In 1957, one of many experiences in jail for civil obedience had a particularly significant impact on Day, leav-ing her "in a state of mental, physical, and even spiritual exhaustion" yet prepared to do it again.[56] It required significant grit to be capable of tak-ing in this self-admittedly excruciating experience and be willing to repeat it. Father Henry Fehren was impressed by Day's grit, noting that she lived "an austere life in the grimmest of conditions, being jailed again and again, never giving up doing the works of mercy, never getting cynical."[57]

Day's involvement in the works of mercy turned her raw energy of opposition to injustice into concrete methods and networks for addressing this injustice. Day became a better "hoper" through this practice: her goals became more specific, her self-knowledge and self-motivation grew, and her personal and communal resources for supporting and directing her energy increased. Day's legacy of love is in part the result of her virtue of hope. The hope of Christians can be strengthened through imitating Day's faith, discernment, courage, presence, and grit.

52. Forest, *All is Grace*, 49.

53. Forest, *All is Grace*, 50.

54. Peter Maurin, a French man who would ultimately mentor her and attempt to fashion her in the mold of past exemplars of justice, provided much of the ideological backbone of Day's organized efforts. Maurin's (and resultantly Day's) personalism em-phasized the personal responsibility of all (rather than the state) to alleviate social ills and take care of others. Day writes in 1958: "We were taught in the Gospel to work from the bottom up, not from the top down. Everything was personalist, we were our broth-ers' keepers, and we were not to pass by our neighbor who has fallen by the wayside and let the State, the all encroaching State, take over, but were to do all we could ourselves" (Day, "Workers of the World Unite." Day's underlying personalist vision was essential to her practice of the works of mercy, as her constant association of "the stranger" with Jesus (Matt 25) sustained her ability to receive others as distinct, valuable persons. In particular, French personalist Emmanuel Mounier informed Maurin's and Day's justice work, especially his emphasis on personal responsibility to shape history (rather than "withdrawal from the world") (Zwick and Zwick, "Emmanuel Mounier").

55. Day, "Letter On Hospices."

56. Forest, *All is Grace*, 207.

57. Fehren quoted in Forest, *All is Grace*, 304–5.

Conclusion

The Road Ahead

The language of love is the only language we can be sure is spoken and understood by God.[1]

—NORTHROP FRYE, 1912–91

What's the Christian life all about? It's about loving God and what God loves. It's about becoming passionate about God and participating in God's passion for a different kind of world, here and now. And the future, including what is beyond our lives? We leave that up to God.[2]

—MARCUS BORG, 1942–2015

I BELIEVE I HAVE offered a hopeful vision of Christian spirituality. Hope has provided a lens through which to view the spiritual life—its movement and its potential. Love has been articulated as a compelling end toward which Christians move as they cultivate their God-given agency. Gratitude, self-care, justice, kindness, and hope are the pathways that should clarify the spiritual life while impacting all of our relationships.

1. Frye, "Double Vision of Language," 220.
2. Borg, *Convictions*, 231.

Receiving the Contents of This Book

I have had in mind American evangelical and mainline Christians as I have written, partly out of personal familiarity with each Christian expression. In my experience, virtue is usually held in suspicion or entirely ignored in these two contexts, due to theological commitments seemingly at odds with a concern for virtue. I don't think this has to be the case. Even without any kind of substantial reformation in either stream, both evangelicals and mainliners can accommodate a vision of the spiritual life as the hopeful movement toward love through virtue.

For example, evangelicals can retain the centrality of the cross but see it as the culmination of a love story, attending to the entirety of this story rather than idolizing—i.e., giving excessive spiritual weight to—the cross. Evangelicals can retain a reverent love for the Bible but read it with an eye for the way love and its virtues are endorsed and embodied.

Evangelicals can maintain the need for conversion and celebrate it as a dramatic shift from death to life while more strongly emphasizing the love-centric life to which one converts (while affirming a God- or grace-enabled personal agency). They can seek to convert others but resist the temptation to simplify the Christian life (e.g. "Just say this prayer"), insisting instead on God's radical and demanding call to the gradual transformation of character. They can worship with enthusiasm but be mindful of the ways worship is transforming individuals into more loving or less loving persons. Evangelicals can relish their personal relationships with Jesus while expressing their love for Jesus not in a private, individualistic way but through their participatory love for others.

Mainliners can insist on inclusivity but pursue not just inclusive political positions but also the virtues that support inclusivity. Similarly, mainliners can continue their justice work but deepen the positive effects of such work through training individuals to be more attentive, responsible, competent, and responsive in all relationships. They can value spiritual diversity and theological spaciousness while insisting on universal love virtues (or at least the universality of love virtues, in some form).

Mainliners can retain their favored liturgical approach but orient it toward love virtues, weekly "rehearsing" the love-centric virtuous life. They can protect authenticity in the sense of creating safe spaces for people, such as for those who have been wounded or those with doubts, while not shying away from a narrative that calls people to become what they are not—accepting the self but also believing in the necessity and liberation of spiritual growth. Mainliners can continue to value ancient spiritual practices while linking them to virtues, lest such practices become merely therapeutic rather than formative.

There are expressions that do not fit these polarities, such as self-identified "progressive" Christians emerging from evangelical contexts. Such progressive-minded Christians may feel that they have broken through to a more loving theology or more loving presentation of that theology. For that matter, evangelicals may laud their own "tough love" approach while decrying the "spineless love" of mainliners. Conversely, mainliners can be quick to assume an overly harsh love on the part of evangelicals while valuing their own more "enlightened" form of love.

Yet both oppositions—and everything in between—will shortchange their religious experience if love is located in stances and doctrines on the one hand or organized efforts on the other. Christians must be *characterized* by love, expressed through and strengthened by ever-developing habits of gratitude, self-care, justice, kindness, and hope. This is hardly a focus on personal righteousness at the expense of those around us with needs. If your virtue does not thrust you into the suffering of others, it is probably not really virtue.

So, with this book in hand—hopefully a perpetual resource for a lifelong project of love cultivation, in whatever Christian stream you find yourself—where do you go from here?

Follow Jesus, the Paradigmatic Compassionate–Participatory Lover

To start with, you follow Jesus. Christians do not simply follow a spiritual growth plan; they follow the ultimate exemplar of love and the virtues. While this model of spiritual growth may be relevant outside of Christianity, the model is distinctly Christ-centered. Jesus loves God and others through collaborating with God's creative love. Jesus's love ought to guide our reflection on what the love-centric virtuous life entails.

Jesus should not be understood primarily as a conveyer of deontological principles, a model for *literal* imitation, a soothing reminder that we are "precious" as we are, or a mechanism by which we gain God's favor. Jesus should be recognized, instead, as the paradigmatic lover, participating in the present and potential goodness of others.

Christian action and formation should then proceed by what William Spohn (following William Lynch and David Tracy) calls the "analogical imagination"—discovering in the "details of parables, encounters, and sayings patterns that normatively guide us in new situations."[3] A hermeneutic informed by my proposed model guides us to look for expressions of compassionate, participatory love in Jesus, attending to the virtues at work and the people involved. It also calls us to creatively participate in Jesus's life and in the lives of others with self-scrutiny, discernment, and a readiness to act.

For example, we might read Jesus's outburst at the temple (Matt 21:12) and interpret this neither as a step on the road to the "real" theologically substantial moment of the cross nor a sanctioning of all our efforts to combat injustice. Instead, we might ask: What healthy emotions are at work in this event and how should we cultivate them? How did Jesus discern this action was fitting? Who is loved by this act and how are they loved? What vision of people and the world informs Jesus's action? What kind of behavior and persons are excluded and included by this act? What steps must I take to move closer to the character required to act in this way? What people—close or distant—suffer in such a way that warrants similar rage (and how do I develop such righteous anger, if I lack it)? As Jesus did in this situation on behalf of the people involved, how might I act in a similar situation for those for whom I am responsible?

To follow Jesus is not just to do what he says. As Richard Burridge points out, the New Testament is not an ethical textbook.[4] To understand Jesus's ethics is to understand his love and virtue. A hermeneutic that starts here need not neglect the spiritual weight of the cross but could perhaps reframe it. For example, the cross can be seen as the exemplary moment of love, one for which Jesus had prepared himself (self-care) and in which Jesus managed, shockingly and movingly, to receive others (gratitude), challenge the powers (justice), forgive while being murdered (kindness), and maintain a commitment to his highest aims (hope).

To follow Jesus is to receive, prepare, fulfill obligations, act supererogatorily, and overcome obstacles to goals in the way he did. Christians' approach to Scripture ought not prioritize authorial intent or original understanding (considering these insofar as they are useful, but not fixating on them) but be driven by a hermeneutic that listens to how God may be clarifying how one ought to cultivate and express love virtues. Such a love hermeneutic emphasizes the continuity of reflection and practice based on the story of Jesus while affirming the needed discontinuity to prevent the living tradition of Christianity from becoming either a traditionless spirituality or a religious fundamentalism.

---

3. Spohn, *Go and Do Likewise*, 50. To think analogically is to "be faithful and creative at the same time" (56).

4. Burridge, *Imitating Jesus*, 19.

Assuming our "hermeneutical situation"[5] is the lifelong movement toward love by means of virtues, how is this virtuous life evident in Jesus?

Jesus was grateful. Jesus receives the tears and cleansing act of a "sinner" (Luke 7:36–50). Jesus welcomes the healing work of "outsiders" whose efforts support the ministry of Jesus (Luke 9:49–50). Jesus, trying to avoid people, is open to the challenge of a mother of a sick child, who appears to successfully alter Jesus's plans and arguably flawed perspective (Mark 7:24–30). Jesus initially resists but ultimately responds to his mother's influence at the wedding of Cana, letting her modify his intended timeline (John 2:1–12). Jesus does not judge an extravagant gift as wasteful but receives it with gratitude (John 12:1–8). Jesus values his ministry but recognizes his limitations while affirming the present and future contributions of others (John 14:12). Jesus upholds children, in their receptivity, as exemplars of true greatness (Matt 18:1–4).

Jesus was self-caring. Jesus goes to the desert to train in virtue and develop self-mastery (Matt 4:1–11). Jesus retreats for solitude and recharging (Luke 4:42). In the midst of anxious disciples facing what they experienced as a severe storm, Jesus naps (Mark 4:35–41). Jesus encourages a readiness for action and a vigilance about one's faithfulness to God (Luke 12:35–39). Jesus regulates his potential irritation and anxiety while also breaking the momentum of the scribes and Pharisees by taking a "time out" to gather his thoughts before evading the potential moral trap of the woman caught in adultery (John 8:1–11). Jesus graphically encourages self-awareness of potential personal obstacles and quick action to remove them (Matt 18:8–9).

Jesus was just. Jesus heals Simon's mother-in-law among many others, physically touching and responding to the varied illness of each (Luke 4:38–40). Jesus shows the fittingness of God's meeting of human needs and implies the significance of human imitation of such fit (Luke 11:12). Jesus confronts Pharisees and lawyers for their neglect and oppression of others (Luke 9:37–54). Jesus is attentive and responsive, not acting out of presumption but giving others, such as the blind Bartimaeus, a voice (Mark 10:46–52). Jesus empathizes to the point of tears, not letting his confidence in his own capabilities overshadow his compassion for those for whom he cares (John 11:28–37). Jesus concludes his justice-oriented sermon on the mount by disparaging good intentions that do not translate to concrete action (Matt 7:24–27).

Jesus was kind. Jesus lauds the confounding generosity of the "prodigal father" (Luke 15:11–32). He encourages love of enemies, offering a second cheek, giving beyond what people request (Luke 6:27–31). Jesus produces an

5. Gadamer, "Language and Hermeneutics," 103.

excessive amount of food for what is already a large crowd (Luke 9:10–17). He promotes the throwing of parties for those who cannot make a reciprocal gesture (Luke 14:12–14). Jesus forgives his killers while being killed (Luke 23:34). Jesus demonstrates the powerful hospitality of addressing people by name, including Mary and Simon (Peter) (John 20:16, Matt 16:17–18). Jesus characterizes himself as a comforting, hospitable presence, willing to extend hospitality not just to close friends but to all who need it (Matt 11:28–30). Jesus magnanimously cures "great crowds" of "lame, the maimed, the blind, the mute, and many others" (Matt 15:29–31).

Jesus was hopeful. Jesus "increased in wisdom," growing in the needed discernment to love others, notably absent when Jesus, with foolish but childlike good intentions, gives his parents the slip (Luke 2:47–52).[6] Jesus consistently articulates his overarching goals (Luke 5:32). Jesus is present to those whose illnesses would cause most to withdraw (Luke 5:12–16). Jesus maintains his commitment to educating and forming his band of disciples, their asinine comments notwithstanding (Luke 9:54). He encourages and demonstrates a fearlessness based on right vision (Luke 12:4). Amidst doubters, Jesus maintains faith in God, himself, his instincts, and his goals (Mark 5:35–43). Jesus is mindful of the future, anticipates challenges, and remains hopeful (and encourages hopefulness in others) for this good future (Matt 24:9–14).

Create a Hope Plan for Spiritual Growth

The process of hope-based virtue cultivation might be considered analogous to the process of learning mathematics: a student may be asked to show his or her work not only for the sake of proof of right process but for his or her own visualization of what he or she is doing. Eventually, such equations can be done in the student's head, without much effort. Similarly, the process of hope becomes internalized. We begin as individuals applying hope theory to being, simply, good "hopers." I suggest two basic steps to initiate this process.

First, familiarize yourself with Snyder's model of hope with simple applications. Pick three goals. The first goal should be something simple that will take place in the next twenty-four hours: cook dinner, go shopping, tuck

---

6. I recognize this moment is traditionally presented as praiseworthy, showing young Jesus with his priorities straight. However, by "filling in the textual gaps" (See Iser, "Asymmetry Between Text and Reader," 89–95), I am sympathizing with his parents, who are not untrusting but genuinely terrified for the well-being of their son. Jesus would hopefully learn that a commitment to God or learning does not, as a rule, trump one's responsibility to parents (though there are of course exceptions).

kids in, etc. Clearly articulate: 1) your goal related to this task in as much detail and specificity as possible; 2) your capability of attaining that goal considering context, personal strengths, experience; 3) your pathways—the steps needed to get there. The second and third goals could be something that will happen within the week and be less easily attainable (e.g., exercise ninety minutes, call three friends, etc.). Doing this will help you become conversant with the three steps in the model.

Then, pick a small number of virtues you wish to cultivate and apply this same model. A methodical outlining of the elements of the model will not only cognitively prepare you for practice but also give concrete steps to practicing virtue in some simple way. I assume that repeated and progressively challenging "plans" will deepen the virtue itself as well as your internalization of the model so that you can eventually cultivate virtue "without notes." Use the three elements of Snyder's model as your guide.

Set virtuous goals. Envision what a more virtuous "you" looks like by observing exemplars of targeted virtues, studying philosophical and psychological definitions of these virtues, and by imagining, as vividly as possible, how such virtues would manifest in and transform your relationships with particular individuals and groups. Set goals but be ready to adjust your goals as your understanding shifts. Create a dialogue between long-term goals and immediate, smaller goals to experience measurable success in goal-pursuit while also constantly stretching and expanding your goals. Invite others to help define, develop, and broaden your formational goals.

Strengthen your agency. Take responsibility for yourself as coauthor of your story, co-shaper of your identity, and co-molder of your brain. Recognize already strong virtues in yourself and find ways to express them, even using such virtues to assist the cultivation of weaker virtues. Rely on others and recognize your fundamental reliance on others, knowing that agency is personal but not individualistic. Pay attention to your personal history, remembering that your past implicates your present and that your present choices have consequences for your future self.

Pave pathways. Experiment with and employ various virtue-cultivating spiritual practices. Imitate the love and virtues of others, whether a famous stranger or a close friend. Practice self-examination to uncover potential obstacles to love and possible antidotal virtues. Develop healthy emotions that, while fleeting, can build more enduring resources like strong connections to others and habitual (virtuous) responses to challenging situations. Recognize the opportunities for practicing virtue in your existing relationships and routines. Consider other existing approaches to moral education and mine them for the resources they can offer your own spiritual journey.[7]

Use Queries to Measure and Incite Growth

Measurement of growth is essential for successful businesses and class-rooms. Such assessment is a way of testing methods for utility and ensuring participants are attaining or moving toward agreed-upon goals. While recognizing the sensitive and personal nature of spirituality and the potential rigidity of categorical assessments, Christians who participate in communities compelled to cultivate and practice love ought to have resources for documenting their own spiritual growth.

The hope model may provide a cohesive framework for this assessment. Start with a thorough self-assessment of the present state of your love virtues, as observed in the context of your varied relationships. Then engage in a group-aided process of goal-setting that articulates small virtuous goals in dialogue with larger ones as well as your present agency, situation, resources, obstacles, etc. This process might involve routine review of your goal "checklist," a readiness to revise, simplify, or stretch goals in light of failure or success, and the ability to particularize goals to different relationships.

You might recognize growth in a number of ways: the feedback of others supporting your growth; feedback from those possible beneficiaries of your growth; your own observations of successful goal attainment; and whether or not your relationships are improving, observable perhaps through increasing success at meeting practical needs, a sense of ease and harmony with others, the extent to which you are being positively shaped by others, or a sense of happiness or delight resulting from such relationships. Such assessment of your love or spirituality requires transparency, the aptitude to discern real virtue from semblances of it, the ability to scrutinize yourself without losing the spontaneous quality of love-centered spirituality, deliberate thought and effort, and a willed dependence on others.

A set of queries (self-reflective questions) could also be a primary resource for individuals and groups attempting to cultivate love virtues. The following sample questions could be modified to fit the needs of participants, answered not simply with yes or no but with numerical assessment, depending on how the questions are posed (e.g. "on a scale of 1–10"), or

7. A good resource for this is Nucci, Narvaez, and Krettenauer, eds., *Handbook of Moral and Character Education.*

nuanced for different relationships (e.g., not just kindness as a whole but kindness toward my child, my neighbor, all incarcerated persons, etc.):

- **Gratitude:** How have I accepted the help of others this week? What are the particular talents of my friends? What are my limitations? What made me say "wow" this week? What did I learn this week about a person, community, or natural or social phenomenon? Who did I thank this week and why? What was I wrong about this week?

- **Self-care:** Where did I show restraint this week? Where did I "treat" myself? What caused me anxiety and stress this week? What physical activities did I do this week and how did they affect me? Where did I experience joy in relationship to doing something I am good at? How did I celebrate myself? How did I voice a need or an opinion to others?

- **Justice:** Whose needs did I notice this week and what did I do about them? How did I help someone grow this week? How did I adjust my assistance or care for another person? What skills did I newly acquire or improve upon that could enhance others' well-being? How did I dismiss, downplay, or ignore others' feelings this week?

- **Kindness:** How did I make others feel special this week? How did I give more than I needed to have given? What actions did I take that others might consider remarkable, inspiring, or elevating? How did I go out of my way to do something for someone else? Where did I give or extend aid without recognition or hope of recognition? How did I let someone who wronged or hurt me off the hook?

- **Hope:** What love goals did I set this week? How did I endure a challenge in one of my relationships? How did I overcome fear(s) for the sake of others? How did I demonstrate unwavering commitment to another person or group this week? How did I keep my overarching religious and love goals at the forefront of my mind?

Reimagining Congregational Life

How might the proposed model impact the way mainliners and evangelicals approach the various facets of their shared ministry and religious experience? While I assume to some extent that local congregations will know better than I how to employ this model in their own context, I offer a few thoughts to spark others' creative application.

Pastoral Leadership

Alan Nelson, writing in the 1990s, postulated a paradigm shift in the role of pastors from "ministers" to "leaders," in light of both American and religious cultural trends. Nelson argued that the emerging model of pastoral leadership was (and arguably still is) moving away from the pastor as primarily a caretaker, manager, provider of spiritual services, and chief "doer" of ministry toward one who leads through vision-casting and empowerment of lay leaders.[8]

My project exhibits a continuity with and expansion upon Nelson's observations. Pastors ought to be hopers, able to see and articulate a possible, good future for their congregations and also guide others toward this future. In addition to Nelson's more functional approach—training lay leaders to fill roles that the pastor may have traditionally been expected to fill—pastors should empower through guidance in virtue. This more fundamental focus can support existing ministries while enabling the creation of new ones, as virtue gives substance and sustaining power to the ministries of a congregation.

Thus, the role of pastor ought to be conceptualized primarily as "love-trainer." Pastors, as love-trainers, are required neither to possess elite knowledge of love nor to demonstrate flawless exemplarity (but should be moving toward these things). They should, however, approach their preaching and pastoral care with the goal of moving congregants toward more receptive, ready, fitting, extravagant, and actualized participation in others. The congregant who seeks guidance for marital conflict ought to be encouraged to consider the virtues of love and discern which are particularly relevant to the situation. Christian education ought to emphasize moral education more than doctrinal knowledge. Sermons should equip people to live virtuously. Pastors should recognize the myriad and often ambiguous ways spiritual growth is conceptualized and redirect people back to the hopeful movement toward love.

A pastor, in the context of some form of mentoring relationship, might ask a congregant: "How do you see the presence or absence of gratitude, self-care, justice, kindness, and hope in your relationships? Which virtues could you focus on to better relate to God? To self? To others—intimate or distant, individuals or communities?" Pastoral care ought to focus primarily on the quality of congregants' relationships, recognizing how essential relationships are to personal well-being and how they provide evidence of the health of one's spirituality.

8. See Nelson, *Leading Your Ministry.*

Small Groups

While there is value in topical or niche small groups, congregations that employ a network of small groups as an essential part of spiritual formation should become training grounds for love. If churches can be considered "schools of love," groups can act as seminars or facilitators of love through mutual discovery and accountability.

I applaud the popular Renovare model of spiritual formation for its depth, comprehensiveness, and presentation of classic Christian resources. Yet while its "six streams" approach operationalizes the spiritual life into manageable domains in an inclusive and interesting manner, it is not all that cohesive of a model.[9] Moreover, like many approaches to spiritual growth, it lacks clarity about where spiritual formation ought to take people. This spaciousness may, however, be intended, and appealing to many.

I propose that the energy and skeletal structure of Renovare should be imitated. The five virtues of love in my model, however, would supplant the six streams, making cultivation of these virtues the focus of such groups. Just as Renovare group reflection and discussion is guided by a series of self-reflective questions, so could virtuous small groups be guided by such questions, in varying degrees of intensity. A contemplative group of four or five might spend an hour reflecting upon each virtue every week while a more casual, family-oriented group might pick one query to guide the evening's discussion. Such queries would provide an outline for discussion but also be an aid to measuring spiritual growth.

Worship

Weekly gatherings of Christians should be a practice by which Christians participate in the present and potential goodness of God: "potential" in the sense that Christians are contributors to the life as well as the ongoing and growing creativity of God. Christian singing, to cite one form of worship, ought to facilitate this collaborative relationship with God.

We sing songs of gratitude, celebrating God's inherent goodness but also the concrete ways we encounter this goodness in the natural world, human creativity, the unfolding of our own personal stories, and in one another—all with a spirit of receptive openness to learning, growing, and changing.

9. The six streams include the "prayer-filled life," the "virtuous life," the "Spirit-empowered life," the "compassionate life," the "Word-centered life," and the "Sacramental life." See Renovaré, "The Six Streams," https://renovare.org/about/ideas/the-six-streams.

We sing songs of self-care, reminding ourselves of our Christian identity, goals, and possible gifts we might offer to others. We also lament with brutal honesty what is not right in our world, relationships, and personal lives, recognizing the necessity of grief in movement toward goals and believing that God welcomes our lament and can "take it."

We sing songs of justice, affirming God's care for every person (including how we might participate in such care for others). We seek God's vision of people and the world so that we might discern our possible role in alleviating personal suffering and systemic injustice.

We sing songs of kindness that emotionally overwhelm us with God's extravagant grace, generosity, and hospitality while letting God guide us to channel such extravagance to others.

We sing songs of hope, affirming what we believe and value, naming our goals, and committing ourselves to move toward these goals despite inevitable obstacles. We listen to God and to each other to discern practical ways to act in the world while believing that God, too, is hopeful, determined, and even gritty.

Aside from music, the sacraments (seen as the means of grace in some traditions), silence, and vocal prayer can be practices of responding to God's invitation to participate in God's love. Churches that are more participatory could occasionally engage in some form of hope exercise in lieu of a sermon (though sermons could remain essential as a pastor's means of vision-casting and instructing, in dialogue with Scripture). This could target individual goals, allowing space for people to work though obstacles to love in their own lives. It could also be a congregational process in which the community seeks a way forward in some area. For example, a ministry leader could guide congregants through some variation of this process:

- What challenge are you facing in the context of some relationship with another person or group?

- First, devise a goal related to your challenge, something slightly out of reach but attainable. If it is a big goal, think of a sub-goal or first step that still feels daunting in itself. Describe in rich detail the goal: what it is, what you are doing, what others are doing, how it feels, how it benefits you or others, what the context is. Try to imagine it vividly enough that you can experience it right now in a compelling manner.

- Next, consider your agency. What makes you capable of attaining this goal? What personal resources do you have? What abilities/strengths do you have? What past, relevant experience? What about friends, family, your church? What power is in you and your circle to actualize this goal? Write down some notes.

- Third, how might you get there? Knowing the goal, and your agency, what steps can you take to realize this goal? What are simple, even basic things you can do, like the clothes you should wear, the people you should contact, the places you need to go?

- Next, consider what obstacles might arise. Maybe current circumstances? Emotional triggers, insecurities, doubts? A person? Past failures? Something outside your control?

- Now revisit agency and pathways. Is there anything to add in light of naming these obstacles that might assist you in overcoming them?

- Finally, commit to implementing the hope plan. Next week we will share our experiences.

Outreach

Spiritual formation is not a luxury that should be discarded to address the urgent needs of those outside our community. Churches with outreach ministries—ministries that attend to nonmembers such as providing free meals or hosting evangelistic events—can maintain such ministries while recognizing the sustenance and enhancement that virtuous love training offers.

An elaborate project with several possible roles for congregants to fill ought to be undergirded by ongoing efforts toward individuals' self-appropriation. A ministry to a marginalized group needs the backing of a virtue of justice that ensures our actions are guided not by a well-intentioned but shallow approach to help "those people" but by a more attentive and responsive approach. Dialogue with religious others, whether done to evangelize or create mutually beneficial interfaith understanding, is enhanced by receptive virtues. Outreach ministries or projects will be enhanced by a hopeful approach insistent on well-defined goals that clarify motivations, guide planning, and increase the efficacy of these ministries.

Perhaps most importantly, outreach should be all-pervasive. If the goal of churches is to cultivate love in community under the tutelage of Jesus, then outreach is simply the extension of such love into every aspect of one's life. While this will frequently be organized and corporate, it will more often be lived out by individuals in their varied relationships.

The continuity between spiritual and natural or personal goals is deepened; work, family, hobbies, chores, bills, regular human interaction with residents of one's city, etc., all become opportunities for participatory love.

I may be able to better serve a marginalized community in my city with the collaboration of like-motivated persons (which I would likely find in my own church). Yet outreach—the conscious and deliberate transference of the spiritual experience of love in gathered Christian community beyond the borders of this community—will most often occur in the more low-key moments of daily life.

Go, Hope and Love

In this book, I have asked to what extent people's religious experience reflects moral growth or an increase in love. I have presented a way of understanding the Christian life that is centered on hope, love, and the virtues. I have suggested a practical conflation of spiritual and moral growth that is united by a traditional, Christological emphasis on love to ensure such growth is neither located in dogmatism, enthusiasm, or activism nor purely and autonomously self-determined but, instead, expressed through our increasing participation in God and others.

    If Christians truly value "love" as the most important element of the Christian experience, they ought to hope for it through cultivating virtues that increase their receptive, ready, fitting, extravagant, and actualizing participation in others. Love unites the virtues. Love clarifies the point of Christian practice(s). Love makes the Christian spiritual life simultaneously much more difficult (love takes work!) and much more compelling (love is the worthiest and most rewarding goal). I have provided one road map to get to love, even if love is always simultaneously achievable and beyond us.

Works Cited

Akin, Lara B., Elizabeth W. Dunn, and Michael I. Norton. "Happiness Runs in a Circular Motion: Evidence for a Positive Feedback Loop Between Prosocial Spending and Happiness." *Journal of Happiness Studies* 13 (2012) 347–55.

Algoe, Sara B. "Find, Remind, and Bind: The Functions of Gratitude in Everyday Relationships." *Social and Personality Psychology Compass* 6 (2012) 455–69.

Algoe, Sara B., and Jonathan Haidt. "Witnessing Excellence in Action: The 'Other-Praising' Emotions of Elevation, Gratitude, and Admiration." *Journal of Positive Psychology* 4 (2009) 105–27.

Anderson, Howard. "'The Moral Example of Desmond Tutu." Episcopal Café, November 26, 2007. http://www.episcopalcafe.com/the_moral_example_of_desmond_tutu/.

Angle, Stephen C. *Sagehood: The Contemporary Significance of Neo-Confucian Philosophy.* Oxford: Oxford University Press, 2009.

Aquinas, Thomas. *Summa Theologica.* http://www.newadvent.org/summa/3.htm.

Aristotle. *Nicomachean Ethics.* Translated by Terence Irwin. 2nd ed. Indianapolis: Hackett, 1999.

Augustine. *Concerning the City of God Against the Pagans.* Translated by Henry Bettenson. London: Penguin, 1972.

Aune, Kristin. "Between Subordination and Sympathy: Evangelical Christians, Masculinity, and Gay Sexuality." In *Contemporary Christianity and LGBT Sexualities*, edited by Stephen Hunt, 40–50. Burlington, VT: Ashgate, 2009.

Austen, Jane. *Sense and Sensibility.* Mineola, NY: Dover, 1996.

Bandura, Albert. "Self-Efficacy: Toward a Unifying Theory of Behavioral Change." *Psychological Review* 84 (1977) 191–215.

Barlow, Rich. "New Episcopal Chaplain a Role Model." *BU Today*, November 18, 2011. https://www.bu.edu/today/2011/new-episcopal-chaplain-a-role-model/.

Bartlett, Monica Y., and David DeSteno. "Gratitude and Prosocial Behavior: Helping When It Costs You." *Psychological Science* 17 (2006) 319–25.

Barton, Ruth Haley. *Sacred Rhythms: Arranging Our Lives for Spiritual Transformation.* Downers Grove, IL: InterVarsity, 2006.

Battle, Michael. "Liberation." In *The Blackwell Companion to Christian Spirituality*, edited by Arthur Holder, 515–31. Malden, MA: Blackwell, 2011.

Beck, Richard. *Unclean: Meditations on Purity, Hospitality, and Morality.* Eugene, OR: Cascade, 2011.

Birkel, Michael L. *Silence and Witness: The Quaker Tradition*. Maryknoll, NY: Orbis, 2004.

Biswas-Diener, Robert. *The Courage Quotient: How Science Can Make You Braver*. San Francisco: Jossey-Bass, 2012.

Boersma, Hans. *Embodiment and Virtue in Gregory of Nyssa: An Anagogical Approach*. Oxford: Oxford University Press, 2013.

Bondi, Roberta C. *To Love as God Loves: Conversations with the Early Church*. Philadelphia: Fortress, 1987.

Bonhoeffer, Dietrich. *Letters and Papers from Prison*. Translated by Eberhard Bethge. New York: The MacMillan, 1953.

Borg, Marcus. *Convictions: How I Learned What Matters Most*. New York: HarperOne, 2014.

Brody, Salena, Stephen C. Wright, Arthur Aron, and Tracy McLaughlin-Volpe. "Compassionate Love for Individuals in Other Social Groups." In *The Science of Compassionate Love: Theory, Research, and Applications*, edited by Beverly Fehr, Susan Sprecher, and Lynn G. Underwood, 3–25. Malden, MA: Wiley-Blackwell, 2008.

Brown, Stephen F. "The Theological Virtue of Faith (IIa IIae, qq 1–16)." In *The Ethics of Aquinas*, edited by Stephen J. Pope, 221–31. Washington, DC: Georgetown University Press, 2002.

Brueggemann, Walter. *The Prophetic Imagination*. 2nd ed. Minneapolis, MN: Fortress, 2001.

Buckingham, Marcus, and Donald O. Clifton. *Now, Discover Your Strengths*. New York: Free Press, 2001.

Buechner, Fredrick. *Telling Secrets*. San Francisco: HarperSanFrancisco, 1991.

———. *Wishful Thinking: A Seeker's ABC*. San Francisco: HarperSanFrancisco, 1993.

Burghardt, Walter J. "Spirituality and Justice." In *Ethics and Spirituality*, edited by Charles E. Curran and Lisa A. Fullam, 183–205. Mawhah, NJ: Paulist, 2014.

Burridge, Richard. *Imitating Jesus: An Inclusive Approach to New Testament Ethics*. Grand Rapids: Eerdmans, 2007.

Campolo, Tony. "The Quiet Revolutionary." *Christianity Today* 35 (February 1991) 22–24.

Cannon, Katie. *Black Womanist Ethics*. Atlanta: Scholars Press, 1988.

Carrette, Jeremy, and Richard King. *Selling Spirituality: The Silent Takeover of Religion*. London and New York: Routledge, 2005.

Cen, Guozhen, and Jun Yu. "Traditional Chinese Philosophies and Their Perspectives on Moral Education." In *Handbook of Moral and Character Education*, edited by Larry Nucci, Darcia Narvaez, and Tobias Krettenauer, 30–42. New York: Routledge, 2014.

Chandler, Diane. *Christian Spiritual Formation: An Integrated Approach*. Downers Grove, IL: Intervarsity, 2014.

Chaudry, Amina. "Interview with Desmond Tutu, Archbishop of Cape Town." *Muslim World* 100 (January 2010) 117–23.

Cheavens, Jennifer S., and Lorie A. Ritschel. "Hope Theory." In *The Handbook of Positive Emotions*, edited by Michele Tugade, Michelle N. Shiota, and Leslie D. Kirby, 396–410. New York: Guilford, 2014.

Chittister, Joan. *Wisdom Distilled From the Daily: Living the Rule of St. Benedict Today*. New York: HarperCollins, 1990.

Clawson, Julie. "Imagination, Hope, and Reconciliation in Ricoeur and Moltmann." *Anglican Theological Review* 95 (Spring 2013) 293–309.

Cleaver, Richard. *Know My Name: A Gay Liberation Theology.* Louisville, KY: Westminster John Knox, 1995.

CNN Wire Staff. "South Africa's Tutu Announces Retirement." CNN, July 22, 2010. http://edition.cnn.com/2010/WORLD/africa/07/22/south.africa.tutu.retires/index.html#fbid=ZeXEgKJ1qcV.

Csikszentmihalyi, Mihaly. *Flow: The Psychology of Optimal Experience.* New York: Harper and Row, 2008.

Davidson, Richard, and Sharon Begley. *The Emotional Life of Your Brain: How Its Unique Patterns Affect the Way You Think, Feel, and Live—and How You Can Change Them.* New York: Penguin, 2012.

Day, Dorothy. *All the Way to Heaven: The Selected Letters of Dorothy Day.* Edited by Robert Ellsberg. Milwaukee, WI: Marquette University Press, 2010.

———. *The Duty of Delight: The Diaries of Dorothy Day.* Edited by Robert Ellsberg. Milwaukee, WI: Marquette University Press, 2008.

———. *From Union Square to Rome.* New York: Arno Press, 1978.

———. "Letter On Hospices." *The Catholic Worker,* January 1948. http://www.catholicworker.org/dorothyday/articles/183.pdf.

———. *The Long Loneliness.* New York: Curtis, 1952.

———. "On Pilgrimage—February 1969." *The Catholic Worker,* February 1969. http://www.catholicworker.org/dorothyday/articles/894.html.

———. "On Pilgrimage—March 1959: The Story of Jack English's First Mass." *The Catholic Worker,* March 1959. http://www.catholicworker.org/dorothyday/articles/750.pdf.

———. "Personalist—Peter Maurin." *The Catholic Worker,* May 1953. http://www.catholicworker.org/dorothyday/articles/170.pdf.

———. "Poverty Without Tears." *The Catholic Worker,* April 1950. http://www.catholicworker.org/dorothyday/articles/230.pdf.

———. "The Scandal of the Works of Mercy." In *Dorothy Day: Writings from Commonweal,* edited by Patrick Jordan, 103–10. Collegeville, MN: Liturgical, 2002.

———. "Workers of the World Unite." *The Catholic Worker,* May 1958. http://www.catholicworker.org/dorothyday/articles/177.html.

DeParle, Jason. "Harder for Americans to Rise from Lower Rungs." *New York Times,* January 4, 2012. http://www.nytimes.com/2012/01/05/us/harder-for-americans-to-rise-from-lower-rungs.html?_r=0.

De Sales, Francis. *Living Love: A Modern Edition of Treatise on the Love of God.* Edited by Bernard Bangley. Brewster, MA: Paraclete, 2003.

Domar, Alice D. *Self-Nurture: Learning to Care for Yourself as Effectively as You Care for Everyone Else.* New York: Penguin, 2001.

Domhoff, William G. "Basics of Studying Power." Who Rules America?, April 2005. http://www2.ucsc.edu/whorulesamerica/methods/studying_power.html.

Duckworth, Angela. *Grit: The Power of Passion and Perseverance.* New York: Scribner, 2016.

Dunn, Elizabeth W., Lara B. Akin, and Michael I. Norton. "Spending Money on Others Promotes Happiness." *Science* 319 (2008) 1687–88.

Dweck, Carol. *Mindset: The New Psychology of Success.* New York: Ballentine, 2006.

Eldridge, John. *Waking the Dead: The Glory of a Heart Fully Alive*. Nashville: Thomas Nelson, 2003.

Emmons, Robert A. *Gratitude Works! A 21-Day Program for Creating Emotional Prosperity*. San Francisco: Jossey-Bass, 2013.

———. *Thanks! How Practicing Gratitude Can Make You Happier*. New York: Houghton Mifflin, 2008.

Emsley, Sarah Baxter. *Jane Austen's Philosophy of the Virtues*. New York: Palgrave Macmillan, 2005.

Fehr, Beverley, Cheryl Harasymchuk, and Susan Sprecher. "Compassionate Love in Romantic Relationships: A Review and Some New Findings." *Journal of Social and Personal Relationships* 31 (2014) 575–600.

Fehr, Beverley, and Susan Sprecher. "Compassionate Love: Conceptual, Measurement, and Relational Issues." In *The Science of Compassionate Love: Theory, Research, and Applications*, edited by Beverly Fehr, Susan Sprecher, and Lynn G. Underwood, 32–42. Malden, MA: Wiley-Blackwell, 2008.

Fehr, Beverley, Susan Sprecher, and Lynn G. Underwood. *The Science of Compassionate Love: Theory, Research, and Applications*. Malden, MA: Wiley-Blackwell, 2008.

Fisher, Kathleen M. "Curiouser and Curiouser: The Virtue of Wonder." *The Journal of Education* 182 (2000) 29–35.

Fishman, Stephen M., and Lucille McCarthy. "The Morality and Politics of Hope: John Dewey and Positive Psychology in Dialogue." *Transactions of the Charles S. Peirce Society* 41 (Summer 2005) 675–701.

Forest, Jim. *All Is Grace: A Biography of Dorothy Day*. Maryknoll, NY: Orbis, 2011.

Foster, Richard. *Celebration of Discipline: The Path to Spiritual Growth*. New York: HarperCollins, 1978.

———. "Spiritual Formation Agenda." *Christianity Today* 53 (January 2009) 29–32.

Fowler, James. *Stages of Faith: The Psychology of Human Development and the Quest for Meaning*. New York: HarperCollins, 1985.

Fredrickson, Barbara. "The Role of Positive Emotions in Positive Psychology: The Broaden-and-Build Theory of Positive Emotions." *American Psychologist* 56 (March 2001) 218–26.

Freire, Paulo. *Pedagogy of the Oppressed*. 20th anniversary ed. New York: Continuum, 1993.

Frye, Northrop. "The Double Vision of Language." In *Literature and the Bible: A Reader*, edited by Jo Carruthers, Mark Knight, and Andrew Tate, 215–21. New York: Routledge, 2014.

Fullam, Lisa. "Humility and Its Moral Epistemological Implications." In *Virtue: Readings in Moral Theology No. 16*, edited by Charles E. Curran and Lisa A. Fullam, 250–74. New York, Paulist, 2011.

Gadamer, Hans-Georg. "Language and Hermeneutics." In *Literature and the Bible: A Reader*, edited by Jo Carruthers, Mark Knight, and Andrew Tate, 94–103. New York: Routledge, 2014.

Garrison, Becky. "Crossing Boundaries: A Transgender Priest Becomes a University Chaplain." *Religion & Politics*, January 3, 2013. http://religionandpolitics. org/2013/01/03/crossing-boundaries-a-transgender-priest-becomes-a-university-chaplain/.

Gates, Jeffery. "Self-Care: A Christian Perspective." *Evangelical Review of Theology* 39 (January 2015) 4–17.

Genovesi, Vincent J. *Expectant Creativity: The Action of Hope in Christian Ethics.* Washington, DC: University Press of America, 1982.

Gerdes, Karen E., Elizabeth A. Segal, Kelly F. Jackson, and Jennifer L. Mullins. "Teaching Empathy: A Framework Rooted in Social Cognitive Neuroscience and Social Justice." *Journal of Social Work Education* 47 (2011) 109–31.

Gilbert, Paul. *The Compassionate Mind: A New Approach to Life's Challenges.* Oakland: New Harbinger, 2009.

Gilligan, Carol. *In a Different Voice.* Cambridge: Harvard University Press, 1982.

———. *Joining the Resistance.* Malden, MA: Polity, 2011.

Goetz, Jennifer L., Dacher Keltner, and Emiliana Simon-Thomas. "Compassion: An Evolutionary Analysis and Empirical Review." *Psychological Bulletin* 136 (2010) 351–74.

Goleman, Daniel. *Emotional Intelligence.* New York: Bantam, 1995.

Grant, Adam. "Goodbye to MBTI, the Fad That Won't Die." *Psychology Today*, September 18, 2013. https://www.psychologytoday.com/blog/give-and-take/201309/ goodbye-mbti-the-fad-won-t-die.

Gregory of Nyssa. *The Life of Moses.* Edited by Everett Ferguson and Abraham J. Malherbe. New York: Paulist, 1978.

Gross, James J. "Emotion Regulation: Conceptual and Empirical Foundations." In *Handbook of Emotion Regulation*, edited by James J. Gross, 3–25. New York: Guilford, 2007.

Gutierrez, Gustavo. *We Drink From Our Own Wells: The Spiritual Journey of a People.* Maryknoll, NY: Orbis, 1984.

Hadewijch. *Hadewijch: The Complete Works.* Translated by Mother Columba Hart. Classics of Western Spirituality. Mahwah, NJ: Paulist, 1980.

Hafiz, Yasmine. "Rev. Cameron Partridge Will Be First Openly Transgender Priest to Preach at Washington National Cathedral." *Huffpost Religion*, June 23, 2014. http:// www.huffingtonpost.com/2014/06/06/transgender-priest-national-cathedral- pride_n_5459762.html.

Haidt, Jonathan. *The Happiness Hypothesis: Finding Modern Truth in Ancient Wisdom.* New York: Basic, 2006.

Hall, David L., and Roger T. Ames. *Thinking Through Confucius.* Albany, NY: Saint University of New York Press, 1987.

Hamrick, William S. *Kindness and the Good Society: Connections of the Heart.* Albany: State University of New York Press, 2002.

Harris, Melanie L. *Gifts of Virtue, Alice Walker, and Womanist Ethics.* New York: Palgrave Macmillan, 2010.

Hauerwas, Stanley. "Character, Narrative, and Growth in the Christian Life." In *The Hauerwas Reader*, edited by John Berkman and Michael Cartwright, 221–54. Durham: Duke University Press, 2001.

———. *The Peaceable Kingdom: A Primer in Christian Ethics.* Notre Dame, IN: University of Notre Dame Press, 1983.

Hauerwas, Stanley, and Charles Pinches. "Courage." In *Virtue: Readings in Moral Theology No. 16*, edited by Charles E. Curran and Lisa A. Fullam, 227–49. New York: Paulist, 2011.

Hauerwas, Stanley, and Jean Vanier. *Living Gently in a Violent World: The Prophetic Witness of Weakness.* Downers Grove, IL: Intervarsity, 2008.

Haws, Charles G. "Suffering, Hope, and Forgiveness: The Ubuntu Theology of Desmond Tutu." *Scottish Journal of Theology* 62 (2009) 477–89.

Herdt, Jennifer. *Putting on Virtue: The Legacy of the Splendid Vices.* Chicago: University of Chicago Press, 2008.

Heyd, David. *Supererogation.* Cambridge Studies in Philosophy. Cambridge: Cambridge University Press, 1982.

Holder, Arthur. "Introduction." In *The Blackwell Companion to Christian Spirituality,* edited by Arthur Holder, 1–11. Malden, MA: Blackwell, 2011.

Howard, Evan. "Three Temptations of Spiritual Formation." *Christianity Today* 46 (December 9, 2002) 46–50.

Isasi-Diaz, Ada Maria. "Spirituality and the Common Good." In *Ethics and Spirituality: Readings in Moral Theology No. 17,* edited by Charles E. Curran and Lisa A. Fullam, 249–57. New York, Paulist, 2014.

Iser, Wolfgang. "Asymmetry Between Text and Reader." In *Literature and the Bible: A Reader,* edited by Jo Carruthers, Mark Knight, and Andrew Tate, 89–95. New York: Routledge, 2014.

Ivanhoe, Philip J. *Confucian Moral Self-Cultivation.* 2nd ed. Indianapolis: Hackett, 2000.

John Climacus. *The Ladder of Divine Ascent.* Edited by Colm Luibheid and Norman Victor Russell. Classics of Western Spirituality. Mahwah, NJ: Paulist, 1982.

John, Oliver P., Laura P. Naumann, and Christopher J. Soto. "Paradigm Shift to the Integrative Big Five Taxonomy: History, Measurement, and Conceptual Issues." In *Handbook of Personality: Theory and Research,* edited by Oliver P. John, Richard W. Robins, and Lawrence A. Pervin, 114–58. 3rd ed. New York: Guilford, 2008.

Johnson, Jan. "Being Present to Others." *Weavings* 12 (Sept/Oct 1997) 27–34.

Julian of Norwich. *Revelations of Divine Love: Short Text and Long Text.* Translated by Elizabeth Spearing. London: Penguin, 1998.

Kabat-Zinn, Jon. "Mindfulness-Based Interventions in Context: Past, Present, and Future." *Clinical Psychology: Science and Practice* 10 (2003) 144–56.

Kabat-Zinn, Jon, and Thich Nhat Hanh. *Full Catastrophe Living: Using the Wisdom of Your Body and Mind to Face Stress, Pain, and Illness.* Rev. ed. New York: Bantam, 2013.

Kannengieser, Charles. "The Spiritual Message of the Great Fathers." In *Christian Spirituality: Origins to the Twelfth Century,* edited by Bernard McGinn, John Meyendorff, and Jean Leclerq, 61–88. World Spirituality 16. New York: Crossroad, 1987.

Karremans, Johan C., Paul A. M. Van Lange, and Rob W. Holland. "Forgiveness and Its Associations with Prosocial Thinking, Feeling, and Doing Beyond the Relationship With the Offender." *Personality and Social Psychology Bulletin* 31 (October 2005) 1315–26.

Keenan, James F. "Proposing Cardinal Virtues." *Theological Studies* 56 (1995) 709–29.

———. "Virtue Ethics and Sexual Ethics." In *Virtue: Readings in Moral Theology No. 16,* edited by Charles E. Curran and Lisa A. Fullam, 117–36. New York: Paulist, 2011.

Keller, Catherine. *On the Mystery: Discerning Divinity in Process.* Minneapolis, MN: Fortress, 2008.

Kelly, Thomas R. *A Testament of Devotion.* New York: HarperCollins, 1941.

Keltner, Dacher. *Born to Be Good: The Science of a Meaningful Life.* New York: W. W. Norton & Company, 2009.

King, Martin Luther, Jr. "Loving Your Enemies." In *Strength to Love*, by Martin Luther King Jr., 43–52. Minneapolis, MN: Fortress, 2010.

———. *Strength to Love*. Minneapolis, MN: Fortress, 2010.

Kogut, Tehlia, and Ilana Ritov. "The 'Identified Victim' Effect: An Identified Group, or Just a Single Individual." *Journal of Behavioral Decision Making* 18 (2005) 157–67.

Krause, Neal, and R. David Hayward. "Religious Involvement and Humility." *The Journal of Positive Psychology* 9 (2014) 254–65.

Kruse, Elliot, Joseph Chancellor, Peter M. Ruberton, and Sonja Lyubomirsky. "An Upward Spiral Between Gratitude and Humility." *Social Psychological and Personality Science* 5 (2014) 805–14.

Lamott, Anne. *Help, Thanks, Wow: The Three Essential Prayers*. New York: Penguin, 2012.

Larkin, Ernest E. "The Three Spiritual Ways." *The Published Articles of Ernest E. Larkin, O. Carm*. http://carmelnet.org/larkin/larkin092.pdf.

Leclercq, Jean. *The Love of Learning and the Desire for God: A Study in Monastic Culture*. New York: Fordham, 1961.

Ledtke, Brian. "Boston U Encourages Students to Get 'Frisky' with '29 Days of Stimulation.'" Campus Reform, February 8, 2016. https://www.campusreform.org/?ID=7260.

Lewis, C. S. "The Weight of Glory." In *The Weight of Glory: And Other Addresses*, 25–46. New York: HarperCollins, 2001.

Li, Chenyang. "The Confucian Concept of Jen and the Feminist Ethics of Care: A Comparative Study." *Hypatia* 9 (Winter 1994) 70–89.

Liebert, Elizabeth. *The Soul of Discernment: A Spiritual Practice for Communities and Institutions*. Louisville, KY: Westminster John Knox, 2015.

Loeb, Paul. "Soul of a Citizen: Rethinking the Limits of Volunteerism." Adapted from *Soul of a Citizen: Living with Conviction in Challenging Times*. New York: St. Martin's Press, 1999.

Lonergan, Bernard. *Method in Theology*. Toronto: University of Toronto Press, 1971.

Lopez, Shane J. *Making Hope Happen: Creating the Future You Want for Yourself and Others*. New York: Simon & Schuster, 2013.

Lovasik, Lawrence G. *The Hidden Power of Kindness: A Practical Handbook for Souls Who Dare to Transform the World, One Deed at a Time*. New York: MacMillan, 1962.

Luskin, Fred. "What Is Forgiveness?" The Greater Good Science Center, August 19, 2010. http://greatergood.berkeley.edu/article/item/what_is_forgiveness.

MacIntyre, Alasdair. *After Virtue*. 3rd ed. Notre Dame: University of Notre Dame Press, 2007.

Mack, Rachel. "Biography: Alice Walker." Americans Who Tell The Truth. http://www.americanswhotellthetruth.org/portraits/alice-walker.

Markoe, Lauren. "Five Questions for Transgender Chaplain Cameron Partridge." *The Washington Post*, July 19, 2013. https://www.washingtonpost.com/national/on-faith/five-questions-for-transgender-chaplain-cameron-partridge/2013/07/19/90d2e63e-f0ac-11e2-bcod-556690a86be2_story.html.

Marks, Nadine F., and Jieun Song. "Compassionate Motivation and Compassionate Acts across the Adult Life Course: Evidence from US National Studies." In *The Science of Compassionate Love: Theory, Research, and Applications*, edited by

Beverly Fehr, Susan Sprecher, and Lynn G. Underwood, 121–58. Malden, MA: Wiley-Blackwell, 2008.

Markway, Barbara. "Seven Types of Self-Care Activities for Coping with Stress." *Psychology Today*, March 16, 2014. https://www.psychologytoday.com/blog/shyness-is-nice/201403/seven-types-self-care-activities-coping-stress.

Martin, Mike W. *Happiness and the Good Life*. Oxford: Oxford University Press, 2012.

McClendon, James William, Jr. *Systematic Theology*. Vol. 1, *Ethics*. Nashville: Abingdon, 1986.

McCullough, Michael E. "Forgiveness: Who Does It and How Do They Do It?" *Current Directions in Psychological Science* 10 (December 2001) 194–97.

McCullough, Michael E., Robert A. Emmons, and Jo-Ann Tsang. "The Grateful Disposition: A Conceptual and Empirical Topography." *Journal of Personality and Social Psychology* 82 (2002) 112–27.

McGinn, Bernard. *The Foundations of Mysticism: Origins to the Fifth Century*. New York: Crossroad, 2004.

McLeod, Saul. "Carl Jung." *Simply Psychology*, 2014. http://www.simplypsychology.org/carl-jung.html.

Meilaender, Gilbert C. *The Theory and Practice of Virtue*. Notre Dame: University of Notre Dame Press, 1984.

Mencius. "Mengzi (Mencius)." In *Readings in Classical Chinese Philosophy*, edited by Philip J. Ivanhoe and Bryan W. Van Norden, 114–59. 2nd ed. Indianapolis: Hackett, 2005.

Merton, Thomas. *Life and Holiness*. New York: Image, 1963.

———. *Thoughts in Solitude*. New York: Farrar, Straus, and Giroux, 1956.

Metz, Johannes B. "The Future *Ex Memoria Passionis*." In *Hope and the Future of Man*, edited by Ewert H. Cousins, 117–30. Philadelphia: Fortress, 1972.

Mikulincer, Mario, Phillip R. Shaver, and Omri Gillath. "A Behavioral Systems Perspective on Compassionate Love." In *The Science of Compassionate Love: Theory, Research, and Applications*, edited by Beverly Fehr, Susan Sprecher, and Lynn G. Underwood, 225–56. Malden, MA: Wiley-Blackwell, 2008.

Milbank, John. *Theology and Social Theory: Beyond Secular Reason*. 2nd ed. Malden, MA: Blackwell, 2006.

Miles, Margaret. *Practicing Christianity: Critical Perspectives for an Embodied Spirituality*. New York: Crossroad, 1988.

Mischel, Walter. *The Marshmallow Test: Mastering Self-Control*. New York: Little, Brown and Company, 2014.

Moltmann, Jurgen. *In the End, the Beginning: The Life of Hope*. Translated by Margaret Kohl. Minneapolis: Fortress, 2004.

———. *Sun of Righteousness Arise! God's Future for Humanity and the Earth*. Translated by Margaret Kohl. Minneapolis: Fortress, 2010.

———. *Theology of Hope: On the Ground and Implications of a Christian Eschatology*. London: SCM, 1967.

Mulholland, Robert. *Invitation to a Journey: A Road Map for Spiritual Formation*. Downers Grove, IL: Intervarsity, 1993.

Neff, Kristen. *Self-Compassion: Stop Beating Yourself Up and Leave Insecurity Behind*. New York: HarperCollins, 2011.

Neff, Lisa A., and Benjamin R. Karney. "Compassionate Love in Early Marriage." In *The Science of Compassionate Love: Theory, Research, and Applications*, edited by

Beverly Fehr, Susan Sprecher, and Lynn G. Underwood, 201–21. Malden, MA: Wiley-Blackwell, 2008.

Nelson, Alan. *Leading Your Ministry: Developing the Mind of a Priest and the Soul of a Prophet*. Nashville, TN: Abingdon, 1996.

Newman, Barbara. "Person to Person: Becoming Present." *Spiritus* 16 (Spring 2016) 99–109.

Noddings, Nel. *Caring: A Relational Approach to Ethics and Moral Education*. 2nd ed. Berkeley: University of California Press, 2013.

Nolan, Albert. "Spiritual Growth and the Option for the Poor." *Church* 1 (1985) 45–48.

Nouwen, Henri. *Reaching Out: The Three Movements of the Spiritual Life*. New York: Doubleday, 1975.

Nucci, Larry, Darcia Narvaez, and Tobias Krettenauer, eds. *Handbook of Moral and Character Education*. New York: Routledge, 2014.

Nygren, Anders. *Apape and Eros*. Translated by Philip S. Watson. New York: Harper and Row, 1969.

Origen. *Commentary on the Song of Songs: Commentary and Homilies*. Translated by R. P. Lawson. Ancient Christian Writers 26. New York: Newman, 1957.

Oswald, Roy M. *Clergy Self-Care: Finding a Balance for Effective Ministry*. Herndon, VA: Alban Institute, 1991.

Outka, Gene H. *Agape: An Ethical Analysis*. New Haven: Yale University Press, 1972.

Palmer, Parker. *Let Your Life Speak*. San Francisco: Jossey-Bass, 2000.

Pannenberg, Wolfhart. *Systematic Theology*. Vol 1. Translated by Geoffrey W. Bromiley. Grand Rapids, MI: Eerdmans, 1991.

Partridge, Cameron. "Other Sheep: A Sermon by Rev. Dr. Cameron Partridge." *Believe Out Loud*, May 10, 2012. https://www.believeoutloud.com/boltoday/20120510/other-sheep-sermon-by-rev-dr-cameron-partridge.

Perrin, David B. *Studying Christian Spirituality*. New York: Routledge, 2007.

Peterson, Christopher, and Martin Seligman. *Character Strengths and Virtues: A Handbook and Classification*. New York: Oxford University Press, 2004.

Plato. *Republic*. Translated by G. M. A. Grube. Indianapolis, IN: Hackett, 1992.

Pope, Stephen J. "Love in Contemporary Christian Ethics." *Journal of Religious Ethics* 23 (Spring 1995) 167–97.

Post, Stephen. "The Purpose of Neighbor-Love." *Journal of Religious Ethics* 18 (Spring 1990) 181–93.

———. *A Theory of Agape: On the Meaning of Christian Love*. London: Associated University Presses, 1990.

Putman, Daniel. "Philosophical Roots of the Concept of Courage." In *The Psychology of Courage: Modern Research on an Ancient Virtue*, edited by Cynthia L. S. Pury and Shane J. Lopez, 9–22. Washington, DC: American Psychological Association, 2010.

Rahner, Karl. *Foundations of Christian Faith: An Introduction to the Idea of Christianity*. Translated by William V. Dych. New York: Seabury, 1978.

Ramsay, Nancy J. "Intersectionality: A Model For Addressing the Complexity of Oppression and Privilege." *Pastoral Psychology* 63 (2014) 453–69.

Rawls, John. *A Theory of Justice*. Oxford: Clarendon, 1972.

Riegle, Rosalie G. *Dorothy Day: Portraits By Those Who Knew Her*. Maryknoll, NY: Orbis, 2003.

Roberts, Hayley. "Implicit Bias and Social Justice." Open Society Foundations, December 18, 2011. https://www.opensocietyfoundations.org/voices/implicit-bias-and-social-justice.

Rodham, Thomas. "Reading Jane Austen as a Moral Philosopher." *Philosophy Now*, Feb/Mar 2016. https://philosophynow.org/issues/94/Reading_Jane_Austen_as_a_Moral_Philosopher.

Rohr, Richard. *Falling Upward: A Spirituality for the Two Halves of Life.* San Francisco: Jossey-Bass, 2011.

————. "My Problem with Religion." *Tikkun* 22 (July/August 2007) 20–22.

————. *The Naked Now: Learning to See as the Mystics See.* New York: Crossroad, 2009.

Scheler, Max. *The Nature of Sympathy.* Translated by Peter Heath. London: Routledge & Kegan Paul, 1954.

Schneiders, Sandra. "Approaches to the Study of Christian Spirituality." In *The Blackwell Companion to Christian Spirituality*, edited by Arthur Holder, 15–33. Malden, MA: Blackwell, 2005.

————. "Theology and Spirituality: Strangers, Rivals, or Partners?" *Horizons* 13 (1986) 253–74.

Schwartz, Barry, and Kenneth Sharpe. *Practical Wisdom: The Right Way to Do the Right Thing.* New York: Riverhead, 2010.

Seligman, Martin E. P. *Flourish: A Visionary New Understanding of Happiness and Well-Being.* New York: Simon & Schuster, 2011.

Sheldon, Kennon M., and Sonja Lyubomirsky. "How to Increase and Sustain Positive Emotion: The Effects of Increasing Gratitude and Visualizing Best Possible Selves." *The Journal of Positive Psychology* 1 (April 2006) 73–82.

Sheldrake, Philip. *Spirituality: A Brief History.* 2nd ed. Malden, MA: Wiley-Blackwell, 2013.

Simon-Thomas, Emiliana. "Meditation Makes Us Act with Compassion." Greater Good Science Center, April 11, 2013. http://greatergood.berkeley.edu/article/item/meditation_causes_compassionate_action.

Small, Deborah A., George Loewenstein, and Paul Slovic. "Sympathy and Callousness: The Impact of Deliberative Thought on Donations to Identifiable and Statistical Victims." *Organization Behavior and Human Decision Processes* 102 (2007) 143–53.

Smith, Pamela A. "Green Lap, Brown Embrace, Blue Body: The Ecospirituality of Alice Walker." In *Cross Currents* 48 (Winter 1998–99) 471–87.

Smith, Tom W. "Loving and Caring in the United States: Trends and Correlates of Empathy, Altruism, and Related Constructs." In *The Science of Compassionate Love: Theory, Research, and Applications*, edited by Beverly Fehr, Susan Sprecher, and Lynn G. Underwood, 81–119. Malden, MA: Wiley-Blackwell, 2008.

Snyder, C. R. "Hypothesis: There Is Hope." In *Handbook of Hope: Theories, Measures, and Applications*, edited by C. R. Snyder, 1–21. San Diego: Academic, 2000.

————. *The Psychology of Hope: You Can Get There From Here.* New York: Simon & Schuster, 1994.

Snyder, C. R., ed. *Handbook of Hope: Theory, Measures, and Applications.* San Diego: Academic, 2000.

Snyder, C. R., Kevin L. Rand, and David R. Sigmon. "Hope Theory: A Member of the Positive Psychology Family." In *Handbook of Positive Psychology*, edited by C. R. Snyder and Shane J. Lopez, 257–76. New York: Oxford University Press, 2002.

Solzhenitsyn, Aleksandr. *The Gulag Archipelago Abridged: An Experiment in Literary Investigation*. New York: Harper & Row, 1985.

Song, C. S. *Jesus, the Crucified People*. Minneapolis, MN: Fortress, 1996.

Spencer, Gregory. *Awaking the Quieter Virtues*. Downers Grove, IL: InterVarsity, 2010.

Spohn, William. "Christian Spirituality and Theological Ethics." In *The Blackwell Companion to Christian Spirituality*, edited by Arthur Holder, 269–85. Malden, MA: Blackwell, 2011.

———. *Go and Do Likewise: Jesus and Ethics*. New York: Continuum, 2007.

Sri, Edward P. "Called to Greatness: The Virtue of Magnanimity." Catholic Education Resource Center. http://www.catholiceducation.org/en/education/virtue-education/called-to-greatness-the-virtue-of-magnanimity.html.

Stanford Encyclopedia of Philosophy. "Personalism." December 2, 2013. http://plato.stanford.edu/entries/personalism/ (accessed July 8, 2016).

Steere, Douglas V. "Introduction." In *Quaker Spirituality: Selected Writings*, edited Douglas V. Steere, 3–53. Classics of Western Spirituality. Mahwah, NJ: Paulist, 1984.

Suttie, Jill. "Can Restorative Justice Help Prisoners to Heal?" Greater Good Science Center, June 9, 2015. https://greatergood.berkeley.edu/article/item/restorative_justice_help_prisoners_heal.

———. "Is Grit the Key to Success?" Greater Good Science Center, May 6, 2016. http://greatergood.berkeley.edu/article/item/is_grit_the_key_to_success.

Symington, Scott H., and Melissa F. Symington. "A Christian Model of Mindfulness: Using Mindfulness Principles to Support Psychological Well-Being, Value-Based Behavior, and the Christian Spiritual Journey." *Journal of Psychology and Christianity* 31 (2012) 71–77.

Teilhard de Chardin, Pierre. *The Divine Milieu*. New York: Harper Perennial Modern Classics, 2001.

———. *The Future of Man*. Translated by Norman Denny. New York: Harper & Row, 1969.

———. *The Phenomenon of Man*. New York: Harper & Row, 1959.

Thérèse of Lisieux. *Sermon in a Sentence: A Treasury of Quotes on the Spiritual Life from St. Thérèse of Lisieux*. Vol 1. Edited by John McClernon. San Francisco: Ignatius, 2002.

Tillich, Paul. *The Courage to Be*. New Haven: Yale University Press, 1952.

Timmerman, John J. "Some Notes on Magnanimity." *Reformed Journal* 29 (Aug 1979) 2–4.

Townes, Emilie M. "Womanist Ethics." In *Dictionary of Feminist Theologies*, edited by Letty M. Russell and J. Shannon Clarkson, 90–91. Louisville, KY: Westminster John Knox, 1996.

Tronto, Joan. *Moral Boundaries: A Political Argument for an Ethic of Care*. New York: Routledge, 1994.

Trueblood, D. Elton. *The Common Ventures of Life: Marriage, Birth, Work and Death*. Waco, TX: Word, 1949.

———. *Essays in Gratitude*. Nashville, TN: Broadman, 1982.

———. *While It Is Day*. New York: Harper & Row, 1974.

———. "William Penn Lecture 1947: A Radical Experiment." *Quaker Pamphlets*. http://www.quaker.org/pamphlets/wpl1947a.html.

Tu, Weiming. *Centrality and Commonality: An Essay on Confucian Religiousness*. New York: State University of New York, 1989.

——. "The Confucian Sage: Exemplar of Personal Knowledge." In *Saints and Virtues*, edited by John Stratton Hawley, 73–86. Berkeley: University of California Press, 1987.

Tugade, Michele M., Michelle N. Shiota, and Leslie D. Kirby, eds. The *Handbook of Positive Emotions*. New York: Guilford, 2014.

Tutu, Desmond. "Christian Witness in South Africa." *Reformed Journal* 35 (October 1985) 10–18.

——. *No Future Without Forgiveness*. New York: Doubleday, 1999.

——. "A Prisoner of Hope." *Christianity Today* 36 (October 1992) 39–41.

Underhill, Evelyn. *Meditations and Prayers*. New York: Longmans Green, 1949.

Underwood, Lynn G. "Compassionate Love: A Framework for Research." In *The Science of Compassionate Love: Theory, Research, and Applications*, edited by Beverly Fehr, Susan Sprecher, and Lynn G. Underwood, 3–25. Malden, MA: Wiley-Blackwell, 2008.

Uslaner, Eric M. *The Moral Foundations of Trust*. Cambridge: Cambridge University Press, 2002.

Vacek, Edward Collins. "Discernment in a Mutual Love Relationship with God: A New Theological Foundation." *Theological Studies* 74 (2013) 683–710.

——. *Love, Human and Divine: The Heart of Christian Ethics*. Washington, DC: Georgetown University Press, 1994.

——. "Scheler's Phenomenology of Love." *The Journal of Religion* 62 (April 1982) 156–77.

Van Tongeren, Daryl R., Don E. Davis, and Joshua N. Hook. "Social Benefits of Humility: Initiating and Maintaining Romantic Relationships." *The Journal of Positive Psychology* 9 (2014) 313–21.

Vanier, Jean. *Becoming Human*. Toronto: House of Anansi Press, 1998.

Volf, Miroslav. *After Our Likeness: The Church as the Image of the Trinity*. Grand Rapids, MI: Eerdmans, 1998.

Von Culin, Katherine R., Eli Tsukayama, and Angela L. Duckworth. "Unpacking Grit: Motivational Correlates of Perseverance and Passion for Long-term Goals." *The Journal of Positive Psychology* 9 (2014) 1–8.

Wadell, Paul J. *Friendship and the Moral Life*. Notre Dame: University of Notre Dame Press, 1989.

Walker, Alice. "Beauty: When the Other Dancer Is the Self." In *In Search of Our Mothers' Gardens*, 384–94. New York: Harcourt Brace Jovanovich, 1983.

——. "In Search of Our Mothers' Gardens." In *In Search of Our Mothers' Gardens*, 231–43. New York: Harcourt Brace Jovanovich, 1983.

——. "Recently I Wrote a Letter." Alice Walker: The Official Website, June 2012, http://alicewalkersgarden.com/2012/07/recently-i-wrote-a-letter/.

Wallis, Jim. *America's Original Sin: Racism, White Privilege, and the Bridge to a New America*. Grand Rapids, MI: Brazos, 2016.

Wang, Yanan. "A Compassionate Judge Sentences a Veteran to 24 Hours in Jail Then Joins Him Behind Bars." *The Washington Post*, April 22, 2016. https://www.washingtonpost.com/news/morning-mix/wp/2016/04/22/a-judge-sentences-a-veteran-to-24-hours-in-jail-then-joins-him-behind-bars/.

Wesley, John. "A Plain Account of Christian Perfection." In *John and Charles Wesley: Selected Writings and Sacred Hymns*, edited by Frank Whaling, 297–377. New York: Paulist, 1981.

Westheimer, Joel, and Joseph Kahne. "What Kind of Citizen? The Politics of Educating for Democracy." *American Educational Research Journal* 41 (Summer 2004) 237–69.

Wheeler, Sondra. *What We Were Made For: Christian Reflections on Love*. San Francisco: John Wiley & Sons, 2007.

Willard, Dallas. *The Divine Conspiracy: Rediscovering Our Hidden Life in God*. New York: HarperCollins, 1997.

William of St. Thierry. "The Nature and Dignity of Love." In Bernard of Clairvaux, *The Love of God and Spiritual Friendship*, edited by James M. Houston, 61–106. Portland, OR: Multnomah, 1983.

Wilson, Jonathan R. *Gospel Virtues: Practicing Faith, Hope, & Love in Uncertain Times*. Eugene, OR: Wipf & Stock, 1998.

Wood, Alex M., Jeffrey J. Froh, Adam W. A. Geraghty. "Gratitude and Well-Being: A Review and Theoretical Integration." *Clinical Psychology Review* 30 (Nov. 2010) 890–905.

Woolman, John. "Considerations on Keeping Negros, Part II." In *The Journal and Major Essays of John Woolman*, edited by Phillips P. Moulton, 210–37. Richmond, IN: Friends United, 1989.

Worthington, Everett L., Jr., and Michael Scherer. "Forgiveness Is an Emotion-Focused Coping Strategy That Can Reduce Health Risks and Promote Resilience." *Psychology & Health* 19 (2004) 385–405.

Wright, N. T. *After You Believe: Why Christian Character Matters*. New York: HarperCollins, 2011.

Yao, Zinzhong. "Jen, Love, and Universality: Three Arguments Concerning Jen in Confucianism." *Asian Philosophy* 5 (Oct 1995) 181–95.

Yeager, John. "'I've Got a Name'—The Power of Positive Salutation." *Positive Psychology News Daily*, February 10, 2007. http://positivepsychologynews.com/news/john-yeager/2007021090.

Yearley, Lee H. *Mencius and Aquinas: Theories of Virtue and Conceptions of Courage*. New York: State University of New York Press, 1990.

Young, Iris Marion. *Justice and the Politics of Difference*. Princeton: Princeton University Press, 1990.

Zakrzewski, Vicki. "How Humility Will Make You the Greatest Person Ever." Greater Good Science Center, January 12, 2016. http://greatergood.berkeley.edu/article/item/humility_will_make_you_greatest_person_ever.

———. "Two Ways to Foster Grit." Greater Good Science Center, May 5, 2014. http://greatergood.berkeley.edu/article/item/two_ways_to_foster_grit.

Zwick, Mark, and Louise Zwick. "Emmanuel Mounier, Personalism, and the Catholic Worker Movement." *Houston Catholic Worker*, August 1, 1999. http://cjd.org/1999/08/01/emmanuel-mounier-personalism-and-the-catholic-worker-movement/.